ALIVE IN CHRIST

GRADE 6

The Word of God in the Old Testament

aliveinchrist.osv.com

OurSundayVisitor

The Subcommittee on the Catechism, United States Conference of Catholic Bishops, has found this catechetical series, copyright 2014, to be in conformity with the *Catechism of the Catholic Church*.

Nihil Obstat
Rev. Fr. Jeremiah L. Payne, S.Th.L.
Censor Librorum, Diocese of Orlando

Imprimatur
✠ Most Rev. John Noonan
Bishop of Orlando
March 26, 2013

Our Sunday Visitor Curriculum Division
Our Sunday Visitor, Inc.
200 Noll Plaza, Huntington, Indiana 46750
1-800-348-2440

Alive in Christ is a registered trademark of Our Sunday Visitor Curriculum Division, Our Sunday Visitor, 200 Noll Plaza, Huntington, Indiana 46750.

For permission to reprint copyrighted materials, grateful acknowledgment is made to the following sources:

English translation of the *Catechism of the Catholic Church for the United States of America* copyright © 1994, United States Catholic Conference, Inc.—Libreria Editrice Vaticana. English translation of the *Catechism of the Catholic Church: Modifications from the Editio Typica copyright* © 1997, United States Catholic Conference, Inc.—Libreria Editrice Vaticana. Used by permission. All rights reserved.

Excerpts from the English translation of *Rite of Christian Initiation of Adults* © 1988, International Commission on English in the Liturgy Corporation (ICEL). All rights reserved. Excerpts from the English translation of *The Roman Missal* © 2010, ICEL. All rights reserved. Published with the approval of the Committee on Divine Worship, United States Conference of Catholic Bishops.

Scripture texts in this work are taken from the *New American Bible, revised edition* © 2010, 1991, 1986, 1970 Confraternity of Christian Doctrine, Washington, D.C., and are used by permission of the copyright owner. All Rights Reserved. No part of the *New American Bible* may be reproduced in any form without permission in writing from the copyright owner.

Excerpts from the *United States Catholic Catechism for Adults*, copyright © 2006, United States Catholic Conference, Inc.—Libreria Editrice Vaticana.

Excerpts from the *General Directory for Catechesis*, Congregation for the Clergy. © 1997, United States Catholic Conference, Inc.—Libreria Editrice Vaticana.

United States Conference of Catholic Bishops, Inc., Washington, D.C.: Hail, Holy Queen and Psalm Prayer (Re-titled: "Evening Prayer") from *Catholic Household Blessings and Prayers*. Translation copyright © 1989 by United States Catholic Conference, Inc.

Excerpts from the English translation of *The Roman Missal* © 2010, International Commission on English in the Liturgy Corporation (ICEL): All rights reserved.

Music selections copyrighted or administered by OCP Publications are used with permission of OCP Publications, 5536 NE Hassalo, Portland, OR 97213. Please refer to songs for specific copyright dates and information.

Additional acknowledgments appear on page 336.

Alive in Christ Parish Grade 6 Student Book
ISBN: 978-1-61278-050-4
Item Number: CU5252

5 6 7 8 9 10   015016   22 21 20 19 18
Webcrafters, Inc., Madison, WI, USA; May 2018; Job# 136094

Contents at a Glance

© Our Sunday Visitor

Contents in Detail

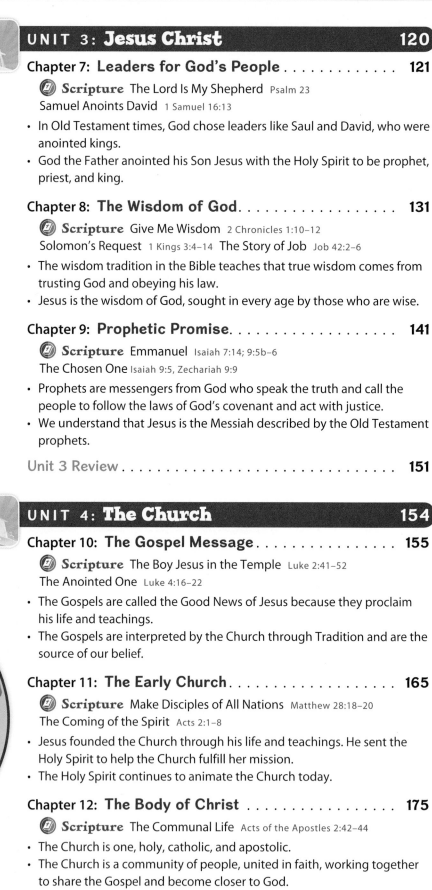

A New Year

 Let Us Pray

Leader: Loving God, you created all that exists and have a plan for each of us. Guide us to hear your voice and know your will.

"Your word is a lamp for my feet,
    a light for my path.
I make a solemn vow
    to observe your righteous judgments."
    Psalm 119:105–106

All: We praise you, O God, for lighting the way and making yourself and your plan known to us.

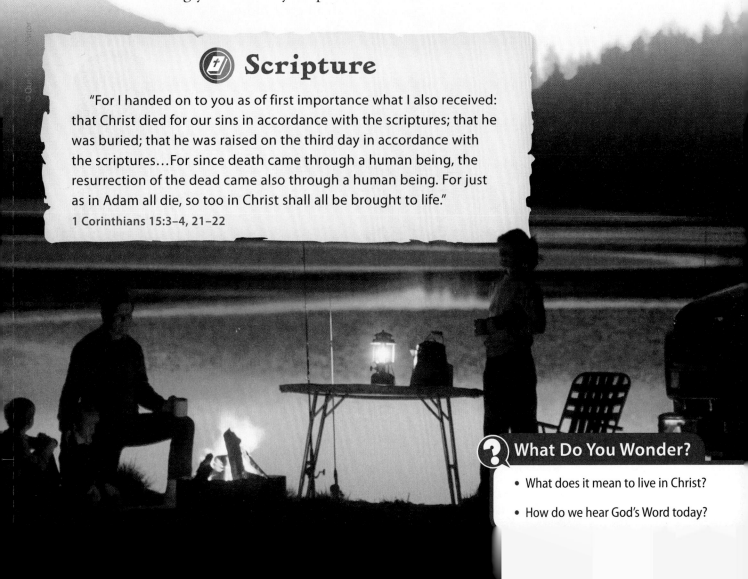

Scripture

"For I handed on to you as of first importance what I also received: that Christ died for our sins in accordance with the scriptures; that he was buried; that he was raised on the third day in accordance with the scriptures…For since death came through a human being, the resurrection of the dead came also through a human being. For just as in Adam all die, so too in Christ shall all be brought to life."

1 Corinthians 15:3–4, 21–22

? What Do You Wonder?

- What does it mean to live in Christ?
- How do we hear God's Word today?

Sixth Grade

Where will this year take us?

A new year is ahead of you. It's sort of like a journey.

This symbol lets you know that the story or reading that follows is from the Bible. In every lesson you will spend time with God's Word in Scripture.

You will visit Egypt, the ancient land of the pharaohs. You will travel through the Holy Land, where kings and prophets lived and where Jesus walked the Earth. And you will set sail with the Apostles as they proclaim the Good News of Jesus to the world. All of this journeying is to help you grow closer to Jesus and the Church.

You will begin and end each lesson with a prayer. Each time you are together, you have the chance to thank God, ask for his help, pray for the needs of others, and praise God for being God. God the Holy Spirit helps you pray.

You will sing songs to praise God and celebrate our faith. During the year, you'll explore the feasts and seasons of the Church year, and you will meet many important Biblical figures as well as Saints of the Church.

Every chapter includes tools to help you interact with what's written and better understand what's being taught. You may be underlining, circling, writing, matching, or more.

The story of God's People recorded in the Bible took place in the Holy Land and its surroundings.

Discovering Our Roots

This year you will be concentrating on the history of God's relationship with his People and the **salvation** that he has offered over the ages. Words highlighted in yellow are Catholic Faith Words. They are important for your understanding of the lesson and our faith. These words are also defined in boxes on the sides of the pages.

You will recall that God is faithful and true to his People throughout history. You will become reacquainted with these people from the Bible, and you will have the chance to meet many new ones. You will learn more about God's Kingdom and his love for his People.

Your family and parish will support you as you discover more about your faith and grow as a member of the Church.

Three times a chapter you'll see the green words like the ones below. This means it's time for an activity. You'll take a break to think about your faith and special people in your life; make connections to what you do at home, with friends, and at Church; and see how living your faith can make a difference.

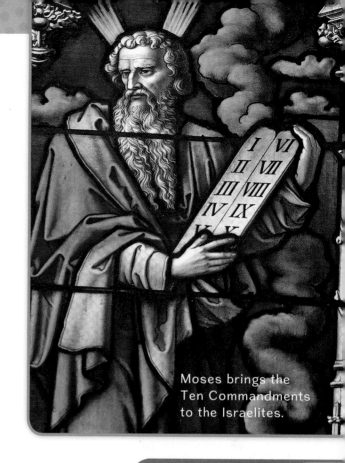

Moses brings the Ten Commandments to the Israelites.

Catholic Faith Words

salvation the loving action of God's forgiveness of sins and the restoration of friendship with him brought by Jesus

 Underline one thing you want to learn more about this year.

Share Your Faith

Reflect What do you know about the Kingdom of God? What did Jesus teach about the Kingdom?

_____

_____

_____

Share In small groups share your thoughts.

Sacred Scripture

The history of salvation begins with creation, reaches its highest point in Christ, and lasts until the end of time. It is the story told in the Bible—the story of God's saving actions for humans—and lived out today.

Important events of salvation history in the Old Testament include:

- God's promise to Abraham
- the Exodus
- the covenant given to Moses
- the Israelites' entering the land of Canaan, and
- the establishment of the Kingdom of Israel under David.

In the New Testament, salvation history is seen as coming together in the life, Death, and Resurrection of Jesus. The Church continues to participate in salvation history.

Another name for the Bible is **Sacred Scripture**. It is the inspired Word of God written by humans. The Catholic canon, or authorized version, of the Bible contains seventy-three books—forty-six in the Old Testament and twenty-seven in the New Testament.

The Old Testament

The first part of the Bible is about God's relationship with the Hebrew people before Jesus was born. It includes the laws, history, and stories of God's People.

The Pentateuch

This is the first five books of the Bible— Genesis, Leviticus, Deuteronomy, Exodus, and Numbers.

The Historical Books

These books include Joshua, Judges, Ruth, 1 Samuel, 2 Samuel, 1 Kings, 2 Kings, 1 Chronicles, 2 Chronicles, Ezra, Nehemiah, Tobit, Judith, Esther, 1 Maccabees, and 2 Maccabees.

The Prophetic Books

These books include Isaiah, Jeremiah, Lamentations, Baruch, Ezekiel, Daniel, Hosea, Joel, Amos, Obadiah, Jonah, Micah, Nahum, Habakkuk, Zephaniah, Haggai, Zechariah, and Malachi.

The Wisdom Books

These books are Job, Ecclesiastes, Sirach, Psalms, Song of Songs (Ecclesiasticus), Proverbs, and Wisdom.

The New Testament

The second part of the Bible tells of God's love for people after the coming of Jesus. It is about the life and teaching of Jesus, his followers, and the early Church.

The **Gospels**—Matthew, Mark, Luke, and John—are the first four books of the New Testament. They tell about Jesus' life on Earth and how he died and rose to save us.

The **Acts of the Apostles** tells how the Church grew after Jesus returned to his Father.

The **Epistles**, or letters, tell Christ's first followers how to live their faith. One reading at Mass comes from a letter of Saint Paul or another early Church leader. The Epistles include Romans, 1 Corinthians, 2 Corinthians, Galatians, Ephesians, Philippians, Colossians, 1 Thessalonians, 2 Thessalonians, 1 Timothy, 2 Timothy, Titus, Philemon, Hebrews, James, 1 Peter, 2 Peter, 1 John, 2 John, 3 John, and Jude.

The **Book of Revelation** is an example of apocalyptic literature. *Apocalyptic* means "revealed" or "unveiled." Apocalyptic writings reveal the secrets of Heaven or the future by an angel or the Risen Christ. They were written to give hope to a suffering people. This form of writing began in Old Testament times and continued through the first century A.D.

© Our Sunday Visitor

Catholic Faith Words

Sacred Scripture another name for the Bible; Sacred Scripture is the inspired Word of God written by humans

Letters from early Church leaders were sent to Christians in several lands.

Connect Your Faith

Identify a Scripture Story Is there a Scripture story that has had a special meaning to you on your journey of faith? Summarize that story to a partner.

Our Catholic Life

Each chapter in your book has an Our Catholic Life section. It builds on what's in the chapter and focuses in a special way on what it means to be Catholic. Text, images, and activities help you better understand how to grow closer to Jesus and the Church.

For each action listed in the left column, add an example of how you can do it. One has been done for you.

Growing as Disciples of Jesus

Know more about our faith	_____
Understand and take part in the Sacraments	_____
Live as Jesus calls us to	_____
Talk and listen to God in prayer	_____
Be an active member of the Church	_____
Help others know Jesus through our words and actions	Spread the Gospel through how we live and act with our families, friends, and others

People of Faith

You will also be introduced to People of Faith, holy women and men who loved God very much and did his work on Earth. They are officially recognized by the Church as Venerables, Blesseds, or Saints.

Live Your Faith

Name someone who is a model of faith for you. Explain why.

_____

_____

_____

_____

 **Let Us Pray**

Pray Together

Every chapter has a prayer page. Over the course of the year, you'll pray in different ways. You may proclaim God's Word, pray for the needs of others, call on the Saints to pray for us, and praise God the Father, Son, and Holy Spirit in words and song.

Gather and begin with the Sign of the Cross.

Leader: Blessed be God.

All: Blessed be God forever.

Leader: Let us pray.

Bow your heads as the leader prays.

All: Amen.

Leader: A reading from the second letter of Timothy.

Read 2 Timothy 3:14–16.

The word of the Lord.

All: Thanks be to God.

 Sing "Alive in Christ"

We are Alive in Christ, We are Alive in Christ
He came to set us free
We are Alive in Christ, We are Alive in Christ
He gave his life for me
We are Alive in Christ, We are Alive in Christ

FAMILY+FAITH
LIVING AND LEARNING TOGETHER

YOUR CHILD LEARNED >>>

This page encourages you to share your faith and identify the many ways you are already living the faith in daily family life.

In this section, you will find a summary of what your child has learned in the chapter.

Scripture

 This introduces you to the opening Scripture, and provides direction for more reading.

Catholics Believe

Bulleted information highlights the main points of doctrine of the Chapter.

People of Faith

Here you meet the holy person featured in People of Faith.

CHILDREN AT THIS AGE >>>

This feature gives you a sense of how your child, at this particular age, will likely be able to understand what is being taught. It suggests ways you can help your child better understand, live, and love their faith.

How They Understand Sixth graders may find themselves at the pinnacle of the elementary school or the lowest level of the middle school pecking order. Eleven and twelve year olds are transitioning into puberty, with its rapid physical and emotional changes.

Children of this age are usually very attached to their peer group and are concerned with social conformity. You may have to help your child see the value in nonconformity when it supports their beliefs and values. They are capable of reaching beyond their personal concerns to be of service and to act for justice. At this age your child does wonder about the future and sometimes can be worried or anxious. Show them in words and example that they can trust in God to take care of them.

CONSIDER THIS >>>

This question invites you to reflect on your own experience and consider how the Church speaks to you on your faith journey.

LET'S TALK >>>

Here you will find some practical questions that prompt discussion about the lesson's content, faith sharing, and making connections with your family life.

- What is your family looking forward to this year? Is there a Scripture passage that speaks to your hopes and goals?

LET'S PRAY >>>

 Encourages family prayer connected to the example of our People of Faith.

Holy men and women, you model faithfulness and trust in God. Pray for us as we journey through this year. Amen.

 For a multimedia glossary of Catholic Faith Words, Sunday readings, seasonal and Saint resources, and chapter activities go to **aliveinchrist.osv.com**.

The Presentation of the Blessed Virgin Mary

 ## Let Us Pray

Leader: Holy Mary, Mother of God
pray for us, as we seek to dedicate our
lives to your Son, Jesus.

"Sing and rejoice, daughter Zion!
Now, I am coming to dwell in
your midst [says] the LORD."
Zechariah 2:14

All: Amen.

Scripture

"Blessed be the God and Father of our Lord Jesus Christ, who has blessed us in Christ with every spiritual blessing in the heavens, as he chose us in him, before the foundation of the world, to be holy and without blemish before him. In love he destined us for adoption to himself through Jesus Christ, in accord with the favor of his will, for the praise of the glory of his grace that he granted us in the beloved."
Ephesians 1:3–6

? What Do You Wonder?

• What are spiritual blessings?

• What does it feel like to know you are blessed?

© Our Sunday Visitor

Presentation of Mary

On November 21 in Ordinary Time, the Church celebrates the feast of the Presentation of the Blessed Virgin Mary. Mary's parents were religious people who practiced the Jewish faith. One Jewish custom was to present a young child in the Temple and dedicate him or her to God's service. According to tradition, Anne and Joachim took Mary to the Temple for this ceremony.

Dedication

Mary has long been honored as a model of faith. We do not know the details of Mary's childhood. But we do know that when she was asked by God to be the Mother of his Son, she said "yes." Her "yes" changed the world. Why was Mary so willing to do as God asked? The Angel Gabriel addressed Mary with these words: "Hail, Mary, full of grace." Mary was filled with God's grace. Her heart was open to fully receive God's life and love.

Ordinary Time

The life and ministry of Jesus are the focus of Ordinary Time.

• In Ordinary Time, the priest wears green vestments.

• Mary and the Saints are also remembered throughout the year in what is known as the sanctoral cycle.

• The priest wears white vestments on Mary's feast days.

This grace and Mary's dedication to God helped her to do his will. The dedication ceremony in the Temple was just the beginning of her journey of faith. As she grew up, she must have spent much time praying and serving others. This made her dedication to God grow even stronger.

You have been dedicated to God through your Baptism. You, too, are called to a life filled with grace, a life of prayer and service. Mary's example will help you as you grow in God's friendship and grace.

Mary said "yes" to being the Mother of God. God asks you to say "yes" to him in your daily life. He asks you to dedicate yourself to him as Mary did.

➜ Who has encouraged you to say "yes" to God?

➜ What are some practical ways to dedicate yourself to God?

Activity

Find Meaning To learn more about what is written in the Bible about dedication, read one of the following passages on each day of the coming week. Write what meaning you get from each passage.

1. Song of Songs 8:6–7

_____

_____

2. Isaiah 44:1–5

_____

_____

3. Colossians 3:1–4

_____

_____

4. Acts 4:32–35

_____

_____

5. Matthew 11:25–30

_____

_____

6. Luke 10:38–42

_____

_____

7. John 17:20–26

_____

_____

People of Faith

Chapter	Person	Feast Day
1	Saint Teresa of Ávila	October 15
2	Saint Fiacre	September 1
3	Blessed Peter To Rot	July 7
4	Saint Monica	August 27
5	Saint Teresa Benedicta	August 9
6	Saint Hilda of Whitby	November 17
7	King Saint Louis IX of France	August 25
8	Saint Thomas Aquinas	January 28
9	Blessed Jacinta Marto	May 13
10	Saint John Neumann	January 5
11	Saint Timothy	January 26
12	Saint Jude	October 28
13	Blessed Pier Giorgio Frassati	July 4
14	Blessed Maria Vicenta	July 30
15	Saint Margaret of Cortona	February 22
16	Saint Rose Philippine Duchesne	November 18
17	Saint Ignatius of Loyola	July 31
18	Saint Henry II	July 13
19	Saint Mary Faustina Kowalska	October 5
20	Saint Charles Borromeo	November 4
21	Saint John the Evangelist	December 27

Honor Mary

 Let Us Pray

Gather and begin with the Sign of the Cross.

Leader: Blessed be God.

All: Blessed be God for ever.

Leader: Let us pray.
Bow your heads as the leader prays.

All: Amen.

Listen to God's Word

Reader: A reading from the prophet Isaiah.
Read Isaiah 61:10–11.

The word of the Lord.

All: Thanks be to God.

After each intercession, the response is Lord, hear our prayer.

Leader: Let us pray the prayer that Jesus taught us.

All: Our Father …

Go Forth!

Leader: Go forth now to follow God's will as Mary did.

All: Thanks be to God.

 Sing "Let It Be Done"

FAMILY+FAITH
LIVING AND LEARNING TOGETHER

TALKING ABOUT ORDINARY TIME >>>

Ordinary Time is the longest season of the Church year. It covers thirty-three to thirty-four Sundays. It is divided into two parts. The first part extends through the weeks between Christmas and Ash Wednesday. The second part begins at the end of the Easter season and extends until the first Sunday of Advent, which begins the next cycle, or a new liturgical year. The liturgical color for the Sundays of Ordinary Time is green. White is the liturgical color for feasts of the Blessed Virgin.

Scripture

Read **Ephesians 3:1–14**, which was written to Gentiles who had recently converted to Christianity. The letter encourages them in their transformation and socialization into God's purposes.

HELPING YOUR CHILD UNDERSTAND >>>

Mary

- At this age, children will be curious about the Jewish religious traditions and rituals that were a part of Mary's formation.

- Usually children at this age will understand that Mary was a woman who had a very close relationship with God.

- As a rule, children at this age are capable of comparing what is being expressed about Mary in different art forms.

CATHOLIC FAMILY CUSTOMS >>>

Feast of the Presentation of Mary

The Feast of the Presentation of Mary occurs on November 21, during the second period of Ordinary Time. It honors the decision of Mary's parents Anne and Joachim to dedicate her, as a child, at the Temple to God's service. The significance of this feast is that Mary was completely dedicated to God throughout her life, as we are called to be.

The Feast of the Presentation of Mary celebrates dedication to God's service, which in our everyday lives occurs through service to others. Your family can celebrate the Presentation of Mary with your own rite of thanksgiving and rededication. On November 21, gather around the family table—set with an image of Mary and a lighted candle, if you wish—and take time to name and appreciate the blessings that God has given your family.

FAMILY PRAYER >>>

Loving Father,

Send your Holy Spirit upon us to guide us to live in love and share the blessings of our Baptism with others. We ask this in the name of your Son, Jesus. Amen.

For a multimedia glossary of Catholic Faith Words, Sunday readings, seasonal and Saint resources, and chapter activities go to **aliveinchrist.osv.com**.

Anticipation

 ## Let Us Pray

Leader: God our Father,
Send us the strength of the Holy Spirit
that we will be without fear to live as your children
always.

"Say to the fearful of heart:
Be strong, do not fear!
Here is your God ..." **Isaiah 35:4a**

All: Amen.

 ## Scripture

"Be patient, therefore, brothers, until the coming of the Lord. See how the farmer waits for the precious fruit of the earth, being patient with it until it receives the early and the late rains. You too must be patient. Make your hearts firm, because the coming of the Lord is at hand. Do not complain, brothers, about one another, that you may not be judged. Behold, the Judge is standing before the gates. Take as an example of hardship and patience, brothers, the prophets who spoke in the name of the Lord." **James 5:7–10**

? What Do You Wonder?

• On a scale of 1–10, how patient are you?

• What do your friends or family members do when they get impatient waiting?

We Look Forward

Advent means "coming." As the diagram shows, Advent celebrates the comings of Jesus.

Advent, the first season of the Church year, is a season of preparation. During the four weeks of Advent, the Church uses purple to remind you to repent and remember that Christ is your king. The season also calls you to trust in God's infinite love by asking forgiveness for your sins, and invites you to reach out to those in need as Jesus did.

Besides preparing to celebrate Jesus, the Son of God, coming into the world as one of us, Advent also helps us anticipate and prepare for the Second Coming of Christ at the end of time.

1. Underline what we prepare for during the season of Advent.

2. Circle what we are called to do during Advent.

The Word became flesh.

In the beginning was the Word.

He lived, died, and rose to new life.

He will come again.

Second Coming

Jesus told his disciples that there would come a day when he would return in glory. "[H]e will send out the angels and gather [his] elect from the four winds, from the end of the earth to the end of the sky" (Mark 13:27).

Jesus' Second Coming will be the last day of human history. On that day, those who have not loved God and neighbor will be forever separated from God's love. Those who have led good lives will be embraced. And all who have died believing in Jesus will rise to greet him. There will come a new Heaven and a new Earth. We look forward to this day, because we will be reunited with our loved ones in God's presence. All will be well.

Prepare for Jesus' Coming

During Advent, the Church directs your attention to the birth of Jesus in the past, his Second Coming in the future, and his presence with you now. As you prepare to celebrate Christmas, also prepare to be ready for Jesus' return in glory at the end of time. No one knows when this will happen. The Second Coming could be tomorrow, or it could be thousands of years from now.

➜ If the Second Coming happened today, what would Jesus' review of your life be like?

At the Center The Season of Advent reminds you to make Jesus the center of your life. With a partner, discuss things you can do to make Jesus the most important part of your daily living. Share your ideas with the group. Choose one thing to do for each week of Advent.

Prepare the Way

A celebration of the Word is a moment of prayer with the Church, using the Scriptures.

 ### Let Us Pray

Gather and pray the Sign of the Cross.

Leader: Our help is in the name of the Lord.

All: Who made Heaven and Earth.

Leader: Let us pray.
Bow your heads as the leader prays.

All: Amen.

Listen to God's Word

Reader 1: A reading from the prophet Isaiah.
Read Isaiah 40:1–5, 9–11.

The word of the Lord.

All: Thanks be to God.

Take a moment of silence to let the Word of God speak to your heart and mind.

Side 1: I will listen for the Word of God; surely the LORD will proclaim peace.

Side 2: To his people, the faithful, those who trust in him.

Side 1: Near indeed is salvation for the loyal; prosperity will fill our land.

Side 2: Love and truth will meet; justice and peace will kiss.
Based on Psalm 85:9–11

Reader 2: A reading from the Second Letter of Peter.
Read 2 Peter 3:8–14.

The word of the Lord.

All: Thanks be to God.

Dialogue

What message of hope do you get from these readings?
What can you do to prepare for Jesus' Second Coming?

Go Forth!

Bow your heads as the leader prays.

Leader: Go forth and prepare a place for Jesus in your heart and make ready for his Second Coming, when all will be called to share in God's infinite, divine love.

All: Thanks be to God.

 Sing "Find Us Ready"

FAMILY+FAITH
LIVING AND LEARNING TOGETHER

TALKING ABOUT ADVENT >>>

The season of Advent, which occurs during the four weeks before Christmas, calls us to live in the past, present, and future of Christian life. We remember God's promise of a Messiah and his coming into history as Jesus, God's only Son. During the days of Advent, we also anticipate Christ's Second Coming at the end of time and long for the fulfillment of God's Reign of justice, love, and peace.

Scripture

 Read **James 5:7–10**, in which James is encouraging the early Church, who believed Jesus was returning soon, to be patient with the wait and to keep Jesus' New Commandment.

HELPING YOUR CHILD UNDERSTAND >>>
Advent

- Children are usually curious about and fascinated with stories, video games, and movies about the end of the world. Remind them of the truth: that we will share in God's love at that time.

- This is a time in children's lives when they are becoming more aware of mortality. It can be frightening for them. They need to hear the message of hope that we, too, have a promise of Resurrection as followers of Christ.

FEASTS OF THE SEASON >>>
Our Lady of Guadalupe
December 12

In the sixteenth century, the Blessed Virgin appeared as Our Lady of Guadalupe to Juan Diego, an Aztec Indian on his way to pursue the things of God. She told him to ask the bishop of Mexico City to build a church on the hill to assist in the conversion of the nation and be a source of consolation to the people. The bishop asked for a sign, which was given in the miraculous appearance of roses on the hill during winter, and the Blessed Virgin's image on Juan Diego's cloak. The times in Mexico were hard for the indigenous groups, and Our Lady of Guadalupe's appearance as one of them is a powerful reminder of God's love for and identification with those who suffer.

FAMILY PRAYER >>>

 Pray this prayer each week during Advent while lighting the Advent wreath.

We know that our Redeemer lives,
And on that final day of days,
His voice shall bid us rise again. Amen.

For a multimedia glossary of Catholic Faith Words, Sunday readings, seasonal and Saint resources, and chapter activities go to **aliveinchrist.osv.com**.

Season of Peace

 Let Us Pray

Leader: Faithful God,
You sent your only Son to bring us the gift of peace.
May we be messengers of peace with our families and
friends.

"And let the peace of Christ control your hearts,
the peace into which you were also called in one
body." **Colossians 3:15**

All: Amen.

 Scripture

"... 'And this will be a sign for you: you will find an infant wrapped
in swaddling clothes and lying in a manger.' And suddenly there was
a multitude of the heavenly host with the angel, praising God
and saying: 'Glory to God in the highest and on
earth peace to those on whom
his favor rests.'" Luke 2:12–14

Young people reenact
a Nativity scene during
a Christmas Eve Mass.

? What Do You Wonder?

- How many ways can you bring peace
  to your family?

- Why can't people live in peace?

© Our Sunday Visitor

Christmas

Christmas is a season of hope and peace.

• During the weeks between Christmas and the Feast of the Baptism of Jesus, you often hear those words—hope and peace—as you listen to the readings and the hymns.

• White or gold vestments, the colors of the Christmas season, invite you to grow in peace and hope.

Jesus, Prince of Peace

As the Jewish people waited for the Messiah, they heard many prophecies. They learned that a virgin would give birth to a son called Immanuel. He would be known as "Wonder-Counselor, God-Hero, Father-Forever, Prince of Peace" (Isaiah 9:5). This child's reign would be vast and forever peaceful (see Isaiah 9:6). Christmas celebrates the arrival of this Prince of Peace.

Message of Peace

When Jesus was born, the heavenly host praised God and proclaimed, "Glory to God in the highest and on earth peace to those on whom his favor rests" (Luke 2:14). After his Resurrection, Jesus greeted people with the words "Peace be with you" (John 20:19). The peace Jesus offers is rooted in the promise that no matter what happens, you can trust that God is always with you.

One way to celebrate Jesus' birth is to commit yourself to peacemaking. You become a peacemaker by settling problems with kindness and justice, by praying for harmony, and by asking God to end conflicts between neighbors and nations. You make the world more peaceful by working for justice in your home, school, and community.

➡ **How can you be a peacemaker?**

Celebrate Peace

 ## Let Us Pray

Gather and pray the Sign of the Cross.

Leader: Blessed be the name of the Lord.

All: Now and forever.

Leader: Let us pray.
Bow your heads in silent prayer. Then listen as the leader prays.

All: Amen.

The Lord's Prayer and Sign of Peace

Leader: At the Savior's command
and formed by divine teaching,
we dare to say:

All: Our Father …

Leader: Let us offer each other a sign of peace.

Go Forth!

Leader: Go forth in peace. May the love and kindness of Jesus be with you as you share his peace with all you meet.

All: Amen.

 Sing "Go Tell It on the Mountain"

FAMILY+FAITH
LIVING AND LEARNING TOGETHER

TALKING ABOUT CHRISTMAS >>>

The Christmas season, which lasts from the Christmas Eve Vigil until the feast of the Baptism of the Lord, is a joy-filled and hopeful season. The liturgical colors of white and gold and the festive decorations in church raise our hearts to hear the angels' message: "Peace to those on whom [God's] favor rests" (**Luke 2:14**).

Scripture

Read **Luke 2:1–14**, in which we see that one function of the angels is as messengers of God. How do you imagine an angel delivered the message from this passage?

HELPING YOUR CHILD UNDERSTAND >>>

Peace

- Usually children this age are aware of the need for peace in the world. In fact, situations of unrest are often unsettling for them.

- Most children at this age are not naturally peacemakers when they are personally involved in a conflict. It is sometimes difficult for them to see options other than what they want or need. They need to be shown various options.

FEASTS OF THE SEASON >>>

Feast of the Solemnity of the Blessed Virgin Mary
January 1

The feast of the Solemnity of the Blessed Virgin Mary, Mother of God, is a Holy Day of Obligation. At some point during the day, gather your family to say prayers for peace by asking for the intercession of Mary and her Son, the Prince of Peace, to bring peace to nations and families torn by conflict.

In the Ukrainian tradition, children gently toss handfuls of wheat (which symbolizes new life in Christ) at their parents, while wishing them a healthy and blessed New Year.

FAMILY PRAYER >>>

Prayer of Saint Francis

Lord, make me an instrument of your peace:

where there is hatred, let me sow love;
where there is injury, pardon;
where there is doubt, faith;
where there is despair, hope;
where there is darkness, light;
where there is sadness, joy.

Amen.

For a multimedia glossary of Catholic Faith Words, Sunday readings, seasonal and Saint resources, and chapter activities go to **aliveinchrist.osv.com**.

Time for Scrutiny

 Let Us Pray

Leader: Lord, God, send your Holy Spirit
that we may come to know you better.
May we come to know what holds us back from
loving you with all our heart.

"… hope in the LORD,
For with the LORD is mercy,
  with him is plenteous redemption …" **Psalm 130:7**

All: May we return to you and ask forgiveness.
Through Christ, our Lord,
Amen.

Scripture

"But this is the covenant I will make with the house of Israel after those days, [says] the LORD: I will place my law within them, and write it upon their hearts; I will be their God, and they shall be my people. They will no longer teach their friends and relatives, 'Know the LORD!' Everyone, from least to greatest, shall know me … for I will forgive their iniquity and no longer remember their sin." **Jeremiah 31:33–34**

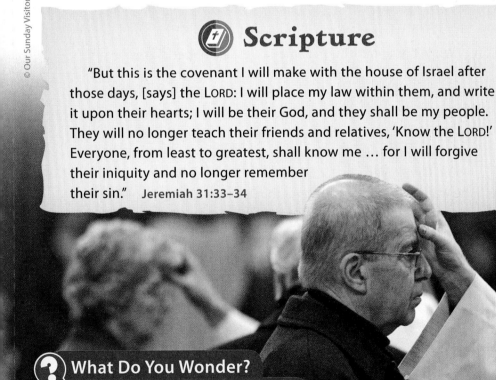

What Do You Wonder?

- How do you know that God loves you?
- How does God forgive you?

Lenten Preparation

Lent begins on Ash Wednesday and ends on the evening of Holy Thursday. Purple, the liturgical color of the season, reminds us that we need to repent. The forty days of Lent are a time to reflect on the sufferings and Death of Jesus. Lent is also a time to prepare to celebrate Jesus' Resurrection on Easter Sunday. Members of the Church dedicate more time to prayer. They perform works of penance, such as fasting, praying, and almsgiving to people who are poor or in need. They also participate in the Sacrament of Reconciliation.

On these Sundays of Lent, we hear important Lenten Gospel accounts: The Woman at the Well (see John 4:3–42), The Man Born Blind (see John 9:1–41), and The Raising of Lazarus from the Dead (see John 11:1–44).

Lent

Prayer is an important part of Lent.

• You pray for faith that you may truly appreciate the wonderful gift of life that Easter brings.

• You pray for hope that you will not let your problems or fears overwhelm you.

• You pray for charity that you will have the generosity to help others in need.

• And you pray for others, including those in your parish preparing for Baptism, asking God to bless them and keep them safe from all harm.

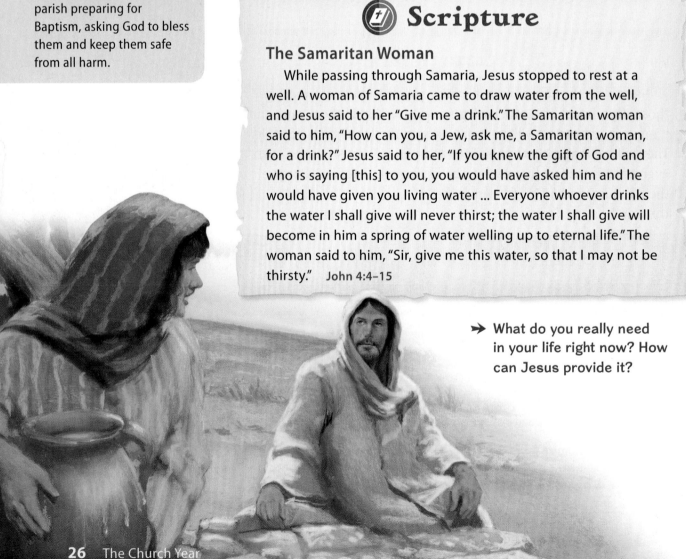

🎵 Scripture

The Samaritan Woman

While passing through Samaria, Jesus stopped to rest at a well. A woman of Samaria came to draw water from the well, and Jesus said to her "Give me a drink." The Samaritan woman said to him, "How can you, a Jew, ask me, a Samaritan woman, for a drink?" Jesus said to her, "If you knew the gift of God and who is saying [this] to you, you would have asked him and he would have given you living water ... Everyone whoever drinks the water I shall give will never thirst; the water I shall give will become in him a spring of water welling up to eternal life." The woman said to him, "Sir, give me this water, so that I may not be thirsty." **John 4:4–15**

➜ **What do you really need in your life right now? How can Jesus provide it?**

Underline what the Church community does during the Scrutinies.

© Our Sunday Visitor

Scrutinies

During Lent, those who will receive the Sacraments of Initiation, the elect, enter a time of reflection to deepen their commitment to follow Christ. To help bring about this process, the Church celebrates rituals called scrutinies. There are scrutinies on the Third, Fourth, and Fifth Sundays of Lent.

During the scrutinies, the elect come forward at Mass. The priest greets them and asks them to kneel. He lays his hands on their heads and prays that God will heal and strengthen them. The community prays with the priest and asks God to protect the elect from evil. The community also asks Jesus to give strength and faith to all his followers.

As the elect prepare for Baptism, Confirmation, and the Eucharist, the entire community is renewed. Each week helps the community to think more deeply about the power of evil in our lives. How are we tempted by evil? What do we need to do in order to reject evil and avoid sin? Through these rituals, the whole Church admits our need for Jesus, our Savior.

Activity

Becoming Members
Write a note to one of the people in your parish who will join the Church this Easter, telling that person that you will pray for him or her in a special way on the scrutiny Sundays.

Celebrate Lent

In this prayer form, a celebration of the Word, you listen to and reflect on God's Word.

 ## Let Us Pray

Gather and pray the Sign of the Cross.

Leader: O Lord, open my lips.

All: That my mouth shall proclaim your praise.

Leader: Lord, grant us your pardon and peace, so that, cleansed of our sins, we may serve you with untroubled hearts. We ask this through Christ our Lord.

All: Amen.

Listen to God's Word

Leader: A reading from the holy Gospel according to Luke. Read Luke 15:1–7.

The Gospel of the Lord.

All: Praise to you, Lord, Jesus Christ.

Dialogue

When have you felt like a lost sheep? Who helped you find your way? When have you helped others find their way?

Prayer of the Faithful

Leader: Let us ask God to make us faithful followers of Jesus.

All: Lord, hear our prayer.

Leader: Let us gather what we ask of God into a single prayer.

All: Our Father …

Penitential Act

Kneel silently as the leader prays.

Leader: Loving Father,
free these young people from whatever could
make them turn from you and help them to
walk in your light.

All: We want to walk with Jesus,
who gave his life for us.
Help us, Father, to follow him.
From the Penitential Act, RCIA.

Go Forth!

Leader: Let us go forth to share Christ's light and peace.

All: Thanks be to God.

 Sing "Through My Fault"

FAMILY+FAITH
LIVING AND LEARNING TOGETHER

TALKING ABOUT LENT >>>

Lent is a forty-day journey that begins on Ash Wednesday. The receiving of ashes on one's forehead marks one's promise to repent or change to grow closer to God and the Church. Lent is a time of inner change for us. It is traditionally a time of penance. During this season, incorporate customs of fasting, prayer, and charity into your family life.

Scripture

 Read **Jeremiah 31:33–34** and reflect on God's covenant and forgiveness. How do family members show forgiveness to one another?

HELPING YOUR CHILD UNDERSTAND >>>
Lent

- Most children at this age understand Lent as a season to "give up" things rather than to change. Help them to first think of something that needs to change, and then find a sacrifice that helps them to remember the deeper need for conversion.

- Many children at this age have developed an appreciation for art. They would likely benefit from reflecting on different art portrayals of Jesus' Passion and Death.

CATHOLIC FAMILY CUSTOMS >>>

Lent is a good time to broaden our awareness of the Sacraments and our shared faith journey. During family prayer time, pray for the children who will be receiving Reconciliation for the first time during Lent. Talk with your children about how this Sacrament helps us make a fresh spiritual start. Also include a prayer for the RCIA candidates in your parish.

FAMILY PRAYER >>>

 Use this as an evening blessing prayer for the family:

May the Lord our God send his Holy Spirit to guide us in our Lenten journey. May he strengthen us to change what needs to be changed in order to be better followers of Jesus. Amen.

For a multimedia glossary of Catholic Faith Words, Sunday readings, seasonal and Saint resources, and chapter activities go to **aliveinchrist.osv.com**.

Triduum

♥ Let Us Pray

Leader: Lord, God, you have saved your People over and over again. We are unworthy and we are grateful. Keep us close to you.

"May your mercy, LORD, be upon us;
   as we put our hope in you." **Psalm 33:22**

All: Amen.

✝ Scripture

"Seek the LORD while he may be found,
   call upon him while he is near.
Let the wicked forsake their way,
   and sinners their thoughts;
Let them turn to the LORD to find mercy;
   to our God, who is generous in forgiving.
   For my thoughts are not your thoughts,
      nor are your ways my ways [says] the LORD." **Isaiah 55:6–8**

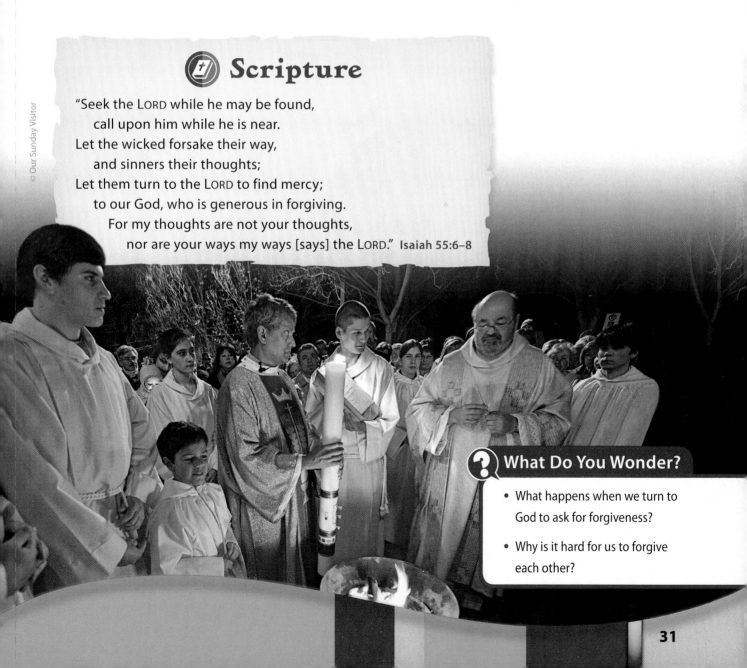

❓ What Do You Wonder?

- What happens when we turn to God to ask for forgiveness?

- Why is it hard for us to forgive each other?

31

From Life to Death; From Death to Life

In the opening chapters of the Bible, stories are told to explore the beginning of the human race and the origin of sin. In the Scripture, God creates our first parents, Adam and Eve, to live in friendship with him forever. Adam and Eve choose instead to violate God's friendship and follow their own path. By doing this, they lose paradise and the Original Holiness God shared with them. Death replaces eternal life as the destiny of humans.

However, God acts in human history to bring his People back to himself. This is seen in key events below, and in the establishment of David's kingdom, and the words of the prophets.

The story of salvation in the Old Testament reaches its fulfillment in the New Testament events also shown below. The history of salvation is fulfilled in Jesus. The stories and events come together in the life of Jesus. The Triduum celebrates the whole of salvation history that culminates in the Paschal Mystery.

➤ **Describe some New Testament accounts that show how Jesus brings salvation.**

Triduum

- The last three days of Holy Week are called the Triduum, a word that means "a period of three days."

- During this time, the Church celebrates the Evening Mass of the Lord's Supper on Holy Thursday, the Lord's Passion on Good Friday, the Easter Vigil on the night of Holy Saturday, and Easter Sunday Mass and Evening Prayer.

- During these three days the entire story of salvation is proclaimed and celebrated in the liturgy.

◄ Adam and Eve's choice

God's promise to Abraham, ▶ Sarah, and all of Israel

Salvation in Christ

The three days of the Easter Triduum summarize and fulfill the Old Testament's story of salvation. By participating in the liturgies on the three most holy days, you are celebrating your own salvation and that of all who live in Christ.

The liturgies of these days help us recall the journey of Jesus' Death and Resurrection. There is much to see, hear, and do at the liturgies of the Triduum, and all of it brings to life the meaning of the events of Jesus' Last Supper, Passion, Death, Resurrection, and Ascension.

Activity

The Three Days Illustrate a triptych that tells the Story of Salvation in words or images in the three panels. Think about how the days are connected and what happens during each.

The Last ▶
Supper

▲ The Resurrection of Jesus

◀ Moses leading the Israelites from slavery to the Promised Land

◀ The Crucifixion of Jesus

Celebrate Triduum

This celebration includes a section from the *Exsultet*, which is proclaimed during the Easter Vigil.

 Let Us Pray

Gather and pray the Sign of the Cross.

Leader: God, come to my assistance.

All: Lord, make haste to help me.

Leader: Glory be to the Father
and to the Son
and to the Holy Spirit,

All: as it was in the beginning
is now, and ever shall be
world without end. Amen.

Leader: Let us pray.
Bow your heads as the leader prays.

All: Amen.

Listen to God's Word

Reader: A reading from the Book of Genesis.
Read Genesis 1:1, 26–31a.

The word of the Lord.

All: Thanks be to God.
Take a few moments of silence to reflect on God's Word.

Dialogue

How do you participate in Jesus' Passion, Death, and Resurrection? How can you live for God in Christ Jesus?

Proclamation

Leader: During the Easter Vigil, a cantor may sing:

Reader: Exult, let them exult, the hosts of heaven,
exult, let Angel ministers of God exult,
let the trumpet of salvation sound aloud our mighty
   King's triumph!
Be glad, let earth be glad, as glory floods her,
ablaze with light from her eternal King,
let all corners of the earth be glad,
knowing an end to gloom and darkness.

Leader: Let us pray.
Bow your heads as the leader prays.

All: Amen.

Go Forth!

Leader: Go forth to glorify the Lord by your life.

All: Thanks be to God.

 Sing "Radiant Light Divine"

FAMILY+FAITH

LIVING OUR CATHOLIC FAITH

TALKING ABOUT TRIDUUM >>>

Holy Week is the holiest week of the Church year. It begins on Palm Sunday and continues until Evening Prayer on Easter Sunday. The Triduum, or "three days," marks the most sacred time of Holy Week. It begins at sundown on Holy Thursday and ends at sundown on Easter Sunday. During these three days, the whole Church fasts and prays with anticipation and hope. On Holy Saturday, the Church gathers in darkness to await the Resurrection of the Light of the World. The Paschal Candle is lit with new fire; its flame is shared with all present. The readings begin with creation and show God's plan for our salvation. The Sacraments of Initiation are a prominent part of the Vigil Service; new members are baptized, confirmed, and given the Eucharist.

Scripture

Read **Isaiah 55:1–11** to learn about Isaiah's rendering of God's covenant as a nourishing experience for hungry and thirsty human beings.

HELPING YOUR CHILD UNDERSTAND >>>

Triduum

- Most children this age come to a better understanding of the meaning of this week if they participate in the liturgies or focus on the symbols.

- At this age, children are often interested in the drama of Holy Week and the Triduum in particular. They may also show an interest in the historical significance and parallels with the Jewish Passover.

CATHOLIC FAMILY CUSTOMS >>>

Holy Saturday

Holy Saturday is a day of waiting, remembering that Christ was in the tomb. Make it a solemn day in your home, a day of quiet and reflection. It is also a day of preparation.

- When all of the Easter foods are prepared, gather as a family to bless them, giving thanks for the food and for Easter.

- At supper, light candles. The Light of Christ precedes us into the dark, chasing away the shadows, replacing darkness with God's mercy and love.

- Have a family member read aloud the words sung during the Easter Vigil (see below).

FAMILY PRAYER >>>

 From the Exsultet

The sanctifying power of this night dispels wickedness, washes faults away, restores innocence to the fallen, and joy to mourners, drives out hatred, fosters concord, and brings down the mighty. ... O truly blessed night, when things of heaven are wed to those of earth, and divine to the human. May this flame be found still burning by the Morning Star ... Amen.

For a multimedia glossary of Catholic Faith Words, Sunday readings, seasonal and Saint resources, and chapter activities go to **aliveinchrist.osv.com**.

Witnesses

 Let Us Pray

Leader: Lord, God, send your Holy Spirit
to give us the courage to witness to others
the Good News of the Resurrection.

"Blessed is [the one]
who comes in the name
of the LORD." **Psalm 118:26a**

All: Amen.

 Scripture

"On the evening of that first day of the week, when the doors were locked, where the disciples were, for fear of the Jews, Jesus came and stood in their midst and said to them, 'Peace be with you.' When he had said this, he showed them his hands and his side. The disciples rejoiced when they saw the Lord. [Jesus] said to them again, 'Peace be with you. As the Father has sent me, so I send you.' And when he had said this, he breathed on them and said to them, 'Receive the holy Spirit. Whose sins you forgive are forgiven them, and whose sins you retain are retained.'" **John 20:19–23**

? What Do You Wonder?

- What do you think the disciples were thinking and feeling when they saw the Risen Christ?

- Why was Jesus' first message about forgiveness?

Sharing the Message

Three days after his death, Jesus rose from the dead. Some faithful women had gone to the tomb, but he was not there. He then appeared to them, saying, "Do not be afraid. Go tell my brothers to go to Galilee, and there they will see me" (**Matthew 28:10**). In the Gospel according to John, Jesus first appears to Mary Magdalene, who reports to the disciples, "I have seen the Lord" (**John 20:18**).

The glorified Jesus also appeared to the disciples on the road to Emmaus and to the eleven Apostles and other followers. The disciples and Apostles who saw the glorified Christ became his witnesses. By their words and actions they spread the news around the world just as Jesus told them to do. (See Acts 1:8.) By gathering to celebrate the Easter message, you are a witness of Jesus' Resurrection today.

➜ How else are you a witness of Jesus' Resurrection today?

➜ How does your parish celebrate Easter?

Easter

- Easter is the Feast of the Resurrection of Jesus.

- It is the oldest and most important celebration in the Church's calendar.

- The Easter Season starts on Easter Sunday and continues until Pentecost, fifty days later.

- The priest wears white vestments during Easter.

Celebrate Easter

 ## Let Us Pray

Gather and begin with the Sign of the Cross.

Leader: Light and peace in Jesus Christ our Lord, Alleluia.

All: Thanks be to God, Alleluia.

Leader: Let us pray.
Bow your heads as the leader prays.

All: Amen.

Listen to God's Word

Leader: A reading from the holy Gospel according to John.
Read John 20:1–9.

The Gospel of the Lord.

All: Praise to you, Lord Jesus Christ.

Go Forth!

Leader: Go forth and live the hope that comes from the Risen Jesus, Alleluia, Alleluia.

All: Thanks be to God, Alleluia, Alleluia.

 Sing "Behold the Glory of God"

FAMILY + FAITH
LIVING AND LEARNING TOGETHER

TALKING ABOUT EASTER >>>

The celebration of the Easter season includes the fifty days following the Triduum. The Easter liturgies reflect the joy of salvation. The Alleluia is sung once again. The words of the hymns celebrate the victory of life over death, love over loss, salvation over sin. The People of God renew their baptismal commitment when they are sprinkled with holy water. The Gospels unpack the meaning of the Easter event and help the assembly to celebrate God's saving power. The People of God are sent out from the Easter celebrations to spread the Good News.

Scripture

 Read **John 20:19–23**, which recounts Jesus' first appearance to the gathered disciples.

HELPING YOUR CHILD UNDERSTAND >>>
Easter

- At this age children are usually very willing to be witnesses; however, they need adult guides or mentors.

- Most children at this age are interested in and capable of researching the cultural practices of Jesus' times regarding death and burial.

- Usually children at this age enjoy the stories and actions of the early Church found in the Acts of the Apostles.

FEASTS OF THE SEASON >>>
Divine Mercy Sunday

Divine Mercy Sunday is the Sunday following Easter. This is a relatively new feast; it was established by Pope Saint John Paul II at the canonization of Saint Mary Faustina Kowalska in 2000. The Gospel read on Divine Mercy Sunday is about the institution of the Sacrament of Reconciliation, one of the great gifts of God's mercy.

FAMILY PRAYER >>>

 Dear Lord,

We want to witness to your Easter message. Show us ways to bring peace to each other and to the places we work and play. Give us the courage to forgive those who have hurt us this week, and open our hearts to ask forgiveness of those whom we may have hurt in word or deed. We ask this in your name. Amen.

For a multimedia glossary of Catholic Faith Words, Sunday readings, seasonal and Saint resources, and chapter activities go to **aliveinchrist.osv.com**.

Ascension

♥ Let Us Pray

Leader: Lord Jesus Christ,
We come before you as your willing disciples.
We want to do your work here on Earth.

"All you peoples, clap your hands;
    shout to God with joyful cries." **Psalm 47:1**

All: Send your Holy Spirit as our guide and helper.
In your name, we pray,
Amen.

✝ Scripture

"'But you will receive power when the holy Spirit has come upon you, and you will be my witnesses in Jerusalem, throughout Judea and Samaria, and to the ends of the earth.' When he had said this, as they were looking on, he was lifted up, and a cloud took him from their sight. While they were looking intently at the sky as he was going, suddenly two men dressed in white garments stood beside them. They said, 'Men of Galilee, why are you standing there looking at the sky? This Jesus who has been taken up from you into heaven will return in the same way as you have seen him going into heaven.'" **Acts 1:8–11**

❓ What Do You Wonder?

- What might the disciples have thought when they saw Jesus ascend to Heaven?

- When will Jesus come again?

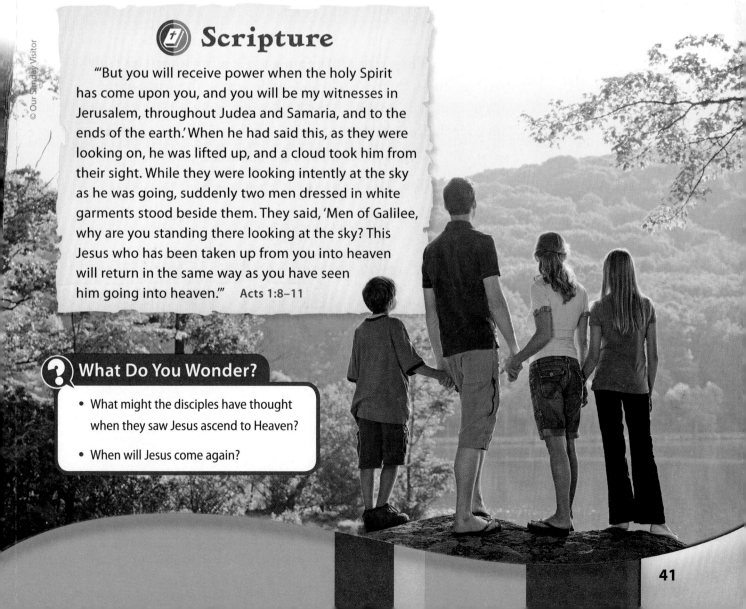

- On the Feast of the Ascension, the Church celebrates Jesus' return to his Father in Heaven.

- Ascension Thursday occurs forty days after Easter. In some dioceses and parishes, it is celebrated on the Seventh Sunday after Easter.

- The priest wears white vestments because it is a feast of Jesus.

- On the Feast of Ascension, the Church is reminded of its mission.

The Commission

On the day of Ascension, Jesus returned to his Father in Heaven to sit at his right hand. The early Church community was left with the promise of the coming of the Holy Spirit, who would strengthen them to go out and continue Christ's work to spread the Good News and help God's Kingdom grow. This continues to be our work today.

Mission

At Baptism, all Catholics are called to mission. Mission means "to be sent." At Confirmation, you are sent to continue God's work. You are not too young to do this. When Jeremiah told God he was too young to be a prophet, God said: "Do not say, 'I am too young.' To whomever I send you, you shall go; whatever I command you, you shall speak. Do not be afraid of them, for I am with you to deliver you" (Jeremiah 1:7–8).

Just as the disciples received the Holy Spirit on Pentecost, you receive the Holy Spirit at Baptism and Confirmation. The Holy Spirit is always there to help and guide you in the work of the mission at home, in school, or with your friends when you reach out to include, to heal, and to stand up for the rights of others.

➜ **How is the Holy Spirit with us on our mission?**

Celebrate the Ascension

 ## Let Us Pray

Gather and begin with the Sign of the Cross.

Renewal of Baptismal Promises

Leader: By water and the Holy Spirit, you received the gifts of faith and new life and were called to mission. Today, let us remember those promises together.

All: Come forward and gather around the water and candle. After each question, answer "I do."

Leader: Do you say "no" to sin, so that you can live always as God's children?
Do you believe in God, the Father almighty?
Do you believe in Jesus Christ, his only Son, our Lord?
Do you believe in the Holy Spirit?
This is our faith. This is the faith of the Church.
We are proud to profess it in Christ Jesus.

All: Amen.

Come forward, dip your finger in the holy water, and make the Sign of the Cross.

Go Forth!

Leader: Loving God, send us forth to bring your love to others. We ask this through Jesus Christ our Lord.

All: Amen.

 Sing "Cry the Gospel"

FAMILY+FAITH
LIVING AND LEARNING TOGETHER

TALKING ABOUT ASCENSION >>>

Catholics celebrate the Feast of Ascension Thursday forty days after Easter. In some dioceses and parishes the feast is moved from Thursday to the seventh Sunday of Easter. The Feast of the Ascension celebrates the Risen Jesus returning to his Father in Heaven. In the United States Ascension Thursday is a Holy Day of Obligation.

Scripture

 Read **Acts 1:8–11**, which describes the Ascension. How do you imagine that Jesus will return?

HELPING YOUR CHILD UNDERSTAND >>>

Ascension

- Usually children this age understand the concept of being sent on a mission.

- For the most part, children this age will appreciate projects aimed at outreach to the poor.

CATHOLIC FAMILY CUSTOMS >>>

Consider having your child earn money doing household tasks. Donate the money or goods purchased with it to an organization that helps the poor. Allow your child to go with you to make the donation.

FAMILY PRAYER >>>

 Pray this prayer together as a family during the days between Ascension Thursday and Pentecost Sunday.

Come, Holy Spirit, fill the hearts of your faithful with the gifts we need to continue the work of Jesus in our daily life. We ask this in his name.

Amen.

 For a multimedia glossary of Catholic Faith Words, Sunday readings, seasonal and Saint resources, and chapter activities go to **aliveinchrist.osv.com**.

Pentecost

 ## Let Us Pray

Leader: Lord, send us the Gifts of the Holy Spirit
that we may grow in unity and in strength
as your followers and witnesses.

All: "I will sing to the LORD all my life;
I will sing praise to my God while I live."
Psalm 104:33

Amen.

 ## Scripture

"At that very moment [Jesus] rejoiced [in] the holy Spirit and said, 'I give you praise, Father, Lord of heaven and earth, for although you have hidden these things from the wise and the learned you have revealed them to the childlike. Yes, Father, such has been your gracious will.'

Then turning to the disciples in private he said, 'Blessed are the eyes that see what you see. For I say to you, many prophets and kings desired to see what you see, but did not see it, and to hear what you hear, but did not hear it.'" **Luke 10:21, 23–24**

? What Do You Wonder?

- Why does God reveal his truths to those who are like children?

- Do you hear and see things differently because of your faith?

Gifts of the Spirit

Pentecost is celebrated fifty days after Easter, when the Church celebrates the day the Holy Spirit came down on the Apostles and Mary. During Pentecost, the Church is also reminded that we continue the mission of Jesus in the world today. The Feast of Pentecost reminds you that, like the Apostles and Mary, you have received gifts from the Holy Spirit through the Sacraments of Baptism and Confirmation. These gifts—wisdom, understanding, counsel, fortitude, knowledge, piety, and fear of the Lord—are lasting qualities that help you grow in your spiritual and moral life, and in your relationships with God and with others. As you use the Gifts of the Holy Spirit, you become more open to the presence of the Holy Spirit in your life.

➤ **What are some ways you have seen others live out the Gifts of the Holy Spirit?**

Led by the Spirit

Those who are led by the Holy Spirit show the Fruits of the Spirit in their lives.

 Describe how each Fruit of the Spirit is seen in your life.

Fruits of the Spirit

Fruit of the Spirit	How it is shown in my words and actions
Charity	_____
Joy	_____
Peace	_____
Patience	_____
Kindness	_____
Goodness	_____
Gentleness	_____
Faithfulness	_____
Modesty	_____
Self-Control	_____
Chastity	_____

Activity

Gifts of the Spirit In the space below, tell how you show in your words and actions the way you share one of these Gifts of the Holy Spirit.

wisdom   understanding   **counsel**   fortitude   **knowledge**   piety   **fear of the Lord**

_____

_____

Celebrate the Holy Spirit

Today you will pray for the Gifts of the Spirit in a celebration of the Word.

 ## Let Us Pray

Gather and sing together the refrain.
Pray the Sign of the Cross together.

Leader: Light and peace in Jesus Christ our Lord, Alleluia.

All: Thanks be to God, Alleluia.

Leader: Let us pray.
Bow your heads as the leader prays.

All: Amen.

Listen to God's Word

Reader: A reading from the Acts of the Apostles.
Read Acts 2:1–11.

The Word of the Lord.

All: Thanks be to God.
Take a moment to listen for the Spirit in the Word of God.

Dialogue

How do you think the Apostles felt on Pentecost?
What examples can you find to illustrate the Gifts of the Holy Spirit alive in the Church today?

Choosing a Gift

Respond to each prayer with these words.

All: Come, Holy Spirit, lead us in the way of Jesus.

Reader: Holy Spirit, let the way of Jesus be our joy and join us on every step of our journey.
Holy Spirit, may we be like trees planted near streams and grow strong in faith, nourished by your gifts.
Holy Spirit, help us always remember that the Father watches over us as we follow the path of his Son.

All: As you proceed to the table, sing "Send Out Your Spirit."

Leader: At the Savior's command
and formed by divine teaching,
we dare to say:

All: Our Father …

Go Forth!

Bow your heads as the leader prays.

Leader: Go forth with the confidence that the Holy Spirit is with you and is giving you what you need to walk the path of faith.

All: Thanks be to God.

 Sing "Send Out Your Spirit"

FAMILY+FAITH
LIVING AND LEARNING TOGETHER

TALKING ABOUT PENTECOST >>>

The Feast of Pentecost marks the end of the Easter Season. It occurs fifty days after Easter. The word Pentecost comes from the Greek word that means "fiftieth day." This feast, which commemorates the coming of the Holy Spirit to the Apostles and the Virgin Mary, is also traditionally celebrated as the birth of the Church. On this day, we celebrate the gifts that the Holy Spirit has given each of us in Baptism and Confirmation, so that we can be strengthened to continue witnessing to the Risen Lord in our daily lives.

Scripture

 Read **Luke 10:21–24**, in which Jesus points out that God reveals his secrets to the young and to those with open minds and hearts. Those secrets are precious to those who know them.

HELPING YOUR CHILD UNDERSTAND >>>

Pentecost

- Most children this age relate very well to the power of the Holy Spirit.

- Usually children are interested in the Gifts and Fruits of the Holy Spirit as they relate to them as individuals.

- Because children this age often experience changes and growth in their friendships, they can relate to the idea of a growing relationship with God.

CATHOLIC FAMILY CUSTOMS >>>

Sealed with the Gifts

Pray together as a family for all who have received Confirmation and been sealed with the Gifts of the Holy Spirit. For nine days, pray a short prayer to the Holy Spirit, each day asking the Holy Spirit to come into their hearts, families, and lives, strengthening in them and us a different Gift or Fruit of the Holy Spirit.

FAMILY PRAYER >>>

During the week between Pentecost and the Feast of the Most Holy Trinity, pray this prayer together daily:

Come Holy Spirit, set our hearts on fire, anoint us with your Spirit.
Guide us to use your gifts
to continue the mission of Jesus.

Amen.

For a multimedia glossary of Catholic Faith Words, Sunday readings, seasonal and Saint resources, and chapter activities go to **aliveinchrist.osv.com**.

Units at a Glance

Revelation

Our Catholic Tradition

- We come to know what God is like from Sacred Scripture and Sacred Tradition. (CCC, 97)

- In both, God reveals himself and his desire for us to live in friendship with him. (CCC, 74, 80)

- Through the accounts of creation and the establishment of the covenant, we learn that God is faithful. (CCC, 346)

- By sending his Son, Jesus, God the Father reveals himself to us in ways we never would have known. (CCC, 151)

Why is it important to study and pray God's written Word in the Old Testament?

Pope Francis celebrates his inaugural Mass inside the Sistine Chapel at the Vatican.

Divine Revelation

Let Us Pray

Leader: Your Word, O Lord, is light and life. Your Word speaks volumes to the heart.

"The word of our God stands forever." Isaiah 40:8

All: Fill us with joy and anticipation for your Word, O Lord. Amen.

Scripture

The LORD's word is upright;
  all his works are trustworthy.
He loves justice and right.
  The earth is full of the mercy of the LORD.
By the LORD's word the heavens were made;
  by the breath of his mouth all their host.
He gathered the waters of the sea as a mound;
  he sets the deep into storage vaults.
Let all the earth fear the LORD;
  let all who dwell in the world show him reverence.
For he spoke, and it came to be,
  commanded, and it stood in place.

Psalm 33:4–9

? What Do You Wonder?

- Why is it important to share stories of faith?

- How can you open your heart to hear God's Word?

God Makes Himself Known

How do we learn about God and his plan?

Stories help families remember what binds them together. Stories can do the same thing for communities and nations. April is a Native American girl who lives with her grandparents in a pueblo near Santa Fe, New Mexico. Her grandparents are introducing April to the traditions of the Navajo people.

The Storyteller

April loved to hear the stories that her grandparents told about the Navajo people. From these colorful tales, she gained knowledge about her roots, respect for all creation, and wisdom for living. Today her grandmother was going to teach her something unique about her people!

Grandmother said, "Our people have always loved stories. They show this by making storyteller figures. Let's make one."

Grandmother continued, "The main figure of the Storyteller is that of a woman. Her mouth is open because she is speaking, and her eyes may be closed as if she is remembering experiences from an earlier time. Attached to the woman are many children. Crowding around the Storyteller, they listen to the stories of history and of the wonders of creation."

➜ **Why is it important for a family or a nation to remember its stories?**

Navajo storyteller dolls are often handmade and shared in families to keep their tradition alive.

© Our Sunday Visitor

Stories of Our Faith

The stories of our Catholic faith are told in the Bible and continued in the Church. Many of the stories in the Bible were passed down orally from generation to generation before God inspired the human authors to write them down. Over a period of more than six centuries, various people wrote the books of the Bible.

The Bible, or **Sacred Scripture**, is God's Word, written by humans acting under the Holy Spirit's inspiration and guidance. The Holy Spirit continues to guide the Church, to preserve and teach God's Revelation. The Church interprets and hands down the message of the Word of God for future generations through her **Sacred Tradition** so all can know and apply God's wisdom to their lives.

Sacred Scripture and Sacred Tradition together are the source of God's **Divine Revelation**, or communication about himself. God, the principal author of the Bible, inspired its human authors.

Learning about God's Plan

By words and actions, God has made himself known gradually and in stages. He gave the Scripture writers the gift of the Holy Spirit to write faithfully about his saving truth.

The Bible presents the story of God's presence and of his loving plan of goodness and actions for his People. After many centuries, God fully revealed his plan of salvation by sending his Son, Jesus, and then, by sending the Holy Spirit as Jesus promised his disciples.

Catholic Faith Words

Sacred Scripture the Word of God written by humans acting under the Holy Spirit's inspiration and guidance; another name for the Bible

Sacred Tradition God's Word to the Church, safeguarded by the Apostles and their successors, the bishops, and handed down verbally—in her Creeds, Sacraments, and other teachings—to future generations

Divine Revelation the process by which God makes himself known. The chief sources of Divine Revelation are Sacred Scripture and Sacred Tradition.

Share Your Faith

Reflect Name one of your favorite Bible stories.

_____

_____

Share this story with a partner. Explain why it is your favorite and what it tells you about God.

Different Types of Writing in the Bible

What are some of the literary forms used in the Bible?

The Bible writers used different literary forms, or styles of writing, to tell the truth God wanted to share with us. Some writers composed poems, and some wrote historical accounts. Others recorded wise sayings or messages from God that had been spoken by the prophets.

Forms are names given to the different styles of writing found in the Bible. Here are some of the different kinds of writing found in the Bible. The descriptions tell the characteristics of the writing style, and the examples are books or stories in the Bible that demonstrate the literary form.

Circle which of these literary forms you like to read. Explain your choices.

Short Stories
Stories told to show how virtuous people live
Example: Joseph and his brothers

Letters
Messages addressed to early Christians by the Apostles and their followers
Example: The Letters of Paul

Apocalyptic Literature
A form of writing that describes the destruction of evil and the coming of God's Reign
Example: The Book of Revelation

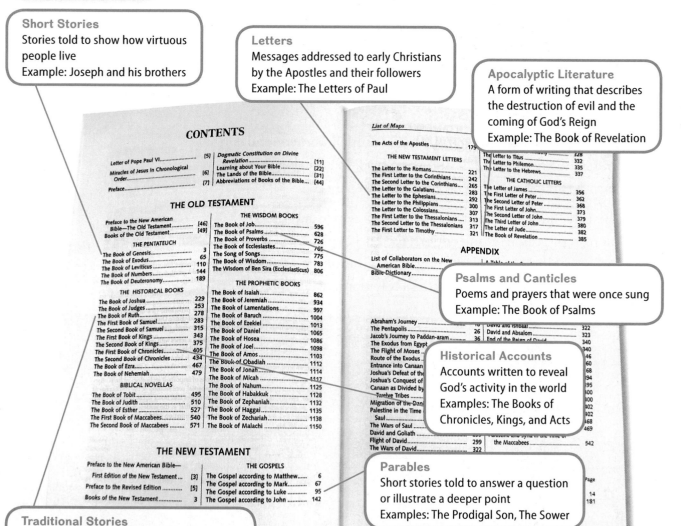

Psalms and Canticles
Poems and prayers that were once sung
Example: The Book of Psalms

Historical Accounts
Accounts written to reveal God's activity in the world
Examples: The Books of Chronicles, Kings, and Acts

Parables
Short stories told to answer a question or illustrate a deeper point
Examples: The Prodigal Son, The Sower

Traditional Stories
Old stories changed and expanded by biblical writers to teach certain truths about God
Example: The Book of Ruth

God's Message

God speaks through all of the literary forms of the Bible. A very important truth of both Scripture and Tradition is that God is faithful and wants you to live with him forever. Scripture and Tradition contain the truths that guide your life. This passage is about one woman's coming to believe in God.

 Scripture

Ruth and Naomi

Naomi and her husband left the land of Judah and settled in Moab. Her husband died and her two sons married women from Moab. Eventually, Naomi's sons also died. So she decided to return to Judah.

Her daughters-in-law, Ruth and Orpah, wanted to go with her, but Naomi told them, "Go back, each of you to your mother's house. May the LORD show you the same kindness as you have shown to the deceased and to me." Orpah went to her home, but Ruth remained.

Ruth said to Naomi, "Do not press me to go back and abandon you! Wherever you go I will go, wherever you lodge I will lodge. Your people shall be my people, and your God, my God."

Based on Ruth 1:1–16

➜ **What does Ruth's decision to remain with Naomi teach you?**

Connect Your Faith

Learn About God Read the passages below. What is the literary form of each passage? What is God's message to you in each passage?

Exodus 19:1–7 _____

_____

Luke 12:16–21 _____

_____

Revelation 11:15–19 _____

_____

Make a commitment to follow this plan for two days this week. How did your reading and prayer apply to your life?

Our Catholic Life

How does the Bible apply to your daily life?

It is important that you make the Bible a part of your daily life. One way to do this is to devote a short time each day to prayer and Bible reading. You may wish to do this in the morning before going to school, or in the evening before going to bed.

The exercise below is based on the Church's practice of *Lectio Divina*, which means "divine reading." It is a reflective reading of Scripture that leads us to prayer.

A Simple Reading Plan

Obtain a list of the Church's Scripture readings for each day from your parish bulletin. Look up the readings for the day.

Begin your time with God with a short prayer, asking the Holy Spirit to guide you.

Open the Bible to the passages indicated for the day.

- The first reading during the week may be from the Old Testament, the Acts of the Apostles, one of the letters in the New Testament, or Revelation.
- On Sundays, the first reading is usually from the Old Testament and the second reading from one of the Letters.
- The final reading is from one of the Gospels. It will tell you about Jesus. Choose one of the readings.

Put yourself into the reading. When the reading is from a Letter, imagine that the Letter is written to you. When you read from the Gospels, imagine that you are a part of the scene.

End your time with a prayer of thanksgiving and praise to God for what you have learned from the Bible.

People of Faith

Saint Teresa of Ávila, 1515-1582

Saint Teresa was born in Spain. After she had been a nun in a Carmelite monastery for twenty years, she dedicated herself to reforming many Carmelite convents, which were not as holy as they could be. One of the first things she did was write new rules based on God's Word in Scripture, particularly the teachings of Jesus and the Commandments. Teresa understood that it was important to listen and learn from God's Word in order to lead a good and holy life. She was serious about God, but also knew it was important to laugh and have fun. She used to dance in the convents to make the other sisters happy.

Discuss: When do you listen and learn from God's Word?

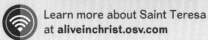

Learn more about Saint Teresa at **aliveinchrist.osv.com**

Live Your Faith

Think about a truth you've learned from the Bible that has helped you know more about who God is or how he wants you to live. Explain, with words or illustration, how knowing this makes a difference in how you act with family or friends.

Let Us Pray

Celebrating the Gift of God's Word

As we begin this new year, we celebrate the gift of God's Word to us in Scripture, an ancient and precious gift that is alive in our lives today.

Gather and begin with the Sign of the Cross.

Leader: We gather to celebrate one of God's gifts to us: his Word written to us in Scripture. **Based on Psalm 19:8–11**

Reader 1: Our treasure is wrapped in brown paper to remind us that this is an old book, one that spans three thousand years. Some parts are so old that they were told even before people knew how to read and write. We wonder what the stories inside this book meant to the first people who heard them. What do the stories in our Bible mean for us today?

Reader 2: Let us praise God for this treasure and its stories of our faith.

All: We do praise and thank God for our Bible.

Reader 3: We think of gold as the most valuable thing there is, but this treasure is more valuable than gold because it is God's Word and guidance for our lives. Even gold cannot buy these things.

Reader 4: Let us praise God for this valuable treasure.

All: We do praise and thank God for our Bible.

Leader: We gather to celebrate one of God's great gifts to us: his Word written to us in Scripture.

Read Matthew 13:1–9.

The Gospel of the Lord.

All: Praise to you, Lord Jesus Christ.

 Sing "Your Words Are Spirit and Life"

FAMILY+FAITH
LIVING AND LEARNING TOGETHER

YOUR CHILD LEARNED >>>

This chapter explains Divine Revelation and that the Bible reveals God's plan of goodness and salvation for us, a plan fulfilled by Jesus.

Scripture

 Read **Psalm 33:4–9** to find out about God's Word and what it means to and for us.

Catholics Believe

- God reveals himself and his plan of salvation through Sacred Scripture, the inspired Word of God written by humans.

- A very important truth of both Sacred Scripture and Sacred Tradition is that God is faithful and wants you to live with him forever.

To learn more, go to the *Catechism of the Catholic Church #51–55, 214* at **usccb.org**.

People of Faith

This week, your child learned about Saint Teresa of Ávila, who was very practical in establishing rules for her convents, based on God's Word.

CHILDREN AT THIS AGE >>>

How They Understand Sacred Scripture Your child is able to understand that Scripture is the inspired Word of God written in human language. His or her growing understanding of history and culture assists your child in placing Scripture in context, and when children this age know about various biblical writers, they are able to see how personality, circumstance, and literary form influenced the style of each book of the Bible.

CONSIDER THIS >>>

When did you last need someone to save you from a situation that you created?

Whatever our age, our words and actions can sometimes get us into situations we cannot fix alone. We need to ask for help. As Catholics, we know that "each of us inherits Original Sin, but it is not a personal fault of ours" (*USCCA, p. 70*). Because of the unity of the human race, everyone is affected by the sin of our first parents [Adam and Eve], just as in turn, humanity is restored to a right relationship with God by Jesus Christ [our Savior].

LET'S TALK >>>

- Ask your child to describe ways God makes himself known to us in our lives.

- Discuss ways your family connects with Sacred Scripture in your parish community and at home.

LET'S PRAY >>>

 Saint Teresa, pray for us that we may follow your example of listening and learning from God's Word, in our hearts and in our homes. Amen.

For a multimedia glossary of Catholic Faith Words, Sunday readings, seasonal and Saint resources, and chapter activities go to **aliveinchrist.osv.com**.

Chapter 1 Review

A **Work with Words** Complete each statement.

1. The Bible writers used different _____ to tell the truth God wanted to share.

2. Scripture and _____ contain truths that guide your life.

3. Sacred Scripture and Sacred Tradition are the sources of God's

   _____.

4. The names of Naomi's two daughters-in-law are _____ and

   _____.

5. What are some ways in which God reveals himself?

   _____

   _____

B **Check Understanding** Circle True if a statement is true, and circle False if a statement is false. Correct each false statement.

6. The process by which God makes himself known to people in Sacred Scripture and Sacred Tradition is called Divine Revelation. **True/False**

   _____

7. The story of Ruth's saving action is found in the Bible. **True/False**

   _____

8. Many stories in the Bible were passed down orally from generation to generation before they were written. **True/False**

   _____

9. One way to make the Bible part of your life is to have daily prayer while fasting. **True/False**

   _____

10. The Holy Spirit helps you open your mind and heart so that you can live the truths of Sacred Scripture and Tradition. **True/False**

    _____

Go to **aliveinchrist.osv.com** for an interactive review.

The Creation Accounts

 **Let Us Pray**

Leader: Gracious Creator, how wonderful your works!
How generous your love!

"May the glory of the LORD endure forever;
may the LORD be glad in his works!" **Psalm 104:31**

All: Loving Father, accept our thanks for all your creation
and for loving us always from beginning to end. Amen.

Scripture

O LORD, our Lord,
how awesome is your name through all the earth!
I will sing of your majesty above the heavens
with the mouths of babes and infants.
When I see your heavens, the work of your fingers,
the moon and stars that you set in place—
What is man that you are mindful of him,
and a son of man that you care for him?
Yet you have made him little less than a god,
crowned him with glory and honor.
You have given him rule over the works of your hands,
put all things at his feet:
All sheep and oxen,
even the beasts of the field,
The birds of the air, the fish of the sea,
and whatever swims the paths of the seas.
Psalm 8:2–3a, 4–9

? What Do You Wonder?

- Where do you see God's glory in the world?

- What do you think it means to be made in the image of God?

In the Beginning

What are the differences between the two creation accounts?

Genesis, the first book of the **Old Testament**, has two accounts of the beginning of the world and how life came to be. Both help answer some of life's most important questions.

Scripture

First Account of Creation

In the beginning, when God created the heavens and the earth, the earth was without form or shape, with darkness over the abyss and a mighty wind sweeping over the waters.

Then God said: Let there be light, and there was light. God saw that the light was good. God then separated the light from the darkness. God called the light "day," and the darkness he called "night."

Genesis 1:1–5

In this account, God separated the waters to create order and boundaries. Then he separated land from water and one kind of plant from another. (See Genesis 1:6–13.)

God created the sun, the moon, and the stars. He created living creatures, releasing birds into the sky and fish into the seas. Then he brought animals into being on the land. God created everything full of goodness. (See Genesis 1:14–25.)

Yet, in addition to all that he had created to fill the Earth, God created one more creature that would be like him and would share in his life and creative work. God created humans, male and female, and placed all of creation in their care. (See Genesis 1:26–30.)

God made humans in his own image and likeness with a **soul** that lives for eternity, or forever, and the ability to love and choose. Because of this, each and every person has value and **human dignity**.

Catholic Faith Words

Old Testament the first part of the Bible, about God's relationship with the Hebrew people before Jesus was born. It includes the laws, history, and stories of God's People.

soul the spiritual part of a human that lives forever

human dignity the worth each person has because he or she is made in the image of God

Underline why God created human life.

A Different Order

The account in the second chapter of Genesis tells you more about God's creation of human life. God creates the man before he creates the other creatures. Then he creates the woman.

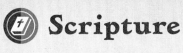 **Scripture**

The Second Account

First God created the heavens and the earth. At that time the earth was like a parched desert, so God made a stream come out of the ground. Then God took some of the clay from the ground and formed a man. God breathed life into the man, and the man came to life.

God planted a wonderful garden called Eden. God asked the man to work in the garden and to take care of it. Soon God saw that it was not good for the man to be alone. So God created more creatures, bringing them to the man to be named. Each creature was good, but none was the right companion for the man. So God caused the man to sleep and removed one of the man's ribs. From this rib, God formed a woman as the man's true partner. **Based on Genesis 2:4–25**

Detail from *The World's First Morning* by Nikos Hadjikyriakos-Ghikas

➥ **What qualities of God are revealed in this passage?**

Share Your Faith

Reflect Think about the two creation accounts. How are they similar? How are they different?

Share With a partner, fill in the Venn diagram with the similarities and the differences between the two accounts. Share your memories of learning about the creation accounts.

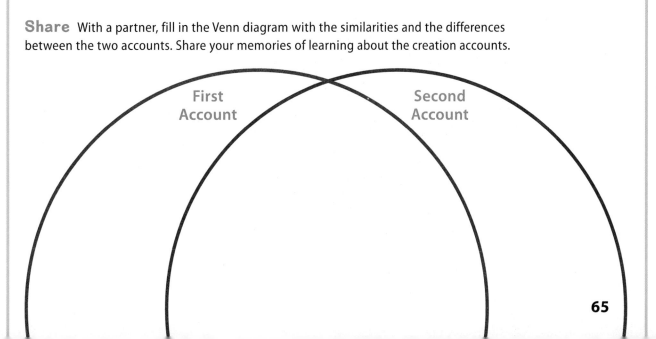

First Account

Second Account

Men and women were created by God to be partners with him and each other.

Lessons of Creation

What are the lessons of the two creation accounts?

In the two creation accounts, we read about how God is the powerful Creator who recognizes the goodness of all that he has made. Both accounts of creation help you understand God's love for humans.

The first creation account tells you that God alone created the universe. In the second creation account, God shows his deep care for the man's loneliness by creating a woman to be the man's true partner. This account shows that men and women were created to work together and share in God's life. Humans are social beings; they need one another. That is why people gather in families and communities. This is all part of God's plan.

Each and every one of us is created in God's image and shares the same human dignity. Therefore, we must respect all life, including protecting the unborn, the elderly, and the sick. This is part of God's plan, too.

Adam and Eve, as our first parents are called, were created by God in a state of **Original Holiness**, or grace. They shared in God's life. They lived in harmony with each other, with God, and with creation. Adam and Eve were pure of heart and generous, and they delighted in caring for the garden.

➡ **What are some ways that men and women work well together to fulfill God's plan?**

Truths about God

The two accounts of creation teach that God alone is the Creator and that humans are his creatures. God is all-powerful, and he created everything that exists. This means that your most important attitude toward God is a response of praise and adoration. God gave you life, embraces you lovingly every day, and gives you everything you need to one day have eternal life—everlasting life with God.

Role of Humans

There are other lessons in the two creation accounts. God placed the man and the woman in charge of the Earth, but that did not mean they could do whatever they wanted. God made them stewards, or caretakers, of creation. They shared in God's **providence**, his loving care for everything that he had made.

You, too, are a responsible steward when you protect the environment and treat other living creatures with kindness. Taking care of yourself—your body, your mind, and your spirit—is another part of caring for creation.

Catholic Faith Words

Original Holiness the state of goodness that humanity enjoyed before our first parents, Adam and Eve, chose to sin against God

providence God's loving care for all things; God's will and plan for creation

Highlight three things we learn about God from the creation accounts.

Connect Your Faith

Write a Haiku A Haiku is a three-line poem. The first line has five syllables. The second line has seven syllables. The third line has five syllables. Create a Haiku poem describing how you see the relationship between God and humans.

_____

_____

Our Catholic Life

How do you demonstrate respect for others?

Human dignity is many things. Most importantly, it is the God-given value and worth of every human. All humans have dignity and worth because all are made in the image and likeness of God. Dignity also means having self-respect and respect for others.

Here are seven ideas to help you respect the human dignity of others.

Check off two ideas you will put into practice this week.

Human Dignity		
D o things together	☐	Work with others. Combine your strengths with their strengths.
I nclude others	☐	Remember that God made us social beings. Make friends and reach out in kindness to others, recognizing that each of us is unique and gifted in our own ways.
G ive acceptance	☐	Welcome others and be patient with them, and with yourself.
N otice what is good	☐	Tell others when they have done something well. Give yourself good feedback, too.
I nvite respect	☐	Respect yourself and others. Avoid putting yourself or others down, and avoid calling yourself or others names.
T ry smiling	☐	Smiling can help you and those around you feel better, even when you face problems.
Y es! Say yes to life	☐	See life as a gift to celebrate. Learn new things. Develop new skills. Meet new people.

People of Faith

Saint Francis of Assisi, 1182–1226 October 4

Saint Francis was the son of a man who sold beautiful cloth. His father wanted Francis to work with him, but Francis wanted to tell people about Jesus. One day while he was praying, Jesus asked him to rebuild the Church. Francis knew that God was calling him to do this special work. Soon other people came to help Francis. He preached the Good News of Jesus and helped make the Church more holy. He helped people to see the beauty of the world by living a simple life and showing kindness to all of God's creatures.

Discuss: How can you be kind to all of God's creatures?

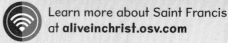

Learn more about Saint Francis at **aliveinchrist.osv.com**

Live Your Faith

Write a Story List four ways that people do God's work every day. Choose one way from the list and write about a person your age who does this.

1. _____

2. _____

3. _____

4. _____

_____

_____

_____

_____

_____

Let Us Pray

Prayer of Adoration

Gather and begin with the Sign of the Cross.

Leader: O LORD, our Lord,
how awesome is your name through all the earth!
You have set your majesty above the heavens!

All: How awesome is your name through all the earth!

Leader: When I see your heavens, the work of your fingers,
the moon and stars that you set in place—

All: How awesome is your name through all the earth!

Leader: What are humans that you are mindful of them,
mere mortals that you care for them?

All: How awesome is your name through all the earth!

Leader: Yet you have made them little less than a god,
crowned them with glory and honor.

All: How awesome is your name through all the earth!
Amen.

Based on Psalm 8:2, 4–6

Leader: Let us pray.

Bow your heads as the
leader prays.

All: Amen.

Sing "Bless the Lord"

Bless the Lord, O my soul,
bless God's holy name.
© 1995, 2002, D. Brennan,
M. Cavallero, K. Roth, and K. Canedo.
Published by spiritandsong.com ®, a division of OCP.
All rights reserved.

FAMILY+FAITH
LIVING AND LEARNING TOGETHER

YOUR CHILD LEARNED >>>

This chapter explains what we learn from the two creation accounts. God alone is the Creator, all he made is good, and humans are made in his image and likeness.

Scripture

 Read **Psalm 8:2–3a, 4–9** to find out about God's love for all creation, especially humans.

Catholics Believe

- The accounts of creation from the Book of Genesis reveal that God alone created the universe.
- God created man and woman in his own image to live in harmony with him for all eternity.

To learn more, go to the *Catechism of the Catholic Church #279–289, 355–361* at **usccb.org**.

People of Faith

This week, your child learned about Saint Fiacre, who is the patron Saint of gardeners.

CHILDREN AT THIS AGE >>>

How They Understand Creation Your child is learning more and more about science and scientific theories. If he or she takes the creation accounts too literally, it may be a struggle to reconcile what he or she has learned about evolution and other scientific processes with what we read in Scripture. On the other hand, children this age are old enough to know and learn that even in Scripture, there are two accounts of creation with notable differences, meaning that the "Word of God" found in the creation accounts is not about how many days creation lasted or in what order things were created, but about how God created everything and created humans in his image.

CONSIDER THIS >>>

What makes a person valuable?

The wonders of creation—roaring ocean waves, mountains, or abundant wildlife—give witness to an awesome Creator. But the truth is that people are God's greatest creation. As Catholics, we know that "the first man and woman were qualitatively different from and superior to all other living creatures on earth. They were uniquely made in the image of God, as are all human beings, their descendants" *(USCCA, p. 67)*.

LET'S TALK >>>

- Ask your child to name two things we learn about God and humans from the biblical creation accounts.
- Talk about how your family trusts in God's providence, his loving care, and his plan for us.

LET'S PRAY >>>

 Dear God, help us always to take good care of the gift of your creation as Saint Fiacre did, by caring for the plants, the animals, and people in it. Amen.

For a multimedia glossary of Catholic Faith Words, Sunday readings, seasonal and Saint resources, and chapter activities go to **aliveinchrist.osv.com**.

Chapter 2 Review

 A **Work with Words** Match each description in Column 1 with the correct term or terms in Column 2.

Column 1

Column 2

1. humans were created to be caretakers of creation

Adam and Eve

2. our first parents, who were created with Original Holiness

first creation account

3. describes how all that God created was good

stewards

4. describes God's creation of man before other creatures, and finally woman as his partner

providence

5. God's loving care for everything; his will and plan for creation

second creation account

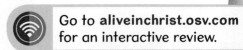

B **Check Understanding** Complete each sentence with the correct term from the Word Bank. Not all terms will be used.

6. God created each human soul to live with him for

_____.

7. The two accounts of creation in the Bible are found in the

Book of _____.

8. God created each person with value and human

_____.

9. Humans are _____; that is, they are made to relate to one another.

10. Because God is the Creator and you are the created, your most important attitude toward God should be

_____.

Word Bank

dignity

social beings

Exodus

Genesis

eternity

independent

praise and adoration

© Our Sunday Visitor

Go to **aliveinchrist.osv.com** for an interactive review.

God's Faithfulness

Let Us Pray

Leader: Faithful God, lead us to faith and deeper faith.
"Praise the LORD, all you nations!
Extol him, all you peoples!
His mercy for us is strong;
the faithfulness of the LORD is forever.
Hallelujah!" **Psalm 117:1–2**

All: Lord of all faithfulness, increase our faith. Help us to be strong enough to depend on you. Amen.

📖 Scripture

May the God of peace himself make you perfectly holy and may you entirely, spirit, soul, and body, be preserved blameless for the coming of our Lord Jesus Christ. The one who calls you is faithful, and he will also accomplish it. **1 Thessalonians 5:23–24**

❓ What Do You Wonder?

- Does the depth of your faith depend on you or on God?

- To you, what is the greatest sign of God's faithfulness?

Humans Turn From God

How does God respond to human disobedience?

As we mature, we learn that all actions have consequences. When we choose sinful things we harm ourselves, others, and our relationship with God. Here is the account of the first time people were tempted by Satan, the enemy of God and his People, and acted selfishly. It is from the Book of Genesis.

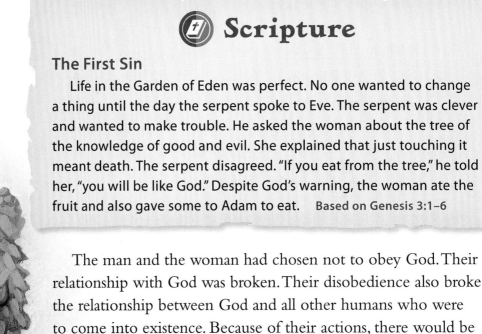

Scripture

The First Sin

Life in the Garden of Eden was perfect. No one wanted to change a thing until the day the serpent spoke to Eve. The serpent was clever and wanted to make trouble. He asked the woman about the tree of the knowledge of good and evil. She explained that just touching it meant death. The serpent disagreed. "If you eat from the tree," he told her, "you will be like God." Despite God's warning, the woman ate the fruit and also gave some to Adam to eat.   **Based on Genesis 3:1–6**

The man and the woman had chosen not to obey God. Their relationship with God was broken. Their disobedience also broke the relationship between God and all other humans who were to come into existence. Because of their actions, there would be hard labor, pain, and death in the world.

Underline what happened as a result of Adam and Eve eating the fruit of the tree. Then discuss what "forbidden fruit" people still eat today.

God Makes a Covenant

The Bible continues to tell the story of the effect of sin and evil in the world. The man and woman remained outside the garden. They had two sons, Cain and Abel. Cain was a farmer, and his brother Abel was a shepherd. Both made offerings to God, but only Abel's offering pleased God. Abel gave his best sheep to God, but Cain gave only poor products from his field. When God told Cain not to be resentful toward his brother, Cain did not listen. In his anger and jealousy, he killed Abel.

Still, God never stopped loving humans, even when they sinned. In the following passage, we learn how God made a **covenant**, or solemn agreement, with humans. God has always remained faithful to his covenant. His **faithfulness** is forever.

© Our Sunday Visitor

Catholic Faith Words

covenant a sacred promise or agreement between God and humans

faithfulness the loyalty and steadfastness that God shows to all humans, even when they sin. God's offer of friendship is never withdrawn.

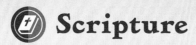

Scripture

The Great Flood

As more people were born, sin continued. God was grieved with humans because of so much evil. He decided to destroy all creatures in a great flood. But Noah was a righteous man. So Noah, his family, and a certain number of creatures were brought to safety in an ark. After the flood, God made a covenant, a solemn, sacred agreement joining God and humans together. His covenant was with Noah and all of creation. As a sign of the covenant, God set a rainbow in the sky. It was a sign of his promise that he would never again destroy the earth with a flood.

Based on Genesis 3:1–24, 4:1–15, 7:1–4, 9:8–11

➥ **How does God show his faithfulness and love?**

Share Your Faith

Reflect Think about God's actions or characteristics that show you his faithfulness to you.

Share With a partner, use two letters of the word *faithful* to begin a word or phrase that states an action or characteristic of God that shows his friendship with you.

Sin and God's Faithfulness

Who is the "New Adam"?

The Book of Genesis gives yet another account of how humans sinned and became separated from one another.

Catholic Faith Words

Original Sin the sin of our first parents, Adam and Eve, which led to the sinful condition of the human race from its beginning

temptation an attraction to sin, those actions and omissions that go against right reason and against God's law

new Adam a title for Jesus. By his obedience to the Father, and willingness to give his life, Jesus made amends for Adam's disobedience, overcame sin, and brought us eternal life.

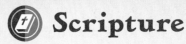

Scripture

The Tower of Babel

In the beginning, everyone spoke the same language. Noah's descendants settled in a beautiful valley. There they decided to build a city and a tower that would reach to the sky. They did this because they were filled with pride and wanted to display their power.

God saw what the people were doing and made their languages different so that no one could understand what anyone else was saying. The place became known as Babel, because it was there that people spoke without being understood. Then God scattered the people all over Earth, and they were unable to communicate with one another because of their different languages. **Based on Genesis 11:1–9**

Free Will

When our first parents, Adam and Eve, disobeyed God, they committed **Original Sin**. Because of their free choice to do wrong, all humans are born with Original Sin. The tendency to sin, as well as suffering and death, are part of the human experience. The **temptation** to sin is part of being human. With God's help, you can overcome temptation.

➡ **What is one temptation that young people your age face today?**

The New Covenant

Through their disobedience, Adam and Eve brought sin and death into the world. Time after time, God's people broke their covenant with him. But an ever-faithful God made a new covenant with humans.

God the Father fully revealed himself and his faithfulness by sending his own Son to teach us and save us. Jesus Christ is the Father's most complete and perfect revelation of his love for his people. The covenant that God made with Noah and with his chosen People, the Israelites, pointed toward Jesus and is fulfilled in him.

The New Adam

Jesus is called the "**new Adam**." Jesus makes amends for the disobedience of Adam. Jesus conquered sin and brought everlasting life. When you were baptized, Jesus, through his Passion, Death, and Resurrection, freed you from Original Sin and brought you into new life, the very life of God.

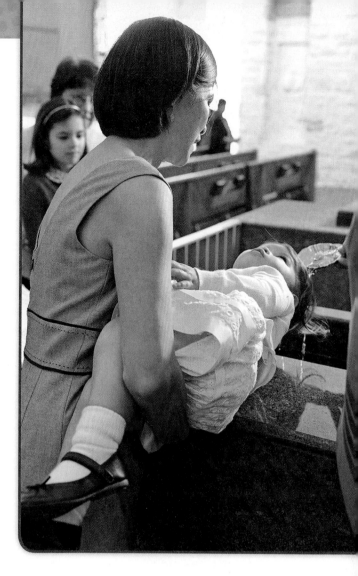

Connect Your Faith

What Have You Learned? Explain one thing you have learned about God the Father through the life, Death, and Resurrection of his Son.

_____

_____

_____

_____

_____

_____

Our Catholic Life

How can you grow in faithfulness?

The statement "God is faithful" has several meanings. First, it means that God honors the covenant that he made with his People; God is loyal. It also means that God is reliable. You can trust what he says. When so much around you is changing and uncertain, only God offers you complete security and certainty.

It is important for others to know that they can count on you. Here are some ways to help you know that you are following God's example of faithfulness.

Add your own examples in the empty bubbles.

You remain loyal to a friend who you know is right, even though your loyalty may cause you to be unpopular.

You believe and act in ways that follow Jesus' example, even though this may result in your being misunderstood and teased.

You place God at the center of your life and keep your heart and mind focused on him.

You tell the truth.

You can be trusted with important responsibilities.

You keep your promises.

People of Faith

Blessed Peter To Rot, 1912–1945

July 7

Blessed Peter To Rot was born on the island of Papua, New Guinea. His parents were among the region's first Catholics. Peter went to Saint Paul's Mission School to become a catechist. Soon, he was a recognized leader and was assigned to the mission in his own village. When the Japanese invaded the island, they forbade Christian worship and all religious gatherings. Blessed Peter was faithful to the Church, even though he was often punished. Finally, he was arrested for practicing his faith. He was put in prison, but he continued to be faithful to God even though he knew he would die because of it.

Discuss: How can you show your faithfulness to God today?

Learn more about Blessed Peter at **aliveinchrist.osv.com**

Live Your Faith

Explain one way that someone you admire has modeled his or her faithfulness in God.

_____

If you were doing an internet search on these traits, what key words would you enter?

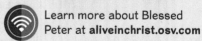

faithfulness and

_____
_____
_____
_____

How would your family describe your faithfulness?

_____
_____
_____
_____

Let Us Pray
Litany of Forgiveness

This litany of forgiveness helps us to reflect on our lives through the eyes of God's constant faithfulness and love. God always believes in us.

Gather and begin with the Sign of the Cross.

Leader: Sometimes life can be confusing. We suffer the consequences of our choices, and we sometimes bear the consequences of others' choices. Yet, one truth is constant.   **Based on Psalm 139**

All: Our God is a compassionate God, always loving us.

Reader 1: Am I too bossy? Do I have to be the center of attention?

All: God is always faithful; God is compassionate and near.

Reader 2: Do I take my family for granted? Do I show them respect?

All: God is always faithful; God is compassionate and near.

Reader 3: Does peer pressure influence many of my decisions? Are my friendships helping me to grow?

All: God is always faithful; God is compassionate and near.

Reader 4: Do I take time to pray? Is Jesus' name important to me?

All: God is always faithful; God is compassionate and near.

Reader 5: Is my school and environment a better place because of me?

All: God is always faithful; God is compassionate and near.
Sit quietly for a time of reflection.

Leader: Loving God, help us to always look to you for hope.

All: God is always faithful; God is compassionate and near.

 Sing "You Are Near"

FAMILY+FAITH
LIVING AND LEARNING TOGETHER

☉ Our Sunday Visitor

YOUR CHILD LEARNED >>>

This chapter teaches that, despite Original Sin and the ongoing struggle of humans tempted to sin, God establishes and remains faithful to his covenant, promising to always love and be there for us.

Scripture

 Read **1 Thessalonians 5:23–24** to find out about God's faithfulness.

Catholics Believe

- God fully revealed his faithfulness to humans by sending his only Son, Jesus, to conquer sin and bring everlasting life.
- Humans have the ability to live in friendship with God.

To learn more, go to the *Catechism of the Catholic Church #396–411, 1468, 1730* at **usccb.org**.

People of Faith

This week, your child learned about Blessed Peter To Rot, a mission leader and native of New Guinea, who was martyred by Japanese invaders in 1945.

CHILDREN AT THIS AGE >>>

How They Understand God's Promises and Faithfulness Keeping one's word is likely very important to your child. Children this age have often developed close friendships based on trust and loyalty. Their emerging understanding of the literary device of foreshadowing helps them to see the ways in which God reveals himself and his plan over time, and how God is faithful to his covenants.

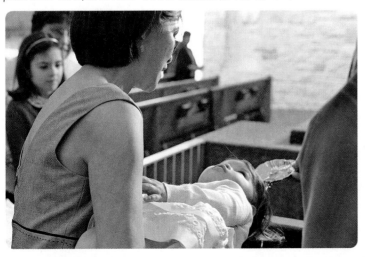

CONSIDER THIS >>>

As a parent, we love our children more than we imagined possible. How do we end each day loving them even more?

An early childhood teacher once said, "With the birth of our first child we learn the depth of our love. When our second is born we learn the breadth of our love." Children come to understand the unconditional love of God by experiencing the unconditional love of a parent. As Catholics, we know that "through the stories of creation in Chapters 1 and 2 of Genesis, God reveals himself as the Creator of all that exists, showing particularly a tender love for the high point of his creation, man and woman" *(USCCA, p. 56).*

LET'S TALK >>>

- Ask your child to explain what God's covenant is.
- Talk about some ways in which your family or close friends have demonstrated faithfulness.

LET'S PRAY >>>

 Dear God, help us to follow Blessed Peter's example of leadership and love by living as your faithful servants. Amen.

 For a multimedia glossary of Catholic Faith Words, Sunday readings, seasonal and Saint resources, and chapter activities go to **aliveinchrist.osv.com**.

Alive in Christ, Grade 6 Chapter 3 **81**

Chapter 3 Review

A **Work with Words** Fill in the circle next to the correct answer.

1. Sin has been present in the world since Adam and Eve chose to _____.
   - ○ resist temptation
   - ○ disobey God
   - ○ name the animals
   - ○ leave the Garden of Eden

2. Cain killed his brother, Abel, because Cain _____.
   - ○ thought his parents favored Abel
   - ○ felt anger and jealousy
   - ○ thought Abel was a bad brother
   - ○ believed Abel had more sheep

3. The sacred agreement that God made with Noah is called a _____.
   - ○ rainbow
   - ○ trust
   - ○ miracle
   - ○ covenant

4. God the Father revealed himself fully by _____.
   - ○ sending his Son, Jesus
   - ○ saving Noah from the flood
   - ○ giving the Ten Commandments
   - ○ creating all things

5. As the new _____, Jesus conquers sin and brings us everlasting life.
   - ○ Adam
   - ○ Noah
   - ○ Abel
   - ○ Moses

6. The covenant God made with the Israelites pointed toward _____.
   - ○ Noah
   - ○ Jesus
   - ○ Adam
   - ○ David

7. Our first parents disobedience to God led to _____, the sinful condition of the whole human race.
   - ○ perfection
   - ○ Original Holiness
   - ○ Original Sin
   - ○ purity

8. God confused the speech of Noah's descendants at _____.
   - ○ Eden
   - ○ Jerusalem
   - ○ Babel
   - ○ Bethlehem

9. As an offering to God, Abel offered the best of his _____.
   - ○ farm products
   - ○ sheep
   - ○ camels
   - ○ cattle

10. Eve ate the fruit from the tree of _____.
    - ○ happiness
    - ○ life
    - ○ blessing
    - ○ knowledge

© Our Sunday Visitor

Go to **aliveinchrist.osv.com** for an interactive review.

A **Work with Words** Solve the puzzle using the clues provided.

Across

4. God's act of bringing all things into being

6. a sacred agreement between God and humans

9. God's forgiveness and friendship

10. time without end; forever

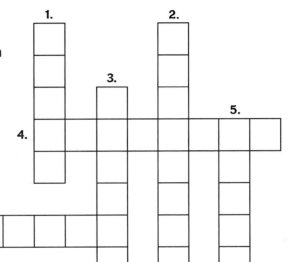
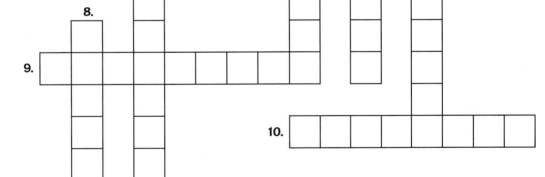

Down

1. the state of holiness in which God created Adam and Eve

2. first part of the Bible

3. attraction to sin

5. first disobedience against God

7. Sacred Scripture and Sacred Tradition

8. God's steadfastness

B Check Understanding Match each description in Column 1 with the correct term in Column 2.

Column 1

Column 2

11. God fully revealed his plan
of salvation by sending him

Original Holiness

12. In the Book of Genesis, the first
creation account tells you that
God created this

rainbow

13. Adam and Eve were created
in a state of this

New Adam

14. This was a sign of God's promise
to Noah

Jesus

15. Because he conquered sin and
death, Jesus is called this

universe

C Make Connections Write a response to each question.

16. What is human dignity?

_____

_____

_____

_____

_____

_____

_____

17. How does Original Sin affect every human?

_____

_____

_____

_____

_____

18. What have you learned about how God reveals himself?

_____

_____

_____

_____

_____

19. What are two ways for you to follow God's example of faithfulness?

_____

_____

_____

_____

_____

20. How do you think reading the Bible helps you as a Catholic?

_____

_____

_____

_____

_____

Trinity

Our Catholic Tradition

- God invites all humans to friendship and love, and we respond with a journey of faith. (CCC, 142)

- The Old Testament reveals the way God acted in the lives of his People to show his saving love. (CCC, 122)

- God the Father continues his saving work by sending his Son, Jesus. Jesus teaches us to love as he loves. (CCC, 293)

- Jesus establishes a new covenant at the Last Supper, and by his Paschal Mystery fulfills the covenant established with the Israelites. (CCC, 613, 762)

What can Abraham and Moses' relationships with God teach you about your relationship with God?

Journeys of Faith

♥ Let Us Pray

Leader: Lord of all faithfulness, keep us faithful to you.

"Trust in the LORD with all your heart,
    on your own intelligence do not rely;
In all your ways be mindful of him,
    and he will make straight your paths."
Proverbs 3:5–6

All: Guide us, O God, on our pilgrimage of faith. Walk with us on our way. This we pray in Jesus' name. In him, may our journey continue. Amen.

📖 Scripture

Be strong and steadfast, for you shall bring this people into the land which the LORD swore to their ancestors he would give them ... It is the LORD who goes before you; he will be with you and will never fail you or forsake you. So do not fear or be dismayed.   **Deuteronomy 31:7–8**

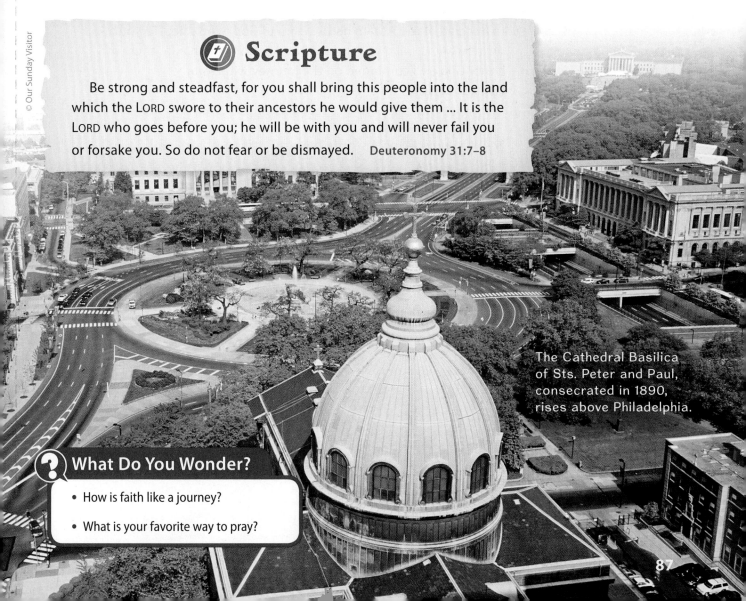

The Cathedral Basilica of Sts. Peter and Paul, consecrated in 1890, rises above Philadelphia.

❓ What Do You Wonder?

- How is faith like a journey?
- What is your favorite way to pray?

Abram and Sarai's Journey

Who is Abraham?

The risks involved in a journey are not so scary if you know that God is with you. Abram and Sarai learned that God was with them always. They remained faithful to God, and he blessed them in many ways.

 **Scripture**

Abram's Call

Abram and Sarai were getting old and had no children. One day God said to Abram, "Go forth from your land, your relatives, and from your father's house to a land that I will show you. I will make of you a great nation, and I will bless you."

As God directed, Abram and Sarai took all of their possessions and set out for the land of Canaan. After traveling through the land to a sacred place, Abram had a vision of God, who said, "To your descendants I will give this land." So Abram built an altar there to honor God and continued on the journey with Sarai.

Based on Genesis 12:1–9

➜ **Why would God's words have surprised Abram and Sarai?**

The Journey Continues

God appeared again to Abram and told him that his descendants would be as numerous as the stars in the sky and that they would have a land of their own. Although he still had no children, Abram put his faith in God. God changed Abram's name to Abraham and Sarai's name to Sarah as a sign of the covenant he made with them.

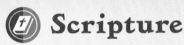 **Scripture**

Abraham's Visitors

One day three men visited Abraham and Sarah. The couple quickly prepared a meal for their guests. The men told Abraham that Sarah would have a son, as God had promised. Sarah was listening and laughed to herself because she was too old to have children. But within a year, Sarah did give birth to a son and named him Isaac, which means "one who laughs." **Based on Genesis 18:1–14; 21:1–6**

➜ **How did God keep his promise to Abraham and Sarah?**

Share Your Faith

Reflect Think about important virtues that people of faith share. Unscramble the letters below to discover three of them.

1. **F I T A H** _____   2. **O P E H** _____   3. **V E L O** _____

Share With a partner, talk about how Abraham and Sarah showed these virtues. Choose one and write one way this virtue is important to us today.

_____

God's Plan of Salvation

What does it mean to have faith?

The journey that began with Abraham continued with his son Isaac and Isaac's son Jacob. These three men are the patriarchs, the male ancestors of Israel who appear in the Book of Genesis both before and after the flood. It is from Jacob that the nation of Israel would take its name. In Genesis, Jacob was renamed *Israel* after wrestling with an angel. The name means "one who struggles with God."

Catholic Faith Words

salvation the loving action of God's forgiveness of sins and the restoration of friendship with him brought by Jesus

Seven Sacraments effective signs of God's life, instituted by Christ and given to the Church. In the celebration of each Sacrament, there are visible signs and Divine actions that give grace and allow us to share in God's work.

faith the Theological Virtue that makes it possible for us to believe in God and the things that he has revealed to us. Faith leads us to obey God. It is both a gift from him and something we choose.

Scripture

The Story of Joseph

Jacob became the father of twelve sons, but Joseph was his favorite. Joseph's brothers were jealous of him and plotted to get rid of him. They sold him to a caravan of travelers, and Joseph became a slave. Because he could interpret dreams, Joseph saved Egypt from starvation during a great famine. Joseph's brothers arrived in Egypt to buy food and were reunited with Joseph, who forgave them and invited them to settle there.

Based on Genesis 37–45

The twelve tribes of Israel are often represented by symbols in art.

God Invites

As seen through the faith stories of Abraham, Sarah, and their descendants, God keeps his promise of **salvation**, of forgiveness of sins and restoration of friendship with him.

You encounter God today through the Bible, the **Seven Sacraments**, and the Church. God's Son, Jesus, is the way of salvation for you. Jesus sent the Holy Spirit to help you on your faith journey. Wherever you go, God the Father is with you.

God invites you to respond to him in the same way that Abraham and Sarah did—with **faith**. This means that you freely choose to believe in God and all that he has revealed. When you respond to God with faith, you offer your heart and mind to him. You begin your own journey of faith, as Abraham and Sarah did. You have faith that God will guide you and keep his promises to you.

Faith and Prayer

God still speaks to people today, and people can communicate with God. This is done through prayer. Prayer begins and ends with listening to God. You can strengthen your faith with prayer, using one of these forms: blessing and adoration, petition for your own needs, intercession (praying for the needs of others), thanksgiving, or praise. You can pray at any time.

➡ **When and where are you most comfortable praying?**

➡ **What helps you listen for God's voice?**

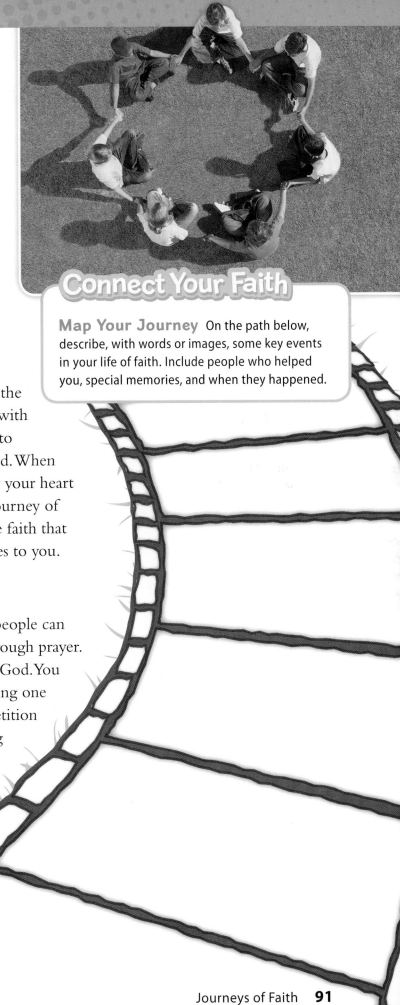

Connect Your Faith

Map Your Journey On the path below, describe, with words or images, some key events in your life of faith. Include people who helped you, special memories, and when they happened.

Our Catholic Life

What are some ways to develop your prayer life?

In the space provided, tell when each prayer form is used during the Mass.

An important way to develop your prayer life is to pray the types of prayers found in the Bible. Because the Bible is God's Word to humans, it contains teaching on prayer that will help you grow as a Catholic. The following examples of prayer will help strengthen your prayer life.

Forms of Prayer

Praise Through this form of prayer, you acknowledge that God is God, giving glory not for what he does, but simply because he is.

- When you praise God, in prayer and in song, you give glory to God as his children.

- You give God praise for his friendship, his kindness, and his goodness.

- _gloria_

Intercession You use this form of prayer to pray for the Church or the whole world.

- You ask God to help someone else.

- You intercede on behalf of others as Jesus intercedes for you with his Father.

- _____

Petition In times of need, you turn to God, ask for his help, and acknowledge that you need him.

- You might pray for God's mercy, forgiveness, and guidance when you are sad, sick, troubled, confused, or in a state of sin.

- You also ask God to help others.

- _reconciliation_

Blessing and Adoration You bless God, who blesses you. You also bless others who are made in God's image.

- A blessing is a prayer of response to all of God's gifts to us.

- Adoration is giving respectful homage to God by honoring the greatness of the Lord.

- _adoration_

Thanksgiving You express your gratitude to God for the good things in your life.

- When you experience some special cause for rejoicing, such as good grades or restored health or a wonderful day, you thank God for it.

- _ucerishc_

People of Faith

August 27

Saint Monica, c. 331–387

Saint Monica lived in North Africa. She was a woman of great faith, and many members of her family became Christian because of her example. Monica had a son named Augustine. In his youth, Augustine led a disgraceful life. Monica wanted him to be baptized, but he refused. For many years, Monica prayed constantly for his conversion. Finally, after much persistence, her prayers were answered. Augustine realized the truth of Christianity and turned his life around. He became a priest and then a bishop as well as one of the great teachers of the faith. Both he and his mother are honored as Saints.

Discuss: Talk about a time when God answered your prayer.

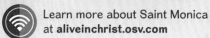

Learn more about Saint Monica at **aliveinchrist.osv.com**

Live Your Faith

Think about which type of prayer you don't pray often, and consider why you don't usually talk to God in this way.

Write a short prayer using this form and pray it during the next week.

© Our Sunday Visitor

♥ Let Us Pray

Guided Reflection

This is a guided scriptural reflection, during which we remember an event in Jesus' life or one of his teachings. We can imagine ourselves in the story.

Gather and begin with the Sign of the Cross.

Leader: We gather today in prayer, attentive once again to God's Word.

Read John 10:14–17, 27–29.

The Word of God is a living word. Although it was written long ago, the Holy Spirit makes God's Word come alive in our own hearts this very day. And so we pray,

All: Holy Spirit, guide us.

Leader: Let us close our eyes, be very still, and imagine.

After the guided reflection:

This Scripture passage reminds us of the care that Jesus gives to those who are on the journey of faith. Let us continue to pray.

Side 1: We thank you, Jesus, the Good Shepherd,

Side 2: for your unceasing care and loving guidance.

Side 1: We trust you.

Side 2: We will always follow you.

All: Thank you for keeping us close to you, in your hands, as one family. Amen.

FAMILY+FAITH
LIVING AND LEARNING TOGETHER

YOUR CHILD LEARNED >>>

This chapter explains how prayer can deepen our faith, and help us trust in God during our journey, just as Abraham and Sarah did.

Scripture

 Read **Deuteronomy 31:8** to find out who will walk with us on our faith journey.

Catholics Believe

- God calls you on a journey of faith toward salvation.
- The path toward salvation is paved with prayer, which allows the Holy Spirit to lead you away from sin.

To learn more, go to the *Catechism of the Catholic Church #176–184, 2558–2565* at **usccb.org**.

People of Faith

This week, your child learned about Saint Monica, whose persistent prayer eventually led to the conversion of her famous son, Saint Augustine.

CHILDREN AT THIS AGE >>>

How They Understand Prayer Your child is probably remarkably more verbally articulate than when he or she was younger, and more capable of true conversation. The implication of this for prayer is that children's ability to use spontaneous, conversational styles of prayer grows if they have been taught how to do this. Because prayer is essentially "conversation with God," children who have been well-formed in prayer can really grow in their prayer lives during this time.

CONSIDER THIS >>>

Where do you spend the most time in prayer: in thanksgiving, asking, or praise?

While we may find our prayer is frequently petition, or asking, prayer is necessary to grow in relationship with God. Using a variety of ways to pray, we can express to God what is in our hearts. As Catholics, we know "the Holy Spirit taught the Church the life of prayer and led her to deeper insights into basic ways of praying: adoration, petition, intercession, thanksgiving, and praise" *(USCCA p. 467)*.

LET'S TALK >>>

- Have your child describe how prayer and the Sacraments are part of our faith journey.
- Share with your child an experience in your life that helped you grow in faith.

LET'S PRAY >>>

 Saint Monica, help us follow your strong example of faith and constant, persistent prayer, especially for members of our family. Amen.

For a multimedia glossary of Catholic Faith Words, Sunday readings, seasonal and Saint resources, and chapter activities go to **aliveinchrist.osv.com**.

Chapter 4 Review

A **Work with Words** Complete each sentence with the correct term from the Word Bank. Terms may be used more than once.

> ### Word Bank
>
> faith   Monica   twelve   salvation
>
> covenant   prayer   Sarah   Isaac
>
> Jerusalem   Joseph   Egypt

1. Abraham's wife was named _Sarah_.

2. Of Jacob's twelve sons, _Joseph_ was his favorite.

3. _Joseph_ was sold into slavery in _Egypt_ by his jealous brothers.

4. _salvation_ is the Theological Virtue that makes it possible for us to believe in God and all that he has revealed.

5. God continues to speak to us today, and we communicate with him through _prayer_.

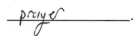

B **Check Understanding** Complete each statement.

6. God promised that he would make a great _covenant_ from Abram and his descendants.

7. Sarah gave birth to a son whose name was _Isaac_.

8. Jacob received the name _Isreal_, which means "one who struggles with God."

9. The journey that God calls you to make is a journey of _faith_.

10. Blessing and adoration, _____, intercession, thanksgiving, and praise are all forms of prayer.

© Our Sunday Visitor

Go to **aliveinchrist.osv.com** for an interactive review.

God's Saving Action

 **Let Us Pray**

Leader: Merciful Savior, we remember your love.
We trust in you.

"The LORD is my light and my salvation;
whom should I fear?" **Psalm 27:1**

All: God who cannot forget us, we give you thanks
for saving us, your people. Amen.

📖 Scripture

Give thanks to the LORD, for he is good,
    his mercy endures forever.
Let Israel say:
    his mercy endures forever.
Let the house of Aaron say,
    his mercy endures forever.
Let those who fear the LORD say,
    his mercy endures forever.
In danger I called on the LORD;
    the LORD answered me and set me free.
The LORD, my strength and might,
    has become my savior.

Psalm 118:1–5, 14

❓ What Do You Wonder?

• What saving act of God does Passover
remember and celebrate?

• What saving act of God does
Eucharist remember and celebrate?

God Delivers His People

How is Moses an instrument of God's action?

God calls ordinary people to accomplish extraordinary things. From biblical times to the present, God has called people where they are to do his work. Moses was one of these people. Through him, you can see God's saving power at work. Through Moses, God delivered the Israelites from slavery to freedom. This was the beginning of the Israelite's journey, called the **Exodus**.

Catholic Faith Words

Exodus the Israelites' journey from slavery in Egypt to freedom in the Promised Land, accomplished and directed by God

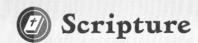

Scripture

Moses

Moses was one of the great leaders of the Hebrew people. He was born after the time of Joseph. The Hebrews were slaves in Egypt then. The pharaoh feared the Hebrews because there were so many of them. They were also strong. The pharaoh ordered every Hebrew baby boy born to be killed.

Moses' mother wanted to save him. She put him in a basket and floated the basket on the Nile River. The pharaoh's daughter found Moses and raised him in the royal palace.

When Moses was grown, he saw an Egyptian hurting a Hebrew. Moses killed the Egyptian, and then he ran away because he knew he would be punished.

Moses found a new home and became a shepherd. One day, he saw a bush that was on fire, but it was not being consumed. As Moses drew close to investigate the bush, God spoke to him.

God told Moses to lead the Hebrews out of Egypt to a wonderful new land. God promised Moses that the pharaoh would send the Hebrews away after God worked many wonders.

Based on Exodus 1—3

Underline how God called Moses.

© Our Sunday Visitor

The Exodus

When Moses was a man, God sent him to the pharaoh to demand freedom for the Hebrews. Moses did as God asked, but the pharaoh refused to listen. God then sent nine plagues to the Egyptians. When the pharaoh still refused, God sent a tenth plague, the angel of death, to kill all of the firstborn Egyptian sons. Pharaoh finally let the Israelites go. They left Egypt to go to the Promised Land.

Based on Exodus 7:1—11:10, 12:29

Share Your Faith

Reflect Recall what you already know about how God called Moses. What qualities did Moses have that helped him answer God's call?

_____

_____

Share In a small group, read and discuss Exodus 3:1–22. What surprises you about God's call? What would you find most difficult if you were Moses?

Memorial Meals

What is the meaning of the Passover meal and the Last Supper?

In the Bible, you read about the Israelites and their descendants, later called Jews, celebrating important events with meals. Two of these meals have very special meaning for us. In the Old Testament, God commands the Jewish people to remember the Exodus by celebrating the Passover meal. In the New Testament, Jesus tells his followers to gather in his memory and remember him in the breaking of bread.

The Passover Meal

Before God sent the final plague, he gave Moses special instructions for the people of Israel. Each family was to kill and eat a lamb and cover the door frame of the home with the lamb's blood. The angel of death would pass over the houses marked with blood, sparing the firstborn sons of the Israelites. On that last night in Egypt, the people had to eat quickly, making bread without yeast to save time.

This great and terrible night is known as the **Passover** of the Lord because it was the night that death passed over the houses of the Israelites. It would be remembered as a new beginning for the people.

Since that time, the Israelites, or Jewish people, have eaten a special meal called the Passover Seder to remember, make present, and celebrate God's saving power. The meal is celebrated around ritual questions and answers about the story of the Israelites' deliverance from slavery in Egypt.

➡ **How does the Passover meal help people remember the Exodus?**

➡ **Explain to a partner why Passover is still celebrated by Jews today.**

Young people read a Haggadah, an order of service, before celebrating the festive meal at a Passover Seder. The meal includes *matzoh* (unleavened bread), *maror* (bitter herbs), and *haroset* (a mix of apples, nuts, and wine).

Jesus Saves

God made a covenant with Moses and the Israelites, an agreement that he would be their God and that they would be his People. When God sent his Son, he made a new covenant with all people forever. This covenant calls for the same kind of faithfulness that the earlier covenant promised. By the grace of the Holy Spirit, you participate in this covenant every time you take part in the Church's Sacraments or make good choices. Because Jesus did God's will even in death, he is our **Savior**. God's saving work is completely fulfilled in Jesus.

Like the other Jews of his time, Jesus celebrated God's saving power at a Passover meal. As Jesus blessed bread and wine at the Last Supper (see Matthew 26:26–30), he told the Apostles that the bread and wine were a sign of the new covenant between God and his People. The bread and wine became Christ's Body and Blood.

The actions of Jesus at the Passover meal mark the new covenant brought about by Jesus' Death and Resurrection, offering salvation to all faithful people. The new sacrifice and holy meal, first celebrated at the Last Supper, is the Eucharist, which is still celebrated today.

© Our Sunday Visitor

Catholic Faith Words

Passover the Jewish holy day that celebrates God's leading the Israelites out of slavery in Egypt

Savior a title for Jesus, who came into the world to save all people who were lost through sin and to lead them back to God the Father

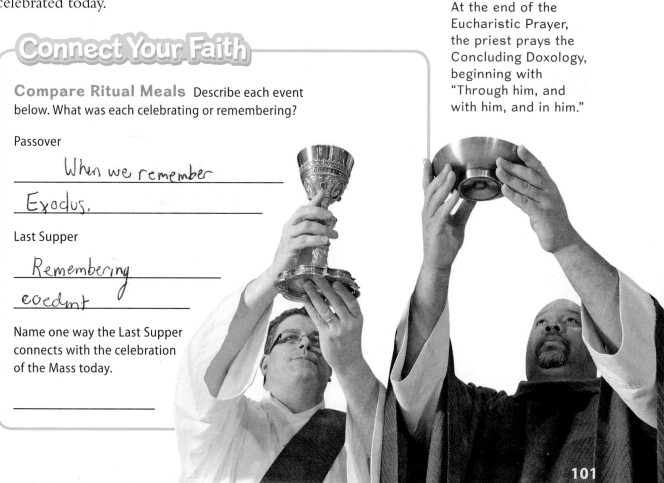

At the end of the Eucharistic Prayer, the priest prays the Concluding Doxology, beginning with "Through him, and with him, and in him."

Connect Your Faith

Compare Ritual Meals Describe each event below. What was each celebrating or remembering?

Passover

When we remember Exodus.

Last Supper

Remembering evedmt

Name one way the Last Supper connects with the celebration of the Mass today.

_____

Our Catholic Life

In what ways do you see God protecting you from evil?

God's saving action is needed to save humans from the power of evil. God calls his People to cooperate with the Holy Spirit in protecting their own lives and those of others from sin and the destruction it causes.

Consider the following suggestions for protecting your life and the lives of others. Use the words in the list to complete the sentences.

Actions that Protect

1. Stay close to God by participating in the Sunday ~~the~~ *eucharist*.

Word List

· · · · · · · · · · ·

freedom

Penance

Eucharist

2. Keep your focus on God, and be aware of his loving presence in your life. Trust that he is leading you to safety.

3. Make the Sacrament of *eucharist* and Reconciliation a regular part of your faith life.

4. Avoid situations in which you are tempted to lie, steal, cheat, disobey rules, or hurt others.

5. Choose your friends wisely. Good friends will help lead you toward *freedom*.

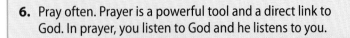

6. Pray often. Prayer is a powerful tool and a direct link to God. In prayer, you listen to God and he listens to you.

People of Faith

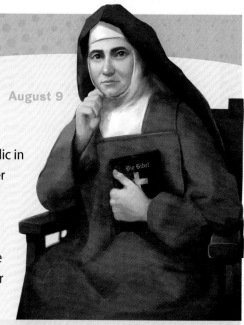

Saint Teresa Benedicta of the Cross, 1891–1942

August 9

Edith Stein was born in Germany to a Jewish family. She grew up celebrating Jewish holidays, such as Passover. Edith became a Catholic in her thirties and entered a convent. She took the religious name Sister Teresa Benedicta of the Cross. During World War II, she moved to the Netherlands. In the Netherlands, the Nazis began persecuting Jews. Because she was of Jewish origin, Edith was arrested and sent to the death camp at Auschwitz, where she was executed. Even though she became a Catholic, she never forgot the lessons she learned from her Jewish mother about the covenant God made with us.

Discuss: What helps you to remain faithful?

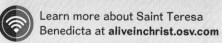

Learn more about Saint Teresa Benedicta at **aliveinchrist.osv.com**

Live Your Faith

Choose three words to describe where you are now on your own journey in life. How can you rely more on God to direct and guide you?

_____   _____   _____

Draw or write inside the GPS screen one way you can ask for more support and direction from family or the Church this week.

Let Us Pray

Prayer of Praise

Gather and begin with the Sign of the Cross.

Leader: When Moses and the Israelites were saved from the Egyptians, they responded in song. May their song be our song.

Reader 1: I will sing to the LORD, for he is gloriously triumphant; horse and chariot he has cast into the sea.
My strength and my refuge is the LORD, and he has become my savior.

All: The Lord shall reign forever and ever.

Reader 2: In your love you led the people you redeemed; in your strength you guided them to your holy dwelling.
You brought them in, you planted them on the mountain that is your own—
The place you made the base of your throne, LORD, the sanctuary, LORD, your hands established.

All: The Lord shall reign forever and ever. **Exodus 15:1–2, 13, 17–18**

Sing "Go Down, Moses"

Refrain: Go down, Moses, Way down in Egypt's land;
tell old Pharaoh: Let my people go.

FAMILY+FAITH
LIVING AND LEARNING TOGETHER

YOUR CHILD LEARNED >>>

This chapter explains how God calls ordinary people to accomplish extraordinary things, and describes the Exodus as the Israelites' journey from slavery in Egypt to freedom.

Scripture

Read **Psalm 118:1–5, 14** as a prayer of remembrance, thanks, and praise.

Catholics Believe

- God rescued the Hebrews from slavery in Egypt and sent his Son to save all people from the power of sin and everlasting death.
- The Passover and the Eucharist celebrate God's saving actions.

To learn more, go to the *Catechism of the Catholic Church #1150–1151, 1339–1340* at **usccb.org**.

People of Faith

This week, your child learned about Saint Teresa Benedicta of the Cross, a Jewish convert who was executed at Auschwitz.

CHILDREN AT THIS AGE >>>

How They Understand God's Saving Action It's hard sometimes even for adults to understand how Jesus' sacrifice was necessary and sufficient for the salvation of humans. Because of his or her emerging independence, your child might be vulnerable to a works-based view of salvation (i.e., I am saved if I do enough good things). Children this age are thinking about identity, and might base their efforts to live the Christian life on whether or not they feel they can do it. Your child needs to know that the grace given to us through God's saving action in Christ empowers us to do God's will.

CONSIDER THIS >>>

Think of some words we use that have multiple meanings, such as break, shape, *and* fire.

Faith is another word that has multiple meanings. As Catholics, we know that "God makes himself known to us through Revelation in order both to give us something and to draw a response from us. Both this gift of God and our response to his Revelation are called *faith*. By faith, we are able to give our minds and hearts to God, to trust in his will, and to follow the direction he gives us" (USCCA p. 37).

LET'S TALK >>>

- Ask your child to tell you about the relationship between the Last Supper and the Mass.
- Talk about special meals your family shares on Church feast days or special occasions. How do you thank God during those times?

LET'S PRAY >>>

Saint Teresa Benedicta, pray for us that we may never forget the promises God has made to us. Amen.

For a multimedia glossary of Catholic Faith Words, Sunday readings, seasonal and Saint resources, and chapter activities go to **aliveinchrist.osv.com**.

Chapter 5 Review

A Work with Words Fill in the circle next to the correct answer.

1. Whom did God send to lead his people out of Egypt?
   - ○ Jesus
   - ● Moses
   - ○ the pharoah

2. What is the Israelites' journey from slavery to freedom called?
   - ○ the ten plagues
   - ○ the pharoah's wrath
   - ● the Exodus

3. What do Passover and Eucharist celebrate?
   - ● God's saving action
   - ○ God's blessed water
   - ○ food from Heaven

4. When was the Last Supper celebrated?
   - ○ at the king's meal
   - ● at the Passover meal
   - ○ at the Exodus meal

5. What is the new sacrifice and holy meal that Jesus celebrated?
   - ○ the Seder
   - ○ a sacrifice
   - ● the Eucharist

B Check Understanding Circle True if a statement is true, and circle False if a statement is false. Correct any false statements.

6. The actions of Jesus at the Passover meal marked a new covenant of salvation. **True**/False

   _____

   _____

7. God sent twelve plagues to the Egyptians. True/**False**

   _____10 plagues_____

   _____

8. One way to preserve your life is to remain independent and trust no one. True/**False**

   _____Trust God_____

   _____

9. God delivered the Hebrews from slavery to freedom on the night of Passover. **True**/False

   _____

   _____

10. At the Last Supper, Jesus blessed bread and water. True/**False**

    _____

    _____

© Our Sunday Visitor

Go to **aliveinchrist.osv.com** for an interactive review.

Living the Covenant

 Let Us Pray

Leader: Teach us, O God, to follow your Commandments.
Help us grow to love others as much as you love us.

"Blessed those whose way is blameless,
who walk by the law of the Lord.
Blessed those who keep his testimonies,
who seek him with all their heart." **Psalm 119:1–2**

All: Teach us, O God, to follow your Commandments.
Help us grow to love others as much as you love us.
Amen.

Scripture

[Jesus said,] "Do not think that I have come to abolish the law or the prophets. I have come not to abolish but to fulfill. Amen, I say to you, until heaven and earth pass away, not the smallest letter or the smallest part of a letter will pass from the law, until all things have taken place. Therefore, whoever breaks one of the least of these commandments and teaches others to do so will be called least in the kingdom of heaven. But whoever obeys and teaches these commandments will be called greatest in the kingdom of heaven." **Matthew 5:17–19**

? What Do You Wonder?

- Why do Christians follow the Ten Commandments given to Israel?

- What is the "New Law" of Jesus?

God's Faithful Presence

What did God give the Israelites when he gave them the Ten Commandments?

An important rule of loving and lasting relationships is fidelity, or "faithful presence." God promised the Hebrews that he would be their faithful God and would protect them always. He also asked the Hebrews to be faithful and obedient to his covenant and to his laws.

The Ten Commandments

As the Israelites traveled through the desert, food began to run out. The people complained to Moses that it would have been better to remain as slaves in Egypt than to die of hunger in the desert! God responded by providing quail and a special food called manna. (See Exodus 16:1–11.)

ⓣ Scripture

The Quail and the Manna

The LORD said to Moses: I have heard the grumbling of the Israelites. Tell them: In the evening twilight you will eat meat, and in the morning you will have your fill of bread, and then you will know that I, the LORD, am your God.

In the evening, quail came up and covered the camp. In the morning there was a layer of dew all about the camp, and when the layer of dew evaporated, fine flakes were on the surface of the wilderness, fine flakes like hoarfrost on the ground. … Moses told [the Israelites], "It is the bread which the LORD has given you to eat."

Exodus 16:11–15

When the water ran out, the people complained again. So God commanded Moses to strike a rock, and water poured out. Even after these miracles, the people of Israel still complained. (See Exodus 17:1–7.)

God wanted the Israelites to be a holy people who would understand his loving relationship with all creation. When the people reached Mount Sinai, the Lord spoke to Moses at the top of the mountain and gave him the law of the covenant. The cornerstone of the law that God gave to Moses is the Ten Commandments. (See Exodus 19:1—20:17.)

God's Laws

God knew that his laws would nourish the Israelites even more than the manna and the quail. He knew that his laws would strengthen their relationships. The Ten Commandments appear in the Bible in both the Book of Exodus and the Book of Deuteronomy. The Ten Commandments are also called the **Decalogue**, which means "ten words." (Go to page 315 for a listing of the Ten Commandments.)

The Commandments reflect the heart of the covenant. The first three Commandments tell how to honor and respect God and his holiness. The other seven Commandments help people respect one another out of love for God. For example, the Fifth Commandment teaches us to respect the lives of all people because of our shared human dignity that comes from being created in God's image.

The Commandments were revealed by God, but they also express the basic law that is written in the human heart. That law, called the **natural moral law**, is unchangeable because it rests on an order that is present in all creation. The natural moral law is based on God's eternal law. It is the law written in your heart that helps you know what is good and what is evil.

God also gave his People other rules, which are contained in the Torah, or the first five books of the Bible. *Torah* means "law" or "doctrine." It contains stories that tell how God wants people to live and be faithful to him.

© Our Sunday Visitor

Catholic Faith Words

Decalogue another name for the Ten Commandments; the summary of laws that God gave to Moses on Mount Sinai. They tell us what must be done to live by God's covenant.

natural moral law rules about goodness that are written in our hearts and are natural to follow. However, our awareness of natural law can be clouded by Original Sin.

Share Your Faith

Reflect Review the Ten Commandments (see page 315). Choose two you think are most challenging for people your age and explain why.

Share With a partner, discuss your ideas and how each Commandment calls us to live.

© Our Sunday Visitor

Jesus' New Law

How do the Ten Commandments relate to the teaching of Jesus?

Even after Moses received the Ten Commandments from God, the people of Israel sometimes chose to disobey God. But their covenant with God helped the Israelites grow as a people as they wandered in the desert for forty years before crossing into the Promised Land. Through the new covenant, all faithful people are promised a place in the **Kingdom of God**.

The Teaching of Jesus

Jesus respected the Ten Commandments and used them as a starting point for his own teaching. When asked about which Commandment was the greatest, Jesus referred to two Commandments, "You shall love the Lord, your God, with all your heart, with all your soul, and with all your mind" and "You shall love your neighbor as yourself." (Matthew 22:37, 39). Together, these two Commandments are called the Great Commandment. Jesus said these two laws included all other Commandments. Later, at the Last Supper, Jesus washed his disciples' feet and told them, "I give you a new commandment: love one another. As I have loved you, so you also should love one another" (John 13:34). Everyone would know they were his disciples if they loved one another.

Catholic Faith Words

Kingdom of God God's rule of peace, justice, and love that exists in Heaven, but has not yet come in its fullness on Earth

New Commandment Jesus' command for his disciples to love one another as he has loved us

---

For those who are faithful to Jesus' **New Commandment**, God promises everlasting life and happiness with him in Heaven. The Holy Spirit was sent to help you believe in Jesus and faithfully live by his New Commandment.

➤ **What do the Ten Commandments, the Great Commandment, and the New Commandment all have in common?**

Connect Your Faith

Commandment Connections Match the words of Jesus, the Son of God, with some of God's "ten words." Then describe the similarities and differences you see.

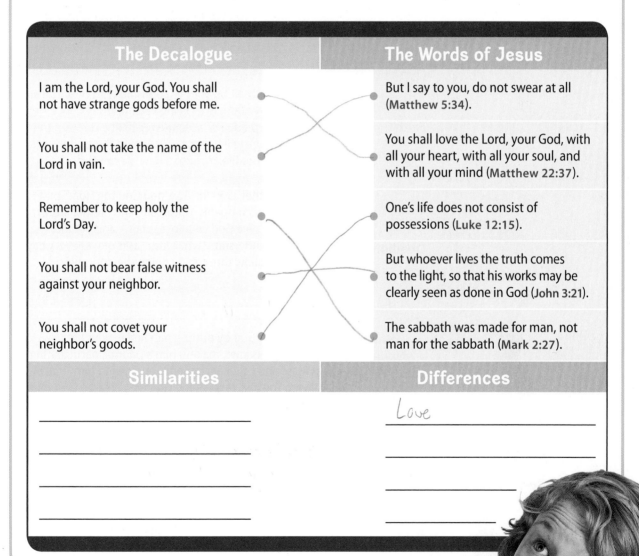

The Decalogue	The Words of Jesus
I am the Lord, your God. You shall not have strange gods before me.	But I say to you, do not swear at all (Matthew 5:34).
You shall not take the name of the Lord in vain.	You shall love the Lord, your God, with all your heart, with all your soul, and with all your mind (Matthew 22:37).
Remember to keep holy the Lord's Day.	One's life does not consist of possessions (Luke 12:15).
You shall not bear false witness against your neighbor.	But whoever lives the truth comes to the light, so that his works may be clearly seen as done in God (John 3:21).
You shall not covet your neighbor's goods.	The sabbath was made for man, not man for the sabbath (Mark 2:27).

Similarities	Differences
_____	Love
_____	_____
_____	_____
_____	_____

111

Our Catholic Life

How can you deepen your friendship with God?

God befriended you first. His love brought you into existence, keeps you alive, and remains with you forever. Being a close friend of God involves being faithful to him. Faith, obedience, respect, and trust are ways to respond to God's friendship and live out the first three Commandments.

 In the spaces below, describe how you would use these ways to live out the Commandments.

The First Three Commandments	
Faith	Your faith is built on your relationship with God. You are asked to have faith in a Divine Person, Jesus Christ. He gives you a pledge of absolute reliability. Through the Holy Spirit, he will be your companion through every minute of your life and into a new life beyond.
Obedience	God the Father, God the Son, and God the Holy Spirit promise you companionship, care, and eternal life. In return, you give God your love, praise, and obedience. You try to understand what Jesus asks of you every day. Then you follow through by doing the right thing. *God will tell you what he wants you to do.*
Respect	You respect God by putting him first in your life, following his laws, making him a priority, participating in Mass and other Sacraments, and giving him time in prayer. You also respect the God who created everyone by respecting the human dignity of everyone. You respond to Jesus by loving others. *I am going to pray every night.*
Trust	You are invited to have a deep friendship with God. You can lean on him as you would lean against a solid rock. If you truly trust him, he will not let you down.

People of Faith

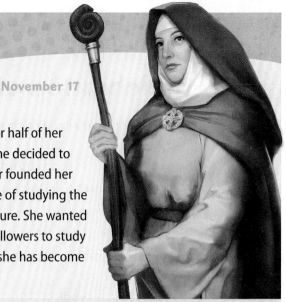

November 17

Saint Hilda of Whitby, 614–680

Saint Hilda of Whitby was a princess who lived in England. For half of her life, she lived at the royal court. When she was thirty-three, she decided to devote the rest of her life to God. She became a nun and later founded her own monastery at Whitby. Because she knew the importance of studying the Bible, everyone who joined her monastery had to read Scripture. She wanted them to read the Bible every day. She also encouraged her followers to study Latin. Because she valued education for both boys and girls, she has become the patron of many schools all over the world.

Discuss: What are some ways the Commandments have guided you in your life?

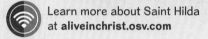

Learn more about Saint Hilda at **aliveinchrist.osv.com**

Live Your Faith

Choose one Commandment that you will focus on following every day this week. Write a short phrase or motto on the scroll that tells how to obey this Commandment.

Let Us Pray

Celebration of the Word

Gather and begin with the Sign of the Cross.

Leader: The Ten Commandments, the Great Commandment, and Jesus' New Commandment help us be faithful to God, ourselves, and others. Imagine that we are gathered with Jesus and the Apostles at the Last Supper. Listen to and reflect on Jesus' words to us.

Reader: A reading from the holy Gospel according to John.

Read John 15:11–17.

The Gospel of the Lord.

All: Praise to you, Lord Jesus Christ.

Leader: We turn our hearts and minds to God and ask him to bless those who love us and those whom we love.

Pray aloud your prayers one by one. After each, respond:

All: Lord, hear the prayer of your faithful ones.

Leader: Let us pray.

Bow your heads as the leader prays.

All: Amen.

 Sing "Love Has Come"

Word of God, enthroned,
dwell in us forevermore.
Love has come to show the way.
Hallelujah, peace be with us.
Love has come to show the way.

YOUR CHILD LEARNED >>>

This chapter teaches the Ten Commandments are laws meant to strengthen the relationship between God and his People, and explains Jesus' New Commandment in relationship to them.

Scripture

 Read **Matthew 5:17–19** to find out what Jesus teaches about God's Commandments.

Catholics Believe

- The Ten Commandments help you stay close to God and in right relationship with others.
- The Ten Commandments are the laws of God's covenant with the Israelites, which was revealed in its fullness in Jesus.

To learn more, go to the *Catechism of the Catholic Church #1949–1953, 1961–1966* at **usccb.org**.

People of Faith

This week, your child learned about Saint Hilda of Whitby, who was known for valuing education and promoting the study of Scripture.

CHILDREN AT THIS AGE >>>

How They Understand God's Commandments Because they are learning to be more independent and feeling more grown up, your child might approach rules with a certain bit of skepticism. It can help to understand that God's laws are given to us as a way to help us be the best that we can be—to find happiness in being and doing exactly what we were made for.

CONSIDER THIS >>>

What is the difference between a medical professional who does what is necessary and one whose actions come from the heart of compassion?

Most of us can think of a time when the compassion of a medical professional helped ease our discomfort. Because Jesus had compassion, he knew that following the Commandments without a heart of love was not enough. Jesus brought a new law centered on love. As Catholics, we know that "in Christ we have been called to a New Covenant and a New Law that fulfills and perfects the Old Law. We also are invited to experience God's love for us and to return that love to God and to our neighbor" *(USCCA p. 325)*.

LET'S TALK >>>

- Ask your child to tell you about the Ten Commandments.
- Together, describe what family life looks like when everyone follows Jesus' New Commandment to love one another as he has loved us.

LET'S PRAY >>>

 Saint Hilda, pray for us that we may follow your example of education and worship by treasuring and studying the Commandments. Amen.

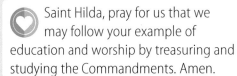 For a multimedia glossary of Catholic Faith Words, Sunday readings, seasonal and Saint resources, and chapter activities go to **aliveinchrist.osv.com**.

Chapter 6 Review

A Work with Words **Complete each statement.**

1. The Ten Commandments are also called the _____ which means "ten words."

2. The Israelites called the first five books of the Bible the

    _____.

3. God asks you for your faith, _____, respect, and trust.

4. The basic law written in your heart is called the _____.

5. The New Commandment that Jesus gave to his followers is

    "_____."

B Check Understanding **Write a brief summary of the chapter that includes the five terms from the Word Bank.**

6–10. _____

_____

_____

_____

_____

_____

_____

_____

_____

_____

_____

_____

_____

_____

Word Bank
fidelity
Torah
Decalogue
Jesus' New Commandment
natural moral law

© Our Sunday Visitor

Go to **aliveinchrist.osv.com** for an interactive review.

A Work with Words **Complete the following statements.**

1. The laws that God first gave to Moses are called the _____, or the Ten Commandments.

2. The Jewish holy day that celebrates God's leading the Israelites out of slavery in Egypt is called _____.

3. _____ is the Theological Virtue that makes it possible for us to believe in God and the things he has revealed to us.

4. During the _____, Jesus turned the bread and wine into his Body and Blood.

5. Directed and accomplished by God, the _____ is the Israelites' journey from slavery in Egypt to freedom in the Promised Land.

B Check Understanding **Match each description in Column 1 with the correct name in Column 2.**

Column 1	Column 2
6. Raised in a palace in Egypt	Joseph
7. Laughed when promised a son	Moses
8. Interpreted dreams	Jacob
9. Had twelve sons	Jesus
10. Taught a new law of love	Sarai

Fill in the circle of the choice that best completes each sentence.

11. The sacrifice and holy meal first shared at the Last Supper is the _____.

    ○ Mass
    ○ Eucharist
    ○ Passover
    ○ Great Feast

12. The natural moral law is based on _____.

    ○ the human heart
    ○ the Scriptures
    ○ God's eternal law
    ○ common sense

13. Jesus taught that the Sabbath was made for _____.

    ○ man
    ○ all creatures
    ○ God
    ○ priests

14. The name Israel means _____.

    ○ "one who laughs"
    ○ "one who struggles with God"
    ○ "one who leads"
    ○ "one who loves God"

15. On the night of the Passover, the people of Israel ate bread without _____.

    ○ water
    ○ butter
    ○ yeast
    ○ any other food

C **Make Connections** Write a response to each question or statement.

16. List three ways that you can be faithful to God in your everyday life.

_____

_____

_____

17. What might you pray for using each of the five forms of prayer?

_____

_____

_____

_____

_____

18. What are some things you can do to respond to God's love?

_____

_____

_____

19. Give an example of a time when God protected you from evil. How did he do so? What did you learn from that experience?

_____

_____

_____

_____

20. What do you think your reaction would be if God called you to serve him far away from home, as he called Abraham and Sarah?

_____

_____

_____

Jesus Christ

Our Catholic Tradition

- During Old Testament times, God chose leaders for his People who were anointed as priests, or prophets, or kings. (CCC, 695)

- The Gospels in the New Testament proclaim that Jesus was also anointed by God to be priest, prophet, and king. (CCC, 783)

- Jesus Christ is the Messiah whom the prophets spoke of, and whom God promised to send to his People. (CCC, 436)

How do the kings and prophets help you to understand what God expects of you?

The prophet Elijah witnesses to God's glory on Mt. Carmel.

Leaders for God's People

 Let Us Pray

Leader: Great and gracious God, be our leader. Lead us always to you.

"I will appoint for you shepherds after my own heart, who will shepherd you wisely and prudently."
Jeremiah 3:15

All: Shepherd us, O God. We are the sheep of your pasture. Lead and we will follow. Amen.

 Scripture

The LORD is my shepherd;
    there is nothing I lack.
In green pastures he makes me lie down;
    to still waters he leads me;
    he restores my soul.
He guides me along right paths
    for the sake of his name …

You anoint my head with oil;
    my cup overflows.
Indeed, goodness and mercy will pursue me
    all the days of my life;
I will dwell in the house of the LORD
    for endless days. Psalm 23

? What Do You Wonder?

- Why did God choose a shepherd like David to be king?

- Why is Jesus called the Good Shepherd when he was not a shepherd?

© Our Sunday Visitor

A New Leader

How did Israel get its first king?

Good leaders are guides who give direction, urge caution when necessary, and manage change. Good leaders earn your trust and make you want to follow them. Moses had many of the qualities of a strong leader, but he died just before the Israelites entered the Promised Land. Who would be their new leader?

The Bible Research Team

Ms. Gomez asked her class to read through the Books of Joshua, Judges, Samuel, and Kings, and to tell who followed Moses as leader.

"I know!" said Jamal. "After Moses died, Joshua led the Israelites into Canaan. God chose Joshua because he was a good military leader and he trusted God." Jamal explained that under Joshua, the people fought the tribes of Canaan and defeated them. After Joshua's death, other heroes were chosen to lead the tribes.

The Period of Judges

"That's where I pick up," Shannon said. "These heroes were called judges. Gideon and Jephthah were military leaders. Other judges, such as Samuel and Deborah, were prophets."

© Our Sunday Visitor

Catholic Faith Words

anoint to use oil to mark someone as chosen for a special purpose. In biblical times, the priests, the kings, and sometimes the prophets were anointed as a sign of God's favor.

Fill in the chart below with the names of two more judges you find in the Book of Judges in the Old Testament.

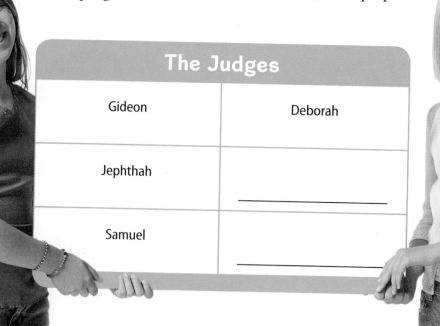

The Judges	
Gideon	Deborah
Jephthah	_____
Samuel	_____

Gracie continued. "Israel wasn't governed by human power, but by God alone. But the people of Israel were not always happy about this. They wanted a human king."

Israel's First King

Justin added, "The last judge of Israel, the prophet Samuel, thought that the Israelites were very foolish to reject God as their only king. Samuel warned the people that the king they wanted would have power over them. But he knew that God would give his People the freedom to find out for themselves."

"So," said Eldon, "God sent Samuel to **anoint** Saul with oil as the first king of Israel. This anointing showed that God chose Saul to be king. Saul was strong, tall, and very handsome. He seemed to be the sort of king that the people of Israel were looking for."

"Was Saul a good king?" Ms. Gomez asked.

"Saul became a great military leader," said Kelly. "But he didn't always obey God's commands, and soon his armies began to be defeated. Saul became angry and lost his popularity with the people."

"Then what happened?" the teacher asked.

"God told Samuel to find someone new to anoint as king," replied Kelly. "I think that's where we ended our research."

➡ Who was Israel's first king?

➡ How was he selected?

Deborah

Gideon

Jephthah

Share Your Faith

Reflect Look up one of the following passages. Then write the qualities of the leader you read about.

Judges 4:1–16 (Deborah) _____

Judges 6:1–24 (Gideon) _____

Judges 11:11–28 (Jephthah) _____

Share With two other students, discuss why the Israelites followed their leaders.

A Line of Kings

Why is Jesus called the Son of David?

God sent Samuel to Bethlehem to look for a king who would replace Saul. Here is the story of how the new king was chosen.

King David

Jesse's seven oldest sons were impressive, but Samuel rejected them all. God had told him not to judge from appearances.

Jesse's youngest son, David, was a humble shepherd, poet, and harp player. Jesse thought David was too young to be chosen as king, but Samuel asked to see him anyway. When the boy arrived, God told Samuel that David was the one who would be king.

 **Scripture**

Samuel anoints David

Then Samuel, with the horn of oil in hand, anointed him in the midst of his brothers, and from that day on, the spirit of the LORD rushed upon David. **1 Samuel 16:13**

© Our Sunday Visitor

David became a leader in Saul's army. (See 1 Samuel 16:21.) Later, after the death of Saul, the men of Judah anointed David as their king. David united the northern and southern tribes under his rule and made Jerusalem their capital. David was a great king who tried to understand God's will. He was a model for other leaders of God's People. (See 2 Samuel 2:1–7.)

Because of David's faithfulness, God renewed the covenant with him. God promised to establish a line of rulers that would start with David. One day, someone from David's house would sit on the royal throne forever. (See 2 Samuel 7:8–17.)

Jesus, Son of David

A thousand years after David ruled, Jesus was born and fulfilled the promises made to David. Christians proclaim Jesus is the King of Kings, and that his reign will last forever.

Jesus was like David in many ways, although David sinned and Jesus was without sin. Jesus' foster father, Joseph, was a descendant of David. Jesus was born in Bethlehem, where David had lived when God called him through Samuel. Like David, Jesus was a shepherd to God's People and called himself the Good Shepherd.

Both David and Jesus were anointed. In fact, the title **Christ** means "anointed one." God the Father anointed his Son with the Holy Spirit to be prophet, priest, and king. Both David and Jesus were great kings, but only Jesus is king for all eternity.

➡ **How is Jesus a shepherd to those who follow him?**

Men of Prayer

Both David and Jesus were men of prayer. David is credited with writing some of the **psalms** you sing today in the Responsorial Psalm during the Liturgy of the Word at Mass. This psalm is called responsorial because the assembly sings a response after each verse. Jesus prayed often to his Father and taught his followers how to pray. The Lord's Prayer that Jesus taught is one of the first prayers all Christians learn today.

© Our Sunday Visitor

Catholic Faith Words

Christ a title for Jesus, the One anointed by God as Messiah

psalms poems and hymns that were first used in the liturgy of the Israelites. Today, the psalms are also prayed and sung in the public prayer of the Church.

Connect Your Faith

Identify Leadership Qualities What qualities of good leaders did David and Jesus have in common?

_____

_____

Which qualities do you see in yourself? Which would you like to strengthen? Why is it important to have strong Catholic leaders?

_____

_____

Our Catholic Life

How does the Church celebrate Jesus as King all year long?

Catholics everywhere think of Jesus Christ as their king and leader. Jesus' kingship is so important that the Church celebrates the feast of Christ the King on the last Sunday of the liturgical year, just before Advent begins.

Honoring Christ as King

A flag has been designed to honor Christ the King. The design includes a blue panel with a gold star, a red panel with a gold cross, and a white panel with a gold crown. These symbols represent Christ's birth, Death, Resurrection, and kingship.

We all need to follow the example of Christ the King. As one of the King's subjects (one who is under his authority), you can follow his example in your attitudes, words, and actions by living according to his teachings all year long. Jesus shows us the way to true happiness and tells us the way to live in God's Kingdom now and always.

© Our Sunday Visitor

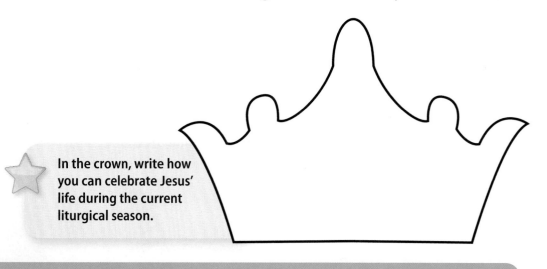

In the crown, write how you can celebrate Jesus' life during the current liturgical season.

The Liturgical Year

Advent the four Sundays of Advent before the Christmas season begins	**Triduum** includes Holy Thursday, Good Friday, and Holy Saturday
Christmas includes Christmas Day, the Feast of the Holy Family, and the Feast of Epiphany	**Pentecost** occurs fifty days after Easter
Ordinary Time I the Sundays between Epiphany and Ash Wednesday	**Easter** includes Easter Sunday, the second through seventh Sundays of Easter, and Pentecost Sunday
Lent includes Ash Wednesday, the five Sundays of Lent, and Passion (or Palm) Sunday	**Ordinary Time II** the Sundays between Pentecost and the first Sunday of Advent

People of Faith

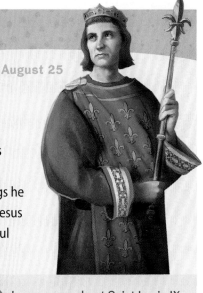

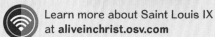

August 25

Saint Louis IX of France, 1214–1270

Jesus is the King of Kings, but earthly kings still rule countries. One king who was both a good ruler and a holy man was King Louis IX of France. King Louis believed that he was the "lieutenant of God on Earth." This meant that he felt responsible for ruling the way he thought Jesus would rule. Among the things he did was to send soldiers to the Holy Land to try to protect the places where Jesus lived and died. He gave a great deal of money to the poor and built a beautiful church to honor God.

Discuss: When you are a leader, how should you act?

Learn more about Saint Louis IX at **aliveinchrist.osv.com**

Live Your Faith

Design a Help Wanted Ad God needs wise men and women to lead his People in every age. Design a Help Wanted ad to let others know what qualities a person must have to be a good leader today.

♥ Let Us Pray

Psalm Prayer of Praise

This psalm prayer from the Old Testament helps us reflect on and gratefully praise God's wonders and works.

Gather and begin with the Sign of the Cross.

Leader: In gratitude, awe and love, we gather, knowing we are in God's presence.

Side 1: Give thanks to the LORD, for God is good. God's love endures forever.

Side 2: Give thanks to God of gods. God's love endures forever.

Reader 1: To God who alone does great wonders,
who by his understanding made the heavens,
his love endures forever.
Who spread out the earth upon the waters,
who made the great lights—
his love endures forever.

All: Give thanks to the LORD, for God is good. God's love endures forever.

Reader 2: To God who brought Israel out from Egypt
with a mighty hand and outstretched arm;
his love endures forever.
To him who led his people through the wilderness;
and gave them land as an inheritance,
his love endures forever.

All: Give thanks to the LORD, for God is good. God's love endures forever. **Based on Psalm 136**

 Sing "Give Thanks to the Lord"

YOUR CHILD LEARNED >>>

This chapter examines the Israelites' request for an earthly king, describes anointing to mark someone as chosen by God for a special purpose, and shows how Jesus is the Anointed One, our King of Kings.

Scripture

 Read **Psalm 23** to find out why the Lord is described as a shepherd.

Catholics Believe

- In Old Testament times, God chose leaders like Saul and David, who were anointed kings.
- God the Father anointed his Son Jesus with the Holy Spirit to be prophet, priest, and king.

To learn more, go to the *Catechism of the Catholic Church #60–64, 218–220, 695* at **usccb.org**.

People of Faith

This week, your child learned about King Louis IX of France. A zealous defender of the faith, Saint Louis sponsored two Crusades to the Holy Land.

CHILDREN AT THIS AGE >>>

How They Understand Leadership Many children want to be leaders. Your child is old enough to recognize the responsibilities that go with leadership in addition to the

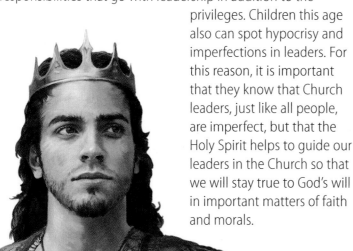

privileges. Children this age also can spot hypocrisy and imperfections in leaders. For this reason, it is important that they know that Church leaders, just like all people, are imperfect, but that the Holy Spirit helps to guide our leaders in the Church so that we will stay true to God's will in important matters of faith and morals.

CONSIDER THIS >>>

Have you ever considered that you were chosen by God to parent your child?

God gives you the grace to raise children in faith. As Catholics, we know that "parents are the primary educators in the faith. Together with them … all members of the family play [a] part in the education of the younger members.… The family is defined as a 'domestic Church,' that is, in every Christian family the different aspects and functions of the life of the entire Church may be reflected: mission; catechesis; witness; prayer etc. Indeed in the same way as the Church, the family 'is a place where the Gospel is transmitted and from which is extends'" (GDC 255).

LET'S TALK >>>

- Ask your child to tell you who King David is and what he and Jesus have in common.
- Talk about leaders, both youth and adults, in your parish who set good examples for the community.

LET'S PRAY >>>

 Dear God, watch over our leaders. Help them follow the example of leadership of Saint Louis IX of France to make decisions that are in accord with your will. Amen.

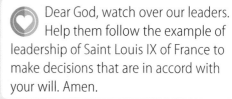 For a multimedia glossary of Catholic Faith Words, Sunday readings, seasonal and Saint resources, and chapter activities go to **aliveinchrist.osv.com**.

Chapter 7 Review

A **Work with Words** Complete each sentence with the correct term from the Word Bank.

Word Bank

Bethlehem	Joshua	psalms	Spirit
forever	Samuel	"anointed one"	Jesus
good	Judges		poor
		Jerusalem	

1. After the death of Moses, _____ led the people of Israel into the Promised Land of Canaan.

2. At the time of the _____, Israel was a nation ruled by God alone.

3. Christians believe that _____ fulfilled the promises made to David.

4. The last judge of Israel was _____. He anointed both Saul and David as kings of Israel.

5. The birthplace of both David and Jesus was _____.

6. Many sung prayers in the Bible are called _____.

7. The word Christ means _____.

8. "Blessed are the _____ in spirit, for theirs is the kingdom of heaven."

9. God promised David that someone from his house would sit on the throne _____.

10. After Samuel anointed David, the _____ of the Lord was with David.

Go to **aliveinchrist.osv.com** for an interactive review.

The Wisdom of God

 **Let Us Pray**

Leader: Teach us your wisdom, O Lord.

"The LORD gives wisdom,
from his mouth come knowledge and
understanding." **Proverbs 2:6**

All: All-knowing God, increase our trust in you, for
such is the beginning of wisdom. Amen.

Scripture

[Solomon prayed to God]: "Give me, therefore, wisdom and knowledge to govern this people..." God then replied to Solomon: Because this has been your wish—you did not ask for riches, treasures, and glory, or the life of those who hate you, or even for a long life for yourself, but you have asked for wisdom and knowledge in order to rule my people over whom I have made you king—wisdom and knowledge are given you.   **2 Chronicles 1:10–12**

? What Do You Wonder?

• What can wisdom help you do?

• Why can we call Jesus the wisdom of God?

God Gives Wisdom

What is wisdom?

God is the source of all wisdom. **Wisdom** is a gift from God that helps us understand his purpose and plan for our lives. Wisdom helps us know what will make us truly happy. Here is the story of a Saint who showed wisdom.

Saint Hildegard of Bingen

Saint Hildegard is an example of a person who used wisdom in the correct way: to glorify God. When she was very young, Hildegard began having visions of light. These visions helped her understand Scripture and other holy writings. A voice told her to share these insights, but she felt unworthy to do so. Eventually, she did write about the visions as a way to lead others to God.

Hildegard was interested in many topics, and she shared her knowledge of them. She wrote about virtues and sins, the nature of the universe, and the history of salvation. She studied the use of plants for medicines and wrote two medical books to share what she had learned.

Hildegard thought music was the best way to honor God, and even better than words for revealing wisdom. She composed over seventy songs, and wrote a play, poems, and letters.

Many people learned from Hildegard's writings and her talks. She traveled and spoke to nobles, scholars, and religious people. She challenged people to show care and compassion.

Underline what Saint Hildegard thought was the best way to honor God.

Wisdom Writing in the Bible

Wisdom was greatly admired by the people of Israel. They believed that if you did what was right, you would prosper; but if you did what was foolish or evil, you would suffer. Several books of the Old Testament contain wisdom writings of the people of Israel: Psalms, Job, Proverbs, Sirach, Ecclesiastes, and Wisdom.

Guides for Living

These books in the Bible offer guides for living. The Book of Proverbs is filled with teachings and short sayings that reflect the traditional insights of the people of Israel. You may have heard some of these proverbs.

Whoever meddles in the quarrel of another
is one who grabs a passing dog by the ears. **Proverbs 26:17**

The way of fools is right in their own eyes,
but those who listen to advice are the wise. **Proverbs 12:15**

Rich and poor have a common bond:
the LORD is the maker of them all. **Proverbs 22:2**

Gray hair is a crown of glory;
it is gained by a life that is just. **Proverbs 16:31**

As face mirrors face in water,
so the heart reflects the person. **Proverbs 27:19**

➤ **Which proverbs have you found to be true in your own life?**

© Our Sunday Visitor

> ## Catholic Faith Words
>
> **wisdom** a gift from God that helps us see God's purpose and plan for our lives. Wisdom leads us to see things as God sees so that we might live holy lives.

Circle the proverbs that sound familiar to you.

Share Your Faith

Reflect Think of someone you know who is wise.

Share In the Book of Proverbs, find a proverb that suits the person you have chosen.

_____

_____

_____

Then read the proverb to the group.

The Wisdom Books

How is God's wisdom shown by Solomon and Job?

The Book of Wisdom, often called the Book of Solomon, teaches in a different way. It is a narrative about the importance of acting wisely.

Solomon, the son of King David, succeeded his father as king. Solomon built a Temple in Jerusalem to give the people of Israel a place where they could worship the one true God. However, Solomon is remembered even more for his wisdom.

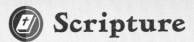

Scripture

Solomon's Request

Solomon asked for God's help. "I am young," he said. "So that I may serve you well, LORD, give me an understanding heart to judge your people and to know right from wrong."

God approved Solomon's request and replied, "Because you have not asked for wealth and power over your enemies, I will grant your request. I give you the wisest heart that has ever been or will ever be, and I will give you wealth, honor, and long life besides." **Based on 1 Kings 3:4–14**

Solomon knew that true wisdom comes from more than human insight. God's laws revealed his purpose and plan. Observing God's laws led to wisdom. Because of his faith, Solomon knew that true human wisdom is a participation in God's own wisdom and goodness.

➤ **What did Solomon ask of God?**

➤ **What gifts should leaders ask for today?**

1 Kings 6–8 describes the building of King Solomon's Temple to God. At its dedication, Solomon said, "I have built this house for the name of the LORD, the God of Israel" (1 Kings 8:20).

A New Way of Seeing

The Books of Wisdom and Proverbs primarily hand down traditional wisdom. Other books, like the Book of Job, challenge popular beliefs. Job was depressed. He was a very good man, yet he was suffering. Some friends told him that his troubles must be his punishment for displeasing God. But Job knew that he was good and demanded to talk to God directly.

God spoke to Job. Revealing all of his creative power and might, he reminded Job of who God is. A terrified Job responded this way:

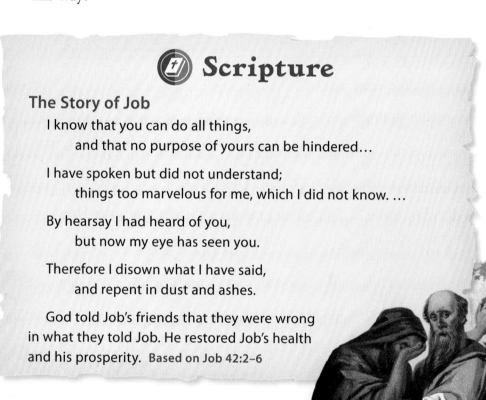

📖 Scripture

The Story of Job

I know that you can do all things,
and that no purpose of yours can be hindered...

I have spoken but did not understand;
things too marvelous for me, which I did not know. ...

By hearsay I had heard of you,
but now my eye has seen you.

Therefore I disown what I have said,
and repent in dust and ashes.

God told Job's friends that they were wrong in what they told Job. He restored Job's health and his prosperity. **Based on Job 42:2–6**

➤ **What is happening in this artwork?**

➤ **What does Job's posture tell you about his attitude toward God?**

Connect Your Faith

Learning from Experience Summarize the story of Job to a partner. Tell what you can learn from Job's experience.

Our Catholic Life

How can you make wise decisions?

You need wisdom when you make important decisions. Before making those important decisions, take time to look for God's wisdom in what you are going to do.

Here are some simple steps you can follow to help you make wise decisions.

1. Find a place where you can pray without distractions.

2. Pray to the Holy Spirit for wisdom and the ability to discover God's will.

3. Ask yourself the following questions:

   - Am I choosing between two things or among many things?

   - How would each decision help me trust God and obey his laws?

   - How would each decision make it harder for me to trust God and obey his laws?

4. Try to remember a Bible passage in which a similar decision had to be made. Think about what happened in the passage.

   - What passage did you choose?

   _____

   _____

   - How did the passage end?

   _____

   _____

   _____

5. If you are still not sure of the choice you should make, discuss the situation with a trusted adult, such as a parent or relative, a priest or parish minister, or a teacher.

6. After making your decision, continue to pray for guidance from the Holy Spirit.

Answer the questions above in the spaces provided.

People of Faith

Saint Thomas Aquinas, 1225–1274

When Saint Thomas Aquinas was a student at the University of Paris in France, the other students called him "the dumb ox" because he was big and didn't talk much. But Thomas ended up being one of the smartest and wisest men in the history of the Church. He wrote a three-part study of Catholic teaching called the *Summa Theologica*. He believed we become wise by the things we learn, but also through our faith in God. Saint Thomas also was a university teacher and a consultant to the Pope. Even today, people study his writings and teaching.

Discuss: What helps you to become wise?

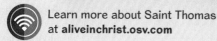

Learn more about Saint Thomas at **aliveinchrist.osv.com**

Live Your Faith

Read James 3:13–18. This passage describes true wisdom that comes from God. In the puzzle below, unscramble each of the clue words. Take the letters that appear in the circle boxes and unscramble them for the final message.

LULF FO MYRCE → F U (l) l   o f   m e r c (y)

NEELTG → G e n t l (e)

DOOG TUSRIF → G o o (d)   F r u (i) (t) (s)

URPE → p u r (e)

LEACEAPEB → p e a c e (a) b l e

MANTOPCIL → (c) (o) (m) p l i (a) (n) t

H e a **V** e n l y   **W** _ _ _ _ _ _

 **Let Us Pray**

Prayer of Praise

Gather and begin with the Sign of the Cross.

Leader: Lord, open our lips.

All: And our mouths will proclaim your praise.

Reader: A reading from the Book of Ecclesiastes.

Read Ecclesiastes 3:1–8.

The word of the Lord.

All: Thanks be to God.

Leader: Let us pray.

Bow your heads as the leader prays.

All: Amen.

 Sing "Holy Spirit"

Holy Spirit,
come into our lives.
Holy Spirit,
make us truly wise.

© 1998, Ken Canedo. Published by OCP.
All rights reserved.

YOUR CHILD LEARNED >>>

This chapter defines wisdom as a gift from God that helps us understand the purpose and plan for our life, and explains how the Wisdom books in the Bible offer a guide for living.

Scripture

 Read **2 Chronicles 1:10–12** to find out what Solomon asked God to give him.

Catholics Believe

- The wisdom tradition in the Bible teaches that true wisdom comes from trusting God and obeying his law.

- Jesus is the wisdom of God, sought in every age by those who are wise.

To learn more, go to the *Catechism of the Catholic Church #156–158, 215–217* at **usccb.org**.

People of Faith

This week, you child learned about Saint Thomas Aquinas. One of the most brilliant men who ever lived, Thomas' study of Catholic teaching, the *Summa Theologica*, is still read today.

CHILDREN AT THIS AGE >>>

How They Understand God's Wisdom Your child is growing in his or her ability to engage in a process of reflection on possible courses of action. This is a by-product of his or her growing skills in the area of abstract reasoning. Your child still might, however, need support in brainstorming alternatives and thinking of all the pros and cons when weighing decisions.

CONSIDER THIS >>>

What is the difference between wise and smart?

Most of us know someone who is "book smart" but does not seem to be wise. Wisdom is a Gift of the Holy Spirit. As Catholics, we know wisdom "enables us to see the world from God's viewpoint, which can help us come to grasp with the purpose and plan of God. It grants us the long-range view of history, examining the present in light of the past and the mystery of the future. It saves us from the illusion that the spirit of the times is our only guide" *(USCCA, p. 208).*

LET'S TALK >>>

- Ask your child to tell you about the wisdom of Solomon.

- Together discuss a time when someone in the family really needed wisdom. What did he or she do?

LET'S PRAY >>>

 Dear God, give us the ability to learn quickly and easily as Saint Thomas Aquinas did. Amen.

For a multimedia glossary of Catholic Faith Words, Sunday readings, seasonal and Saint resources, and chapter activities go to **aliveinchrist.osv.com**.

© Our Sunday Visitor

Chapter 8 Review

A **Work with Words** Match each description in Column 1 with the correct term in Column 2.

Column 1

1. A very good man who suffered
2. A very wise man
3. A wisdom book
4. Restored Job's prosperity
5. Also called Book of Solomon

Column 2

God

Book of Wisdom

Book of Ecclesiastes

Job

Solomon

B **Check Understanding** Fill in the circle next to the correct answer.

6. The wisdom tradition in the Bible is contained primarily in the _____ books.
   - ○ prophetic
   - ○ wisdom
   - ○ historical
   - ○ poetical

7. _____ is useless without a reverent trust in God and respect for his law.
   - ○ Fasting
   - ○ Human wisdom
   - ○ A good deed
   - ○ Prayer

8. One of the greatest examples of a wise person in the Old Testament is _____.
   - ○ Samson
   - ○ Pharaoh
   - ○ Solomon
   - ○ Esau

9. The Book of _____ is an example of wisdom literature.
   - ○ Proverbs
   - ○ Micah
   - ○ Genesis
   - ○ Exodus

10. The greatest way Jesus showed us God's wisdom is through his life, Death, and _____.
    - ○ good deeds
    - ○ good example
    - ○ prayers
    - ○ Resurrection

© Our Sunday Visitor

Go to **aliveinchrist.osv.com** for an interactive review.

Prophetic Promise

 Let Us Pray

Leader: With great mercy, the Lord keeps promises; the Lord fulfills all prophecies.

"Let your mercy come to me, LORD, salvation in accord with your promise."
Psalm 119:41

All: Send, O Lord, the Promise of Ages to dwell as guest-in-our-hearts and so to draw all creation home to you. Amen.

Scripture

The Lord himself will give you a sign; the young woman, pregnant and about to bear a son, shall name him Emmanuel. They name him Wonder-Counselor, God-Hero, Father-Forever, Prince of Peace. His dominion is vast and forever peaceful, Upon David's throne, and over his kingdom, which he confirms and sustains By judgment and justice, both now and forever. The zeal of the LORD of hosts will do this! Based on **Isaiah 7:14; 9:5b–6**

What Do You Wonder?

• Why did God send prophets to the Chosen People?

• Do we still need prophets? How can you act as a prophet?

God's Messengers

What message did the prophets bring to the people?

To be heard and understood is a gift. When a parent, teacher, or friend pays attention to what you have to say, you know that you are valued. When someone will not listen to you, it can be very difficult. Beginning around the time of the kings of Israel, God called certain people to speak the truth to the people and to summon them back to God. These people were called prophets. A **prophet** reminds people to be faithful to the covenant.

One person at the royal court, writing after the death of Solomon, might have written a letter like this one.

Catholic Faith Words

prophet a messenger from God who speaks the truth and calls the people to follow the laws of God's covenant and act with justice

exile the time when Judah, the southern kingdom, was conquered by the Babylonians (586 B.C.). As a result, the people of Judah were sent into Babylon, away from their homeland.

The Disturber of Israel

Dear Cousin Abi,

So much has been happening here at the royal court. The Kingdom has split in two, with Israel in the north and Judah in the south. But the big news is about prophets.

Since the Kingdom has been divided, there have been many false prophets. They speak for money or personal gain. And the court prophets just try to please their Kings.

Recently, however, a prophet named Elijah appeared in Israel. He has warned of years of drought to come. King Ahab called Elijah "the disturber of Israel." But Elijah replied that the true disturber of Israel is King Ahab's own household, because his family members worship idols.

What Elijah says is true. The people and rulers are turning away from God. I hope people listen to Elijah soon.

Your loving cousin,
Hanani

Underline why King Ahab is the true disturber of Israel.

© Our Sunday Visitor

Repentance and Restoration

The people did not listen to Elijah. God continued to send prophets, but the people still did not change their ways. Jerusalem fell to the Babylonians in 586 B.C. Many of the people of Judah were sent into **exile** far away.

The prophet Ezekiel saw the exile of the people of Israel as God's correction of their wrongdoings. In a prophecy called the Vision of the Dry Bones, Ezekiel shared a picture of the exile and what would come after it. The people understood the prophecy to mean that God would restore them to their land.

Melchizedek, Abraham, and Moses are featured on the north portal of Chartres Cathedral in France.

Who Are We?

Prophets in the north

- Amos criticized those who were wealthy for ignoring those who were poor.

- Hosea called the people of Israel unfaithful because they had other gods.

- Micah urged people to turn from their sinful ways back to God.

- Despite all the warnings, the people did not repent, and the Assyrians conquered Israel, the northern kingdom, in 721 B.C.

The great prophets in the south

- Isaiah's prophecies predicted punishment for the kingdom.

- Jeremiah predicted destruction if the people did not repent.

Share Your Faith

Reflect Read one of the passages below, and think about what the prophet means.

Isaiah 3:1–8

Hosea 12:1–4

Jeremiah 19:10–11

Amos 8:4–12

Ezekiel 37:1–14

Micah 3:9–12, 6:8

Share Act out what the message of one of these prophets is for your life or our world today.

Message of a Messiah

Who is the promised Messiah?

The prophets continued to speak to the people even after the Israelites returned to their homeland. Many of the prophetic messages told the people that God would send a **Messiah**, God's anointed or chosen one, to save them. Christians believe that these prophecies of a Messiah tell about Jesus.

© Our Sunday Visitor

Catholic Faith Words

Messiah the promised one who would lead God's People. The word Messiah means "God's anointed," or "God's chosen one." Jesus is the Messiah.

Incarnation the mystery that the Son of God took on human nature in order to save all people

The birth and life of Jesus fulfilled the prophecies of a Messiah coming to the Israelites.

 Scripture

The Chosen One

For a child is born to us, a son is given us; upon his shoulder dominion rests.

They name him Wonder-Counselor, God-Hero, Father-Forever, Prince of Peace.

Isaiah 9:5

Exult greatly, O daughter Zion! Shout for joy, O daughter Jerusalem!

Behold: your king is coming to you, a just savior is he,

Humble, and riding on a donkey, on a colt, the foal of a donkey.

Zechariah 9:9

Underline the similarities and circle the differences between these two prophecies.

Jesus the Christ

We hear these readings at Mass during Advent when we prepare to celebrate the **Incarnation**. During the Christmas season, we remember the meaning of Jesus' name: "God saves." Jesus can save us because he is both God and man, Divine and human. He shares our humanity in all things except sin.

When Jesus began teaching and healing, many believed that he was the promised one. Jesus is called *Christ*, a word meaning "anointed one" or "Messiah." In time, his followers also came to understand that Jesus was the Son of God. Through Jesus and in the Holy Spirit, all people share in God's promise of eternal life.

God still needs messengers to call people to be faithful and turn away from evil. Here are stories about two messengers.

Saint Paul

Saint Paul was one of Jesus' followers who traveled and told people about Jesus. When he left a place, he would write letters to the people there. The letters taught the new Christians more about Jesus, how to follow him, and ways to live in love and God's grace. Paul's messages still speak God's Word to us today. We read from his letters during many Masses.

Dorothy Day

When Dorothy Day was thirty, she became a Catholic. Together with her spiritual adviser, Peter Maurin, she founded the Catholic Worker movement. She started soup kitchens for those who were homeless. Until her death in 1980, she chose to live in poverty and was a witness to Jesus' message of love for all who are poor and homeless. Dorothy Day called for "a revolution of the heart… which must start with each one of us."

➥ **What qualities did Saint Paul and Dorothy Day have in common?**

Dorothy Day

Connect Your Faith

Find the Message Write two words that describe each person's message.

Saint Paul _____

Dorothy Day _____

Who in your community has shared a similar message?
Tell a partner how you have responded to one of these messages.

Our Catholic Life

What does it take to stand strong as the prophets in the Bible did?

The prophets in the Bible gave the people the messages God wanted them to hear. In this way, they helped people know God's will. However, sometimes he called prophets to deliver messages that the people did not want to hear: Stop hurting others! Help those who are poor! Repent of your sins and follow God's laws!

The prophets had to stand up for what they believed, and so do you. Perhaps one day you will have to stand up for someone who is being teased or mistreated. You may have to decide whether to go along with the crowd or go your own way. Like the prophets, you might be rejected or made fun of. Practicing right actions will help you prepare to stand up for what is right when the time comes.

Steps to Standing Strong

1. **KNOW WHAT YOU BELIEVE** Learn God's Word and follow it. He gives you wisdom and the knowledge of what is right and true.

   "With all prayer and supplication, pray at every opportunity in the Spirit. To that end, be watchful with all perseverance and supplication for all the holy ones and also for me, that speech may be given me to open my mouth to make known with boldness the mystery of the gospel" (Ephesians 6:18–19).

2. **PRAY FOR GOD'S HELP** Ask God to help you stand strong when you are pressured to give in.

   "So humble yourselves under the mighty hand of God, that he may exalt you in due time. Cast all your worries upon him because he cares for you" (1 Peter 5:6–7).

3. **TRUST GOD** Have faith that God will give you strength and help you say the right words at the right time.

   "The fear of the Lord is the beginning of wisdom; prudent are all who practice it. His praise endures forever" (Psalm 111:10).

4. **HAVE THE PROPER ATTITUDE** Follow the example of the prophets and of Jesus, all of whom displayed the attitude of humility.

   "Do not worry about how you are to speak or what you are to say. You will be given at that moment what you are to say. For it will not be you who speak but the Spirit of your Father speaking through you" (Matthew 10:19–20).

People of Faith

Blessed Jacinta Marto, 1910 –1920

May 13

Blessed Jacinta Marto was a modern-day prophet. Mary appeared to Jacinta, her brother Francisco, and their cousin Lúcia dos Santos at Fátima, Portugal. Mary gave them a message from Jesus, asking them to tell the world to repent and obey God's laws. She also told the children to say the Rosary and make sacrifices like giving up their lunches. Jacinta obeyed happily. Town officials, however, told Jacinta to stop speaking about the things that Mary had said. Even though she was threatened, she remained brave and continued to spread the message.

Discuss: How do you obey God's laws?

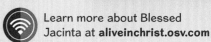

Learn more about Blessed Jacinta at **aliveinchrist.osv.com**

Live Your Faith

Read the Canticle of Mary in Luke 1:46–55. Write your own poem, modeling it on Mary's canticle. In your poem, describe one thing that God the Father, the Son, and the Holy Spirit are accomplishing in your life and in the world around you.

Let Us Pray

Prayer of Reflection

A prayer of reflection allows you to remember the things you have learned and consider how Jesus' words and actions affect you and the way you live each day. Reflective prayer helps us to quiet our bodies and minds and open our hearts to God's presence.

All: Sing "Sacred Silence"

Sacred silence, holy ocean,
gentle water, washing over me.
Help me listen, Holy Spirit,
come and speak to me.

Text © 2003, Tom Booth, Jenny Pixler and Anthony Kuner. © 2003, Tom Booth and Jenny Pixler. Published by spiritandsong.com® a division of OCP. All rights reserved.

Gather and begin with the Sign of the Cross.

Leader: We gather today in thanks. We've learned about the work of Jesus the Messiah, the Promised One as Isaiah tells us.

Read Isaiah 9:5.

The word of the Lord.

All: Thanks be to God.

Leader: During this prayer time, let us rest in God's love, grateful to the Father for sending his Son, Jesus, the greatest of the prophets.

Reflect on the Scripture passage. Be aware of how much God loves you, and listen for what his gift of Jesus means to you.

Leader: As we gratefully end these moments of reflective prayer, and at the Savior's command and formed by divine teaching, we dare to say:

All: Our Father, who art in heaven…

FAMILY+FAITH
LIVING AND LEARNING TOGETHER

YOUR CHILD LEARNED >>>

This chapter teaches that Jesus is the Messiah, God's promised one, and identifies prophets as messengers from God who speak the truth and call people to justice, and who are still needed today.

Scripture

 Read **Isaiah 7:14; 9:5b–6** to find out what the prophet Isaiah had to say about Emmanuel.

Catholics Believe

- Prophets are messengers from God who speak the truth and call the people to follow the laws of God's covenant and act with justice
- We understand that Jesus is the Messiah described by the Old Testament prophets.

To learn more, go to the *Catechism of the Catholic Church #709–714, 2581–2584* at **usccb.org**.

People of Faith

This week, your child learned about Blessed Jacinta Marto, one of the three children to whom Mary appeared at Fátima. Jacinta is remembered for her happiness and obedience to God.

CHILDREN AT THIS AGE >>>

How They Understand the Prophets Because they have grown in their ability to understand the various eras in Scripture, sixth-graders might think of prophets as people who foresaw the future. This is a part of what prophets did, but prophecy means more than this; it is sharing God's Word with others. Understanding this can help your child begin to grasp and live out our anointing at Baptism to share in Christ's mission as "priest, prophet, and king."

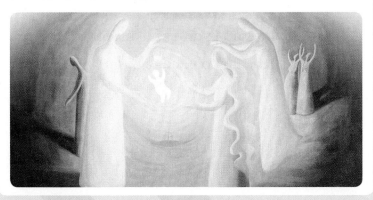

CONSIDER THIS >>>

Have you ever tried to pound a nail with something other than a hammer?

Life is easier when we use things for their created purpose. The prophets warned against unfaithfulness (people living not according to their purpose). As Catholics, we know that "though God is totally other, hidden, glorious, and wondrous, he communicates himself to us through creation and reveals himself through the prophets and above all in Jesus Christ, whom we meet in the Church, especially in Scripture and the Sacraments. In these many ways, God speaks to our hearts where we may welcome his loving presence" (USCCA p. 51).

LET'S TALK >>>

- Ask your child to tell you about why God sent prophets to his People.
- Discuss some of the messages of the biblical prophets and how they apply to your family today.

LET'S PRAY >>>

 Dear God, help us to be happy to follow the example of Blessed Jacinta and obey God's laws.

For a multimedia glossary of Catholic Faith Words, Sunday readings, seasonal and Saint resources, and chapter activities go to **aliveinchrist.osv.com**.

Chapter 9 Review

A Work with Words **Fill in the circle with the correct answer.**

1. King Ahab called _____ the "disturber of Israel."

- ○ Elijah
- ○ Isaiah
- ○ Jeremiah
- ○ Hosea

2. When the Israelites were taken to Babylon, they were living in _____.

- ○ Egypt
- ○ Assyria
- ○ Palestine
- ○ exile

3. The _____ communicated God's truth and call people to follow his law.

- ○ foreigners
- ○ prophets
- ○ kings
- ○ Canaanites

4. Many of the biblical prophets told of the coming of a _____, the one anointed, or chosen, by God.

- ○ man
- ○ woman
- ○ missionary
- ○ Messiah

5. _____ is not one of the steps to standing up for what you believe.

- ○ Knowing what you believe
- ○ Praying for God's help
- ○ Trusting only your own understanding
- ○ Having the proper attitude

B Check Understanding **Complete each statement.**

6. _____ wrote letters telling people how to live good lives.

7. The name _____ means "God saves."

8. The Assyrians conquered _____ in 721 B.C.

9. _____ prophesied punishment for the Northern Kingdom.

10. The _____ is the mystery that the Son of God took on human nature in order to save all people.

Go to **aliveinchrist.osv.com** for an interactive review.

Unit Review

A **Work with Words** Unscramble each of the clue words. Copy the letters in the numbered cells to the empty cells with the same number. Then use the phrase you have unscrambled in a sentence about the biblical prophets.

1. L E S A M U
   ☐ ☐ ☐ ☐ ☐ ☐
   3   9   6

2. H E J L I A
   ☐ ☐ ☐ ☐ ☐ ☐
   5

3. A I S A H I
   ☐ ☐ ☐ ☐ ☐ ☐
     4

4. A M J E I H E R
   ☐ ☐ ☐ ☐ ☐ ☐ ☐ ☐
       7   1

5. R E Z H A H A I C
   ☐ ☐ ☐ ☐ ☐ ☐ ☐ ☐ ☐
     2   8

☐ ☐ ☐ ☐ ☐ **N** **G** ☐ ☐ ☐
1   2   3   4   5   6   7   4

F ☐ **O** ☐   **G** **O** **D**
    8   9

_____

_____

_____

_____

B Check Understanding Match each description in Column 1 with the correct word in Column 2.

Column 1

Column 2

6. An understanding of God's purpose and plan

prophet

7. To mark with oil to show someone is chosen for a special purpose

Messiah

8. A messenger from God to the people

psalm

9. Poem or hymn used for worshipping God

wisdom

10. Title meaning "God's anointed"

anoint

Complete each sentence with the correct term from the Word Bank.

Word Bank

| Saint Paul | Elijah | Dorothy Day |
| Samuel | David | Isaiah |

11. _____ wrote letters to early Christian communities about living in love and God's grace.

12. _____ was a founder of the Catholic Worker movement.

13. _____ was the second king of Israel.

14. The prophet who anointed the first two kings of Israel was _____.

15. _____ was the prophet who was called "the disturber of Israel."

C **Make Connections** Write a response to each question or statement.

16. Choose your favorite proverb and describe what it means to you.

_____

_____

_____

_____

17. How do you think practicing right actions will help you prepare to stand up for what is right?

_____

_____

_____

18. How can knowing God's Word help you make wise decisions?

_____

_____

_____

19. Choose a prophet and explain how his message speaks to us today.

_____

_____

20. Describe a time when you felt like Job. How did God's wisdom help you?

_____

_____

_____

_____

UNIT 4

The Church

Our Catholic Tradition

- Jesus founded the Church and built it on Peter and the Apostles. (CCC, 857)

- The Church's mission and work is rooted in the Gospel, the Good News of God's Kingdom and his saving love. (CCC, 768)

- Jesus sent the Holy Spirit to give life to the Church and help us spread the Good News. (CCC, 798)

- All Church members share the Gospel with others, and together we become closer to the Triune God. (CCC, 738)

How does the Holy Spirit continue to guide the Church and help you be a witness for the Gospel?

CHAPTER 10

The Gospel Message

Let Us Pray

Leader: God our Father, we give you thanks for the Good News of our salvation.

"How beautiful upon the
mountains are the feet of
the one bringing good news,
Announcing peace, bearing good
news, announcing salvation, saying to
Zion, 'Your God is King!'" Isaiah 52:7

All: Loving God, open our ears, our minds, and our hearts to hear the Good News. Amen.

📖 Scripture

"Son, why have you done this to us?" Mary said to Jesus. "Your father and I have been looking for you with great anxiety."

"Why were you looking for me?" Jesus asked. "Did you not know that I must be in my Father's house?"

Jesus returned with his family to Nazareth and was obedient. He grew in age, wisdom, and favor.

Based on Luke 2:41–52

❓ What Do You Wonder?

- What is Jesus' "Gospel," his Good News?

- How did the Good News spread, and how can you help it continue to spread?

Jesus is the Good News

What Good News did Jesus share?

Jesus began to share his message as a faithful Jewish boy who knew the Hebrew story of faith. As the Scripture account of Jesus in the Temple as a young boy tells, he already understood that he had a unique role to play. In the Temple, he spent time listening to the teachers and asking questions.

Many years passed before Jesus, now a grown man, began his public ministry, proclaiming that "This is the time of fulfillment. The kingdom of God is at hand. Repent, and believe in the gospel" (Mark 1:15).

One day, Jesus would be revealed to all of his followers as the **Redeemer** who would give his life for all and save the human race from the slavery of sin.

→ **How could Jesus know so early who he was and what his role would be?**

© Our Sunday Visitor

Catholic Faith Words

Redeemer a title for Jesus, because by his Death on the Cross, he "bought back" the human race from the slavery of sin

Sabbath the seventh day of the week in the Jewish calendar. It is still observed by Jews as a day of rest, prayer, and worship.

Not long after he began his public ministry, Jesus went to the synagogue in Nazareth on the **Sabbath**, a day of rest, prayer, and worship, to read Scripture and to worship God.

 # Scripture

The Anointed One

On this Sabbath, Jesus was invited to read from the scroll of the prophet Isaiah. He read about the promised one, God's anointed.

"The Spirit of the Lord is upon me,
because he has anointed me
    to bring glad tidings to the poor.
He has sent me to proclaim liberty to captives
    and recovery of sight to the blind,
    to let the oppressed go free,
and to proclaim a year acceptable to the Lord."

After reading, Jesus said, "Today this scripture passage is fulfilled in your hearing."

Everyone was amazed. "Isn't this the son of Joseph?" they asked.

Based on Luke 4:16–22

1. Underline what Jesus said God had sent him to do.

2. Explain which of these things sounds hardest to you.

Share Your Faith

Reflect Imagine that you are one of the people in the synagogue, listening to Jesus.

Share With a partner, make up an ending for the story that tells what you think the people did in response to Jesus' announcement.

_____

_____

_____

_____

Then read Luke 4:28–30 to find out what really happened.

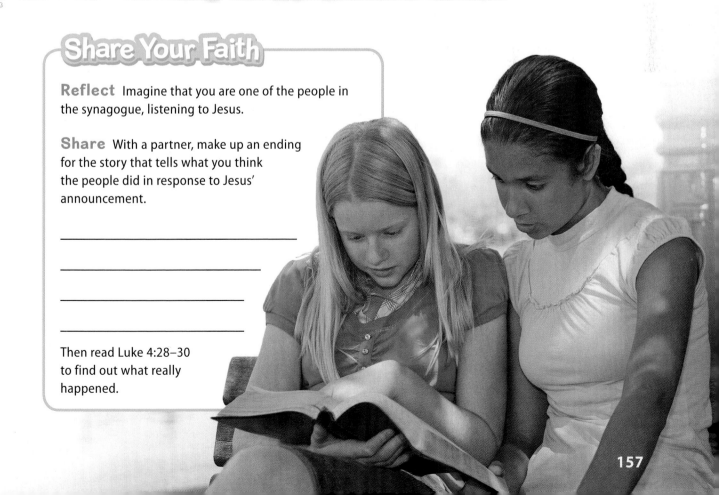

The Gospels

How did Jesus' Good News spread after his Ascension?

There were no reporters or historians taking notes when Jesus lived on Earth. The words Jesus spoke and the events of his life were handed down through oral tradition, by word of mouth.

After Jesus' Death and Resurrection, the Apostles and other followers of Jesus told people what they had experienced. Their stories were written down after a time and became the **Gospel**. The word *gospel* means "Good News." The Gospels are part of the **New Testament** of the Bible. They are the foundation of the Church's faith.

Catholic Faith Words

Gospel a word that means "Good News." The Gospel message is the Good News of God's Kingdom and his saving love.

New Testament the second part of the Bible, about the life and teaching of Jesus, his followers, and the early Church

Church the community of all baptized people who believe in God and follow Jesus. The word is often used for the Catholic Church because we trace our origins back to the Apostles.

The Gospel according to Matthew ▶ comes first in the New Testament. It was written after A.D. 72 and it is named for the Apostle Matthew, a former tax collector. This Gospel was written for Jewish Christians, and begins with a list of Jesus' ancestors. It includes many stories of healing and parables.

© Our Sunday Visitor

ST. MATTHEW

◀ **The Gospel according to Mark** probably came first, before A.D. 72. It is traditionally attributed to John Mark, a companion of Paul and Peter. This Gospel starts with the ministry of John the Baptist. Almost all of what the evangelist wrote is also in the Gospels according to Matthew and Luke.

ST. MARK

The Gospel according to Luke was also written after A.D. 72. The author was probably a companion of Paul. He wrote for ▶ Christians who were not Jewish, and he started his Gospel with the announcement of Jesus' birth. More than half of this Gospel is unique from the other Gospels.

The Church and the Gospels

After Jesus' Death and Resurrection, the Holy Spirit moved the Apostles and other followers of Jesus to announce the Good News to the world. They proclaimed that Jesus is the Son of the living God. By his Paschal Mystery, we are offered the gift of new life. The enthusiasm of Jesus' followers led many people to join them in believing in Jesus. Communities of prayer and worship started to emerge, and so the **Church** grew.

Over time, many names and images have been used to describe the Church.

- The Church is a worldwide **assembly**, or convocation, of all those who believe in the Good News of Jesus.

- The Church is the **Sacrament** of salvation. She proclaims and lives the Gospel in the world. The Church is the sign and instrument in Christ of the communion of God and humans. She is a visible and effective sign of God's love for the world.

- The Church is the **Body of Christ**. Christ is the head of the body. Through the Spirit and his actions in the Sacraments, Christ establishes the community of believers as his own Body. All members try to imitate Jesus as they continue his work in the world.

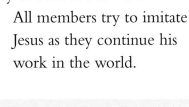

Connect Your Faith

Describe the Church Look up the Bible passages listed below. Write a description of the image of the Church in each passage. On a separate sheet of paper, design one of the images.

John 10:1–11 _____

_____

John 15:1–10 _____

_____

Revelation 21:2–3 _____

_____

The Gospel according to John was written near the end of the first century A.D. The author, probably a disciple of the Apostle John, wrote to a community of believers, probably in Asia Minor. This Gospel stands apart from the other three because so much of its content is not found anywhere else. ▶

Our Catholic Life

How does living in love demonstrate the Good News of Jesus?

Living the Good News involves loving others. You could stand in a school hallway and tell others about Jesus, or you could set up a website and announce the Good News from there. But one of the best ways to share the Good News of Jesus is to love and care about people as he loves and cares about them.

1. Circle the descriptions of love that best describe you.

2. Underline the descriptions of love in which you need to grow.

How to Live Love

1 Corinthians 13:4–8 gives an excellent description of what love is. Each description is actually something you can do or be.

Search It

Love **is patient.**

is kind.

is not jealous.

is not pompous.

is not inflated.

is not rude.

does not seek its own interests.

is not quick-tempered.

does not brood over injury.

does not rejoice over wrongdoing.

rejoices with the truth.

bears all things.

believes all things.

hopes all things.

endures all things.

never fails.

People of Faith

January 5

Saint John Neumann, 1811—1860

Saint John Neumann knew his vocation was to become a priest. However, he couldn't be ordained in his native country of the Czech Republic. So he came to the United States. Soon after his arrival, he was ordained a priest. He was sent to serve European immigrants, mostly Germans, in New York. Feeling a deeper call, he joined the Redemptorist Order and established many schools. Later, Saint John was named bishop of Philadelphia. He encouraged religious orders to settle in the area. He also built a number of new parishes and began building a cathedral.

Discuss: How do you respond to God's call to serve others?

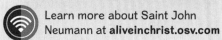

Learn more about Saint John Neumann at **aliveinchrist.osv.com**

Live Your Faith

The Church and You Create an image of the Church today that shows how you live as a member of the Body of Christ.

Let Us Pray

Prayer of Intercession

This prayer follows the format of the Prayer of the Faithful, from the Mass. We come before God, trusting he will care for the needs of others.

Gather and begin with the Sign of the Cross.

Leader: We gather, knowing our God loves us and hears us. We entrust to God our needs and the needs of all the world.

Reader 1: God of the ages, we look to you to guide all leaders to seek your truth.

All: Hear our prayer.

Reader 2: God of the suffering, hear us, we pray. Comfort your people, hold us to you.

All: Hear our prayer.

Reader 3: God of the searching, hear us, we pray. Guide us in safety and lead us home.

All: Hear our prayer.

Reader 4: God of the broken, hear us, we pray. Nourish our hungers and heal our hearts.

All: Hear our prayer.

Reader 5: God of all people, unite all nations and bring us peace.

All: Hear our prayer.

Leader: Loving Father, we know you are with us always. Send your Spirit to strengthen us to live out your Son's Good News.

All: Amen.

 Sing "Hear Our Prayer"

FAMILY + FAITH
LIVING AND LEARNING TOGETHER

© Our Sunday Visitor

YOUR CHILD LEARNED >>>

This chapter recalls some of the images that describe the Church, presents the four Gospels, and examines the ways in which Jesus shared the Good News of salvation.

Scripture

Read **Mark 1:15** to find out about the important announcement Jesus makes.

Catholics Believe

- The Gospels are called the Good News of Jesus because they proclaim his life and teachings.
- They are interpreted by the Church through Tradition and are the source of our belief.

To learn more, go to the *Catechism of the Catholic Church #109–119, 124–127* at **usccb.org**.

People of Faith

This week, your child learned about Saint John Neumann, who emigrated from the Czech Republic to the United States, and who served European immigrants as a priest.

CHILDREN AT THIS AGE >>>

How They Understand the Gospel Your child may recall that there is a Gospel reading at Mass, but might not have paid a great deal of attention to the passages up until now. He or she might also need some guidance on living the Gospel in everyday life. However, the sixth-grader's emerging abstract reasoning skills might make it easier to see the connections between the principles we profess as Catholics and the actions we take in our communities and schools.

CONSIDER THIS >>>

Do you think seeing a commercial repeatedly influences what you think about that product?

When we read or hear something repeatedly, we come to know it by heart. It becomes part of us. It can influence our motivations and our actions. As Catholics, we know that "if we want to know Jesus, we should know the Scripture. This is certainly true about the Gospels… which were written 'that you may [come to] believe that Jesus is the Messiah, the Son of God, and that through this belief you may have life in his name' (Jn 20:31)" *(USCCA, p. 79)*.

LET'S TALK >>>

- Ask your child to name the four Gospels and tell why they are important to the Church.
- Share what is most important to you in Jesus' message, and how you have shared that with others by words and actions.

LET'S PRAY >>>

 Saint John, pray for us that we may respond to God as he calls us to serve him and other people. Amen.

 For a multimedia glossary of Catholic Faith Words, Sunday readings, seasonal and Saint resources, and chapter activities go to **aliveinchrist.osv.com**.

Chapter 10 Review

A **Work with Words** Fill in the circle next to the correct answer.

1. _____ is a title for Jesus because by his death he "bought back" the human race from the slavery of sin.
   - ○ Rabbi
   - ○ Redeemer
   - ○ Incarnate One
   - ○ High priest

2. Reading from the scroll of Isaiah, Jesus announced that he was _____.
   - ○ God's anointed
   - ○ God's ruler of Israel
   - ○ God's priest for the Temple
   - ○ God's friend

3. There are _____ Gospels in the New Testament, the second part of the Bible.
   - ○ five
   - ○ seven
   - ○ three
   - ○ four

4. The Church is a worldwide _____.
   - ○ building
   - ○ assembly
   - ○ government
   - ○ country

5. An image of the Church with Christ as her head is the _____.
   - ○ assembly
   - ○ Sacraments
   - ○ Body of Christ
   - ○ olive tree

B **Check Understanding** Circle the word that best completes the sentence.

6. The Church is a visible sign of God's (love, power) for the world.

7. Jesus came to establish God's (creation, Kingdom) for all people.

8. Jesus went to the synagogue in (Nazareth, Jericho) to read the Scriptures and worship God.

9. When Jesus was a young boy, he and his family went to Jerusalem for the feast of (Passover, Pentecost).

10. The word (Redeemer, Gospel) means "Good News."

© Our Sunday Visitor

Go to **aliveinchrist.osv.com** for an interactive review.

The Early Church

 Let Us Pray

Leader: Renew us in your Spirit, O Lord.

"Send forth your spirit, they are created
and you renew the face of the earth."

Psalm 104:30

All: O Holy Spirit, inspire us; enflame us with your
love; help us embrace the mission of sharing
the Good News. Amen.

Scripture

Then Jesus approached and said to [his disciples], "All power in
heaven and on earth has been given to me. Go, therefore, and make
disciples of all nations, baptizing them in the name of the
Father, and of the Son, and of the holy Spirit, teaching
them to observe all that I have commanded you. And
behold, I am with you always, until the end of the age."

Matthew 28:18–20

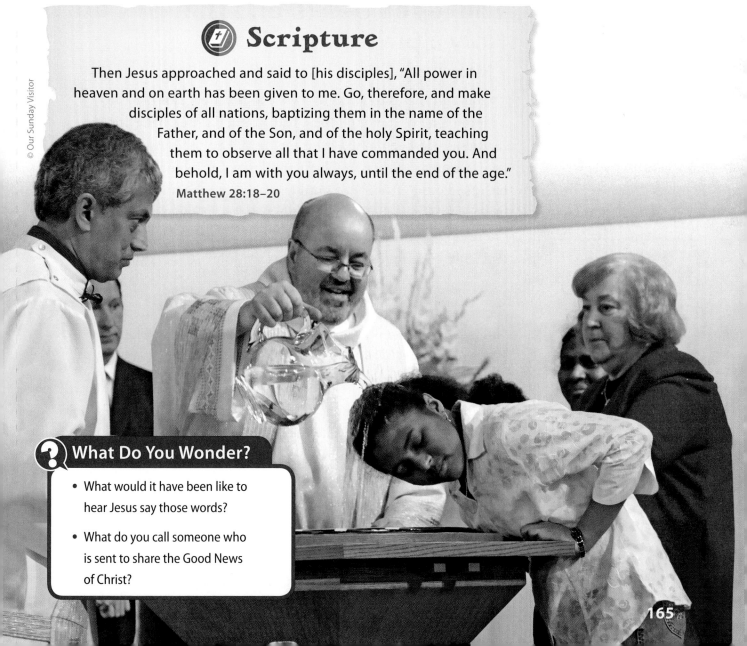

? What Do You Wonder?

- What would it have been like to hear Jesus say those words?

- What do you call someone who is sent to share the Good News of Christ?

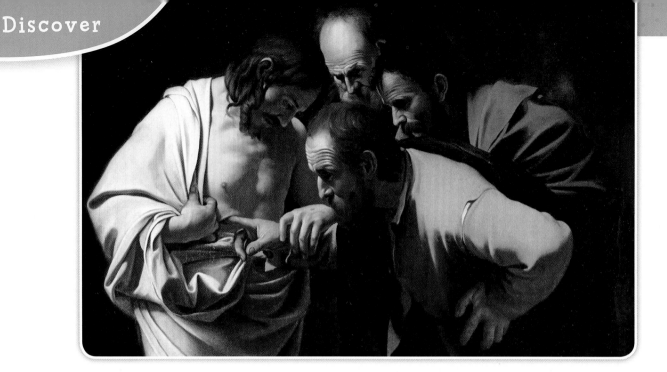

The Risen Jesus and the Holy Spirit

What happened after Jesus died?

Catholic Faith Words

Holy Trinity the mystery of one God in three Divine Persons: Father, Son, and Holy Spirit

The Apostles did not know what to do after Jesus died. In addition, one of them, Thomas, had a difficult time believing that Jesus had been raised from the dead. The other Apostles had spoken to the Risen Christ and knew his Resurrection to be a true event. It was not until Jesus entered the room without using a door and showed the wounds in his hands and side that "doubting Thomas" came to a fuller faith and realized that Jesus had truly been raised and was alive. (See John 20:24–29.)

Jesus appeared to the Apostles on another occasion. He told them that they would be his witnesses to the ends of the Earth, and promised to send the Holy Spirit, one of the three Divine Persons in the **Holy Trinity**. Then suddenly, Jesus was gone. He ascended to his Father in Heaven. (See Acts 1:1–12.)

After Jesus' Ascension, the Apostles remained in Jerusalem as Jesus had told them to. While they waited, they elected Matthias to replace Judas. Matthias had been with Jesus ever since John had baptized Jesus in the Jordan River. Mary, Jesus' mother, was also with the Apostles. She prayed with them and gave them hope. (See Acts 1:13–26.)

➔ What do you think the Apostles felt after Jesus' death?

➔ What gave them hope?

Scripture

The Coming of the Spirit

When the time for Pentecost was fulfilled, they were all in one place together. And suddenly there came from the sky a noise like a strong driving wind, and it filled the entire house in which they were. Then there appeared to them tongues as of fire, which parted and came to rest on each one of them. And they were filled with the holy Spirit and began to speak in different tongues, as the Spirit enabled them to proclaim.

Now there were devout Jews from every nation under heaven staying in Jerusalem. At this sound, they gathered in a large crowd, but they were confused because each one heard them speaking in his own language. They were astounded, and in amazement they asked, "Are not all these people who are speaking Galileans? Then how does each of us hear them in his own native language?"   Acts 2:1–8

Highlight the effect the Holy Spirit had on the Apostles.

Share Your Faith

Reflect Imagine that you are with the disciples on Pentecost. What are your thoughts?

Share With a partner list two gifts that the world needs from the Holy Spirit today in order to make communication better between different groups.

_____   _____

In the space below, write a short prayer of petition for one of those gifts.

_____

_____

The Church's Work

How does the Church carry out her mission?

The Apostles were excited. Jesus had given them a **mission** to spread the Gospel. Even though they had not known what would happen next, the Holy Spirit had filled them with courage and helped them to know what to say. Although Jesus wasn't physically present, they had his Spirit to guide and inspire them.

The Early Church

The story of the early Church is told in the Acts of the Apostles, the fifth book of the New Testament. Here you read how the Spirit transformed the Apostle Peter, a humble fisherman, into a powerful leader. Jesus had called Peter to be one of his first disciples. The special authority that Jesus gave to Peter made this Apostle first among the early leaders in the Church.

Unlike Peter, Paul was not a disciple of Jesus during the time when Jesus physically lived on Earth. On the road to Damascus, Paul met the Risen Christ and heard the voice of Jesus. He became a Christian and then a missionary. Missionaries are people who devote themselves to bringing the Good News to other people. Because Paul was chosen by Jesus and had met the Risen Lord, he is called an Apostle. On three journeys through Asia Minor and Greece, Paul proclaimed the Gospel to Jews and non-Jews.

➔ **Discuss how the mission of the Church today is similar to the mission of the early Church.**

© Our Sunday Visitor

Catholic Faith Words

mission a job or purpose. The Church's mission is to announce the Good News of God's Kingdom.

Apostolic Succession the term used to describe how the authority and power to lead and teach the Church is passed down from the Apostles to their successors, the bishops

The Apostle Peter became the first Pope of the Church.

Leaders and Martyrs

Many powerful leaders, including Roman emperors, feared the spread of the Good News and saw the emerging Christian Church as a threat to their power and influence. When Christians refused to renounce their belief in Jesus, they were often executed for standing up for their beliefs. Called martyrs, they suffered death in witness to their faith in Jesus. Both Peter and Paul were martyred.

The Church Today

Like the early Christians, Catholics today are baptized, and they gather for the Eucharist. They also pray over those who are sick, encourage the confession of sin, and promote faithful marriages. Some even sacrifice their lives as witnesses for Jesus, just as the early Christians did.

The Church is built on the lasting foundation of the Apostles. **Apostolic Succession** means that the bishops, in a direct line of succession from the Apostles, receive the authority and power of Jesus to lead and teach the Church. Therefore, bishops, united with the Pope, share in the mission of the Apostles. The first among the bishops is the Pope, who is Peter's successor and the visible head of the Church.

Pope Saint Pius X, reigned 1903–1914

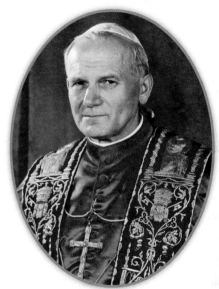

Pope Saint John Paul II, reigned 1978–2005

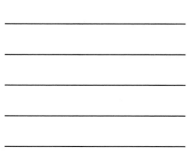

Name Similarities Name three ways the early Church was like the Church today.

_____

_____

_____

_____

_____

_____

_____

_____

Pope Francis, reigned 2013–present

Pope Benedict XVI, reigned 2005–2013

Our Catholic Life

How can you be a good witness for Jesus?

Witnesses are people who are called to testify about something they know or something they have seen or heard. You may have seen television shows or movies in which witnesses are called to provide evidence or information in a trial.

In the same way, God calls you to testify to your belief in Jesus. This means that as a follower of Jesus and as a member of the Catholic Church, you are called to be Jesus' witness in what you do and say in your daily life. Here is some helpful advice.

In the space provided, tell how you can use these ideas to be a faithful witness for Jesus.

Be a Good Witness

Be faithful. Follow the examples of the martyrs and Saints who were faithful and loyal to Jesus. These heroes of the faith were steady in their commitment to him, true to their word, and reliable in their actions.	_____ _____ _____ _____
Remember that Jesus is loyal to you. There will be times when your faith in Jesus will be tested. At these times, it may be easier to steal, cheat, be lazy, and betray Jesus than to be loyal to him. That is when you need to remind yourself that Jesus is the most loyal friend you have in the world.	_____ _____ _____ _____
Stay in touch with Jesus. It is difficult to be a friend to someone with whom you seldom talk. And it is hard to be a witness to Jesus when you seldom speak to him or take time to listen to the Holy Spirit. Make a habit of reading the Bible and praying daily.	_____ _____ _____ _____

People of Faith

Saint Timothy, 17–80

Saint Timothy traveled with Saint Paul, helping spread Christianity through Asia Minor and Greece. His story is told in the Book of Acts. His mother and grandmother probably were Christians as well, since Paul says they were pious and faithful. Timothy may have first heard about Jesus from them. Paul says that Timothy knew the Bible very well. He became a bishop in a city in Turkey and was stoned to death when he tried to stop some people from worshipping an idol. Saint Paul wrote two letters to Saint Timothy, which are in the New Testament.

Discuss: Who first told you about Jesus?

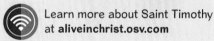

Learn more about Saint Timothy at **aliveinchrist.osv.com**

Live Your Faith

Write What You Believe When the early Christians witnessed to their faith, they told people what they believed. On a card, write a statement of your faith. Start by filling in the spaces below with what you believe about God the Father, Jesus the Son, the Holy Spirit, and the Church.

God the Father _____

_____

_____

God the Son _____

_____

_____

God the Holy Spirit _____

_____

_____

the Church _____

_____

_____

From the above ideas, write a summary statement on your card. Then decorate it with symbols of your faith in Jesus.

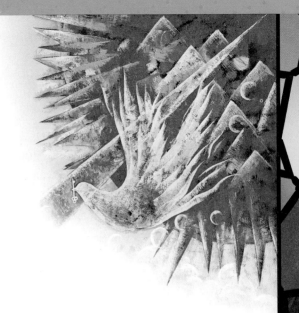

♥ Let Us Pray

Prayer of Petition

Gather and begin with the
Sign of the Cross.

Leader: Spirit of God, come
to our assistance.

All: Lord, make haste to help us.

Reader: Read John 14:23–27.

Side 1: Come, Holy Spirit, fill the
hearts of your faithful, and
kindle in us the fire of your love.

Side 2: Send forth your Spirit and we shall be created,
and you will renew the face of the Earth.

Side 1: Lord, by the light of the Holy Spirit, you have taught the
hearts of the faithful.

Side 2: In the same Spirit, help us choose what is right and always
rejoice in your consolation.

All: We ask this through Christ our Lord. Amen.

Leader: Let us pray.

Bow your heads as the leader prays.

All: Amen.

 Sing "Spirit, Come Down"
Spirit, Spirit, Spirit,
come down from Heaven.
Spirit, Spirit,
and seal us with your love.

FAMILY+FAITH
LIVING AND LEARNING TOGETHER

YOUR CHILD LEARNED >>>

This chapter is about the appearances of the Risen Jesus, Pentecost, and the story of the early Church told in the Acts of the Apostles.

Scripture

 Read the **Acts of the Apostles 2:1–4** to find out what happened on Pentecost.

Catholics Believe

- Jesus founded the Church through his life and teachings. He sent the Holy Spirit to help the Church fulfill her mission.

- The Holy Spirit continues to animate the Church today.

To learn more, go to the *Catechism of the Catholic Church #763–768, 849–854* at **usccb.org**.

People of Faith

This week, your child learned about Saint Timothy. He traveled with Saint Paul and served as a bishop in Turkey. He lived his life as a witness to his faith in Jesus.

CHILDREN AT THIS AGE >>>

How They Understand Church History Your child might not yet know a lot about the history of the Church. This is a great time to start learning about it, since children this age have a clearer concept of various time periods. Seeing the Church throughout history can also help to strengthen a sixth-grader's own identity, which is in development at this time, as he or she identifies with being Catholic.

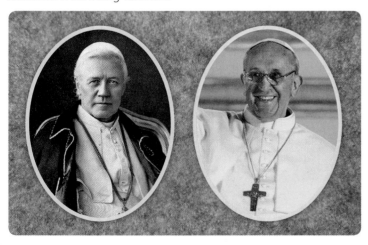

CONSIDER THIS >>>

How necessary is a good leader in achieving a goal?

Good leadership helps us to become and achieve more than we can imagine. Before Jesus ascended into Heaven, he knew the Apostles would need a guide to help them lead. He promised to send the HolySpirit. As Catholics, we know that "beginning with the gifts of the Spirit at Pentecost, the disciples became dynamic missionaries. He filled those disciples with the gift of courage so that nothing stopped them from proclaiming the love of Christ for all people" *(USCCA, p. 103).*

LET'S TALK >>>

- Ask your child to describe what happened at Pentecost, the coming of the Holy Spirit, and how the Church began.

- Share about a time when someone shared their faith openly and what impact that had on you.

LET'S PRAY >>>

 Saint Timothy, pray for us that we teach the world about Jesus as you did. Amen.

 For a multimedia glossary of Catholic Faith Words, Sunday readings, seasonal and Saint resources, and chapter activities go to **aliveinchrist.osv.com**.

Chapter 11 Review

A **Work with Words** Circle True if a statement is true, and circle False if a statement is false. Correct any false statements.

1. The Pope is the invisible head of the Church. **True/False**

   _____

   _____

2. The first leader Jesus chose for his disciples was Peter. **True/False**

   _____

   _____

3. A missionary is one sent to proclaim the Good News of Jesus. **True/False**

   _____

   _____

4. The story of the first generation of the Church is told in the Acts of the Apostles. **True/False**

   _____

   _____

5. A rabbi is one who suffers death as a witness to his or her faith. **True/False**

   _____

   _____

B **Check Understanding** Fill in the circle next to the correct answer.

6. Christians of the first century participated in Baptism and _____.
   - ○ the Eucharist
   - ○ sacrifices
   - ○ tithing
   - ○ holy wars

7. The _____ are the successors of the Apostles.
   - ○ deacon
   - ○ priest
   - ○ missionary
   - ○ Pope and bishops

8. Paul, chosen by Jesus and knowing the Risen Lord, is called _____.
   - ○ a disciple
   - ○ an Apostle
   - ○ a follower
   - ○ the Pope

9. On the day of _____, the Apostles spoke in different languages.
   - ○ Passover
   - ○ the Sabbath
   - ○ Pentecost
   - ○ Atonement

10. _____ found it difficult to believe in the Resurrection.
    - ○ Thomas
    - ○ John
    - ○ Matthew
    - ○ Peter

 Go to **aliveinchrist.osv.com** for an interactive review.

© Our Sunday Visitor

The Body of Christ

Let Us Pray

Leader: You are our shepherd, O God;
we are the flock you tend.

"For he is our God,
we are the people he shepherds,
the sheep in his hands." **Psalm 95:7**

All: Gracious God, keep us one in love, holy at heart, open
to all, and united in faith. Amen.

Scripture

They devoted themselves to the teaching of the apostles and to
the communal life, to the breaking of the bread and to the prayers.
Awe came upon everyone, and many wonders and signs were done
through the apostles. All who believed were together and had all
things in common. **Acts of the Apostles 2:42–44**

? What Do You Wonder?

• Do the people in your parish feel like
they are close?

• How did the disciples communicate
with the early Church communities?

Keeping in Touch

How is God's message shared?

People have always needed to communicate. Over the years, they have shared thoughts and instructions in many fashions. Today, the Church uses many ways to communicate God's truths.

Sharing God's Word Today

God's message to us has not changed over the centuries. However, the ways we receive and share it have.

Today, the Church encourages bishops, priests, and others to use modern information technology to do her work. In the United States, almost every parish, religious order, and diocese has a website that shares vital information with God's People. Blogs, videos, and other forms of social media can also play a positive role in instructing and informing Catholics. After the resignation of Pope Benedict XVI in 2013, millions around the world waited for news of the Papal Conclave and the election of a new Pope. Social media networks were quick to report the election of Pope Francis and share his first messages to the Catholic faithful.

Even though the Church supports technology, it is still important to recognize traditional ways of teaching, such as sermons and personal interaction. The basic message, what Pope Benedict XVI called "God's loving care for all people in Christ," should be presented faithfully. This will give a "soul" to the Internet and be a fitting use for social media.

© Our Sunday Visitor

Catholic Faith Words

Epistles letters written by Paul and several of the other Apostles to new Christian communities that they established. There are twenty-one letters in the New Testament.

Letters of the New Testament

In the early Church two thousand years ago, communicating long distance was much different from the way it is now. Until the 1900s, people communicated primarily by letter. It may be difficult to imagine a world without television, Internet, or cell phones. But your great-grandparents waited months for letters to arrive from other countries to hear news of their families.

The Apostles and many disciples took long journeys to spread the Word of Jesus, and they started many new Christian communities. When they moved on, many of them wrote letters, or **Epistles**, to the new groups. God spoke through these letters, and many of them are now part of the New Testament. The letters of Paul, Peter, James, John, and Jude tell the story of how the Apostles and others planted the seeds of Christianity.

A seller in St. Peter's Square at the Vatican holds a newspaper announcing the election of Pope Francis.

Share Your Faith

Reflect Read these passages to the right and put a checkmark by your favorite. What message does God have for you in that passage today?

Share your favorite passage with a partner. Explain your choice.

☐ Pray without ceasing … give thanks, for this is the will of God for you in Christ Jesus. **1 Thessalonians 5:16–18**

☐ As each one has received a gift, use it to serve one another as good stewards of God's varied grace. **1 Peter 4:10**

☐ For just as a body without a spirit is dead, so also faith without works is dead. **James 2:26**

☐ Let us love one another, because love is of God; everyone who loves is begotten by God and knows God. **1 John 4:7**

Marks of the Church

What do the Marks of the Church mean?

The Church is the community of all baptized people who believe in God and follow Jesus. The Letters of the New Testament show that the Church is one, holy, catholic, and apostolic. These four distinguishing characteristics are the **Marks of the Church** that have identified the Church from her beginning. You hear these Marks when you profess the Nicene Creed at Mass: "I believe in one, holy, catholic and apostolic Church."

One

Paul taught that the faithful are like many parts of one body, with Jesus as the head. Each part relies on the other parts to work well together. Paul is telling you that even though people are different, we all can work together in unity as the **Body of Christ**. In fact, the Church is made up of many different people from all over the world who acknowledge one Lord, confess one faith, and celebrate one Baptism.

1. Underline one time we hear the Marks of the Church.

2. Explain in your own words what it means to be one.

© Our Sunday Visitor

What Scripture Says...

One	Holy	Catholic	Apostolic
"As a body is one though it has many parts, and all the parts of the body, though many, are one body, so also Christ." 1 Corinthians 12:12	"Do you not know that you are the temple of God, and that the Spirit of God dwells in you?" 1 Corinthians 3:16	"And [God] put all things beneath [Christ's] feet and gave him as head over all things to the church, which is his body, the fullness of the one who fills all things in every way." Ephesians 1:22–23	"So then you are no longer strangers and sojourners, but you are fellow citizens with the holy ones and members of the household of God, built upon the foundation of the apostles and prophets, with Christ Jesus himself as the capstone." Ephesians 2:19–20

Holy

The Church is holy because she is set apart for God and his purposes, and God is holy. Christ gave himself up to make the Church holy and gave the gift of the Holy Spirit to give her life. The Spirit fills the Body of Christ, giving the Church life and uniting her members. Thus the Church is called the Temple of the Holy Spirit. The presence of God's Spirit in each person doesn't mean that members of the Church are not sinners. Members can avoid sin with the help of the Holy Spirit who dwells within them or, if they sin, can accept the divine forgiveness available through the Church.

Catholic

The word *catholic* means "containing the whole," or "universal." The Church is catholic because through Christ she proclaims the fullness of faith and provides everything you need for salvation. Her mission is to all people of the world.

Apostolic

The Church is apostolic because the teaching authority of the Church comes directly from Jesus and his chosen Apostles. The bishops of the Church are direct successors of the Apostles.

Catholic Faith Words

Marks of the Church the essential characteristics that distinguish Christ's Church and her mission: one, holy, catholic, and apostolic

Body of Christ a name for the Church of which Christ is the head. All the baptized are members of the body.

Connect Your Faith

A Letter to Paul Read 1 Thessalonians 5:12–22. Imagine that Paul has written one of the messages in this passage to your group. Answer him below, and tell him how the group has been following his requests.

Dear Paul,

_____

_____

_____

_____

Your friend,

Our Catholic Life

How do the members of the Church live out their faith?

The Church is often described as the Body of Christ. The Church lives in Christ and for Christ. You can view the Church as one large body with many local churches all over the world. You can also view the Church as individuals, all working together to make the body function. You are one of these individuals. You are the hands, mouth, ears, and feet of Jesus in the world.

The Church truly comes alive when members like you are living their faith. The New Testament letters offer some good advice to Church members.

1. Match the advice with its explanation in the chart below.

2. Draw a star next to the piece of advice you most need right now.

Advice from the New Testament

Beatitudes		Meaning
Love one another	● ●	This is one important way in which the Church expresses and lives out her faith.
Worship God	● ●	Put on the armor of God to fight against evil. This is God's protection for you against evil and sin.
Use your gifts for others	● ●	Jesus said that everyone would know we are his disciples if we do this for one another.
Be strong and courageous in your faith	● ●	God has given you these things, and he intends that you use them to help others. To do this, you must first think of yourself as a good, valuable, and beloved child of God. Then you can look around and see that you are surrounded by other children of God.

People of Faith

October 28

Saint Jude, First Century

Most of the Epistles in the Bible were written by Saint Paul, but one was written by Saint Jude. He calls himself a "slave of Jesus Christ and a brother of James." We know that his brother was a relative of Jesus, maybe a cousin, so Saint Jude was one of Jesus' cousins, too. In his letter, he tells us to be careful of people who lie. He also reminds us that the Church is a community of people. But most of all, he wants us to do whatever Jesus wants, just like a slave would do for a master.

Discuss: How do you do what Jesus would want?

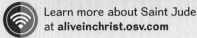

Learn more about Saint Jude at **aliveinchrist.osv.com**

Live Your Faith

Consider Romans 12:9–21 tells you how you can act as Jesus did toward others and build up the Church. Unscramble the words to complete descriptions of love.

1. Let love be **S E R E N I C** _____ .

2. **T H E A** _____ what is evil.

3. Hold on to what is **O D G O** _____ .

4. Love one another with **L A U T M U** _____ affection.

5. Show **R H O O N** _____ to one another.

6. Contribute to the **D S E N E** _____ of others.

7. Exercise **T Y I S O H T A L I P** _____ .

8. **J R E E C I O** _____ with those who **E J C I E R O** _____ .

9. **E P W E** _____ with those who **P W E E** _____ .

10. Do not be **T G H A H U Y** _____

Respond Which attitudes or actions do you find harder than others? Choose one to focus on this week.

Let Us Pray

Baptismal Promises

Gather and begin with the Sign of the Cross.

Leader: Joined together as one community, we are called to one faith.

Reader: A reading from the Letter to the Ephesians.

Read Ephesians 4:1–6.

The word of the Lord.

All: Thanks be to God.

Leader: Let us renew the faith of our Baptism.
Do you believe in God the Father?

All: I do.

Leader: Do you believe in Jesus Christ, his only Son?

All: I do.

Leader: Do you believe in the Holy Spirit, the Lord and giver of life?

All: I do.

Leader: Let us pray.

Bow your heads
as the leader prays.

All: Amen.

Sing "Yes, Lord,
I Believe/Sí Señor Yo Creo"
© 2011, John Burland. All rights reserved.

YOUR CHILD LEARNED >>>

This chapter identifies and explains the Marks of the Church and reflects on passages from the Epistles about the early Christian community.

Scripture

 Read **Acts of the Apostles 2:42–44** to find out about the early Church community.

Catholics Believe

- The Church is one, holy, catholic, and apostolic.
- The Church is a community of people, united in faith, working together to share the Gospel and become closer to God.

To learn more, go to the *Catechism of the Catholic Church* *#811–813, 830–831* at **usccb.org**.

People of Faith

This week, your child learned about Saint Jude, who was both Jesus' follower and one of his cousins.

CHILDREN AT THIS AGE >>>

How They Understand the Church Community At this age, your child is more able to participate in the larger parish community. He or she can assist in the liturgy (as a choir member, altar server, greeter, etc.) or help with a service project. Still, children this age are most likely to associate the community with their group of peers. Therefore, it is important that your child foster friendships in the parish through middle school activities or, in smaller parishes with no middle school youth group, through arranged activities between families.

CONSIDER THIS >>>

Whom do you rely on to support and encourage you in challenging times?

When we find ourselves struggling we often long for someone to give us an answer, someone who can tell us what is right or what we need to survive. As Catholics, we look to the Church to teach us what God intends. "The Church is built upon the foundation of the Apostles, who were chosen by Christ himself, and at whose head he placed Peter. The entire community of Christians received the Apostles' proclamation of the Gospel, and so the Church in her entirety is called 'apostolic'" (*USCCA, p. 132*).

LET'S TALK >>>

- Ask your child to tell you two things about the New Testament letters.
- Discuss what advice your family can benefit from most right now.

LET'S PRAY >>>

 Dear God, give us your grace so that we can serve you faithfully like Saint Jude. Amen.

For a multimedia glossary of Catholic Faith Words, Sunday readings, seasonal and Saint resources, and chapter activities go to **aliveinchrist.osv.com**.

Chapter 12 Review

A **Work with Words** Complete each sentence with the correct term from the Word Bank. Not all terms will be used.

> ### Word Bank
>
> | | | | |
> |---|---|---|---|
> | apostolic | letters | faith | communities |
> | belief | Christ | holy | love |
> | universal | Spirit | salvation | local |

1. The four Marks of the Church indicate that it is one, holy, catholic, and

   _____.

2. Paul taught that the faithful are like many parts of one body, with

   _____ as the head.

3. The word *catholic* means _____.

4. New Testament _____ were written to tell Christian communities how to follow Jesus.

5. A creed is a statement of _____.

6. Let us love one another, because "_____ is of God."

7. The presence of the Holy Spirit and the love of Christ make the Church

   _____.

8. Through Christ, the Church proclaims the fullness of _____.

9. "Do you not know that you are the temple of God, and that the

   _____ of God dwells in you?"

10. The Apostles and many disciples spread the Word of Jesus and started new Christian

    _____.

Go to **aliveinchrist.osv.com** for an interactive review.

A **Work with Words** Fill in the circle of the choice that best completes the sentence.

1. A letter in the New Testament written by Paul or another Apostle is called _____.

   ○ an Epistle
   ○ a psalm
   ○ a Gospel

2. The four Marks of the Church are one, _____, catholic, and apostolic.

   ○ loving
   ○ holy
   ○ righteous

3. _____ is the seventh day of the week in the Jewish calendar.

   ○ Sunday
   ○ The Sabbath
   ○ Purim

4. A formal statement of what is believed is called a _____.

   ○ testimony
   ○ witness
   ○ creed

5. Peter's successor and visible head of the Church is the _____.

   ○ Pope
   ○ disciple
   ○ priest

6. The Gospel that begins with the creation of the world is _____.

   ○ the Gospel according to Mark
   ○ the Gospel according to Luke
   ○ the Gospel according to John

7. The New Testament is about the story of Jesus, his followers, and _____.

   ○ the last days
   ○ the early Church
   ○ science

8. The one image that is not used to describe the Church is _____.

   ○ a chariot
   ○ the Body of Christ
   ○ a Sacrament

9. Paul was on the road to _____ when he met the Risen Christ.

   ○ Jerusalem
   ○ Damascus
   ○ Nazareth

10. The phrase "faith without works is dead" is found in _____.

    ○ The First Letter of John
    ○ The First Letter of Peter
    ○ The Letter of James

B Check Understanding Match each description in Column 1 with the correct term in Column 2.

Column 1   Column 2

11. Prophet whose words Jesus read in   Matthias
    the synagogue at Nazareth

12. Part of the Bible that includes the   universal
    Gospels

13. Apostle who replaced Judas   Isaiah

14. Day the Holy Spirit came to the   Pentecost
    Apostles

15. Meaning of the word *catholic*   New Testament

C Make Connections Write a response to each question or statement.

16. What gifts has God given you that you can use to help others?

    _____

    _____

    _____

    _____

    _____

    _____

17. What can you do to be a faithful witness for Jesus and fulfill
    the Church's mission?

    _____

    _____

    _____

    _____

    _____

    _____

18. What do you think the Scripture phrase "love never fails" means?

_____

_____

_____

_____

_____

_____

19. What picture or image would you use to describe the Church? Why?

_____

_____

_____

_____

_____

_____

20. Describe one of the four Marks of the Church in your own words.

_____

_____

_____

_____

_____

_____

Morality

Our Catholic Tradition

- Catholic morality is rooted in the Great Commandment, Jesus' New Commandment, and the Beatitudes. (CCC, 1984, 2055)

- Our conscience helps us to know what is right and wrong, and to know when we have sinned or been unjust. (CCC, 1778)

- In the Sacrament of Penance and Reconciliation God's forgiveness is given through the Church to those who have sincere sorrow and confess their sins. (CCC, 1422)

How do the Ten Commandments and the Precepts of the Church help you to live a life of charity, justice, and peace?

The Great Commandment

 ## Let Us Pray

Leader: Loving God, help me to cherish and follow
your law.

"The law of the LORD is perfect,
refreshing the soul.
The precepts of the LORD are right,
rejoicing the heart." **Psalm 19:8a, 9a**

All: Loving God, help me to cherish and follow your law.

Scripture

[A scribe asked Jesus], "Which is the first of all the commandments?"
Jesus replied, "The first is this: 'Hear, O Israel! The Lord our God is Lord
alone! You shall love the Lord your God with all your heart, with all
your soul, with all your mind, and with all your strength.' The second
is this: 'You shall love your neighbor as yourself.' There is no other
commandment greater than these." **Mark 12:28–31**

? What Do You Wonder?

• What does it look like when someone loves God
with all his or her heart, mind, and strength?

• Why is it sometimes so hard to love your neighbor?

Ephesians 2:19–22 tells us that we are "citizens... in the household of God... through [Jesus] the structure is held together; In him you are built into a dwelling place of God in the Spirit."

Old Law and New Law

What is the New Law?

Christians understand the Law of the Old Testament as the first step and a preparation for the New Law to be revealed by Jesus. The Old Law is summed up in the Ten Commandments. These Commandments are necessary to follow because they are the Word of God, and they will endure forever.

The great prophets of Israel, such as Isaiah and Jeremiah, tried to call the people back to the wisdom of God's Law and remind them of God's covenant of love with them. God revealed through the prophets that a new day would come when the Law would be fulfilled. This is how God spoke through the prophet Jeremiah.

Jeremiah

 Scripture

The Covenant

"But this is the covenant I will make with the house of Israel after those days—[says] the LORD. I will place my law within them, and write it upon their hearts; I will be their God, and they shall be my people. They will no longer teach their friends and relatives, 'Know the LORD!' Everyone, from least to greatest, shall know me—[says] the LORD—for I will forgive their iniquity and no longer remember their sin." Jeremiah 31:33–34

 Underline the law God has written in our hearts.

The Law Fulfilled

The people of Israel followed the Law of Moses, which included the Ten Commandments and other regulations. When Jesus came, he interpreted the Law in a new way.

© Our Sunday Visitor

Scripture

The Transfiguration of Jesus

One day, Jesus invited Peter, James, and John to pray with him on a high mountain. While Jesus prayed, he suddenly became radiant with light. Moses and Elijah appeared and spoke with him. A voice from heaven said, "This is my beloved Son, with whom I am well pleased; listen to him." The disciples were frightened, but Jesus reassured them. **Based on Matthew 17:1–8**

> ### Catholic Faith Words
>
> **Transfiguration** the revelation of Jesus in glory to the Apostles Peter, James, and John

This event is known as the **Transfiguration**, in which Jesus was revealed in glory to the Apostles Peter, James, and John as the fulfillment of the Law, represented by Moses, and of the prophets, represented by Elijah. God also showed that he had given his Son authority and that Jesus' words are true forever.

➡ **How would you have reacted if you had been there that day?**

Share Your Faith

Reflect The Law taught the Jewish people how to live in right relationship with God. Christians believe that Jesus is the perfect example of this. How are you living in right relationship with God right now? What could you be doing differently?

_____

_____

_____

Share Discuss with a partner some times when it is difficult to live by the Law.

Jesus Teaches

How does Jesus call you to live?

The Pharisees once asked Jesus which Commandment was the greatest. Jesus responded with a simple answer. His reply combines two teachings found in the Old Law.

Catholic Faith Words

morality living in right relationship with God, yourself, and others. It is putting your beliefs into action.

Beatitudes teachings of Jesus that show the way to true happiness and tell the way to live in God's Kingdom now and always

charity the Theological Virtue of love. It directs us to love God above all things and our neighbor as ourselves, for the love of God.

Precepts of the Church some of the minimum requirements given by Church leaders for deepening your relationship with God and the Church

Underline the foundation of Jesus' teachings.

The Greatest Commandment

"You shall love the Lord, your God, with all your heart, with all your soul, and with all your mind. This is the greatest and the first commandment. The second is like it: You shall love your neighbor as yourself. The whole law and the prophets depend on these two commandments." Matthew 22:37–40

This is known as the Great Commandment. Jesus told his followers that he did not come to change the Law of Moses, but to fulfill it. His words and the authority with which he spoke stirred up a great deal of interest. Catholic **morality**, which teaches us to live in a right relationship with God, ourselves, and others, is rooted in the Great Commandment, his Sermon on the Mount, and his New Commandment to love as he loves.

Jesus' teachings about living in and for God's Kingdom are called the **Beatitudes**. The Beatitudes are more than laws; they are a call to a holy way of life, a sign of God's Kingdom, and a source of hope. (See Matthew 5:3–12.)

Freedom to Love

As often happens today, many people in Jesus' day equated happiness with trouble-free lives, security, and wealth. Jesus calls you to a form of happiness that is greater than any happiness that material things can give. To help you follow this path, the Holy Spirit empowers you with a willing heart, self-discipline, strength to pray, and the courage to keep your eyes focused on God.

Jesus brings a law of freedom. It sets you free to love God and others—to live the Great Commandment. The virtue of **charity** is a gift of the Holy Spirit, prompting you to live with love toward all. Charity allows you to show God's love to those who need it most—children, those who are poor and in need, and even your enemies. Charity is the only way of life for a Christian.

The Church's Precepts

The Church offers you guidance for living a moral life. The **Precepts of the Church**, for example, describe some important duties of Catholics. The Precepts are rooted in the love of Christ. They can help you grow in your love of God and neighbor. The Precepts are listed on page 317 in the Our Catholic Tradition section of your book.

As you practice living the Beatitudes and strengthening yourself through the Spirit's gift of charity, you will live the Precepts out of love, rather than from a sense of duty.

© Our Sunday Visitor

Connect Your Faith

Tell About a Christ-like Person Think of a person who is a good example of the life of a true Christian. Create a word map telling all the Christ-like qualities of this person.

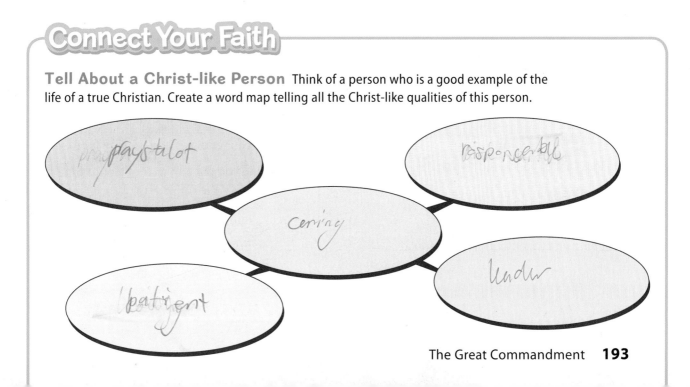

Our Catholic Life

What does it mean to keep the Great Commandment?

Jesus wants you to love God first and then to love your neighbor as you love yourself. He said that the Law and the prophets rest on these two Commandments.

Here are some ways to keep the Great Commandment.

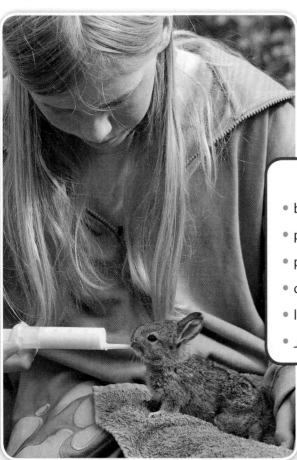

Add your own ideas to the lists.

You can love God by ...

- being faithful to God's laws.
- participating at Mass.
- praying often.
- caring for creation.
- loving your neighbor as you love yourself.
- _helping others_

You can love your neighbor by ...

- respecting and caring for members of your family.
- being a good friend to others.
- loving your enemies and praying for them.
- showing compassion or concern for others' troubles.
- being kind, patient, gentle, and humble.
- acting justly.
- forgiving when you are hurt.
- _helping out_

You can love yourself by ...

- taking care of your body.
- educating your mind.
- practicing the virtue of chastity.
- keeping your heart and spirit free to love.
- avoiding tobacco products and illegal drugs.
- _getting enough sleep_

People of Faith

Blessed Pier Giorgio Frassati, 1901–1925

Blessed Pier Giorgio Frassati was a young Italian who loved the outdoors, his friends, and having fun. But he also was deeply involved in works of charity. He would give his train money to the poor and then have to run home in time for dinner. Sometimes he even gave his coat to beggars. He lived his whole life following the Great Commandment. When he was only twenty-four, he contracted polio and died. At his funeral, hundreds of people he had helped came to pray. Pope Saint John Paul II called him "a man of the Beatitudes."

Discuss: What Beatitude do you find the easiest to live?

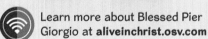 Learn more about Blessed Pier Giorgio at **aliveinchrist.osv.com**

Live Your Faith

Tell what Catholic morality means when it comes to your relationship with:

God

pray to God.

Don't say God's name in vain

thanking God

Yourself

taking care of yourself

don't hurt yourself

Others

be kind!

help out

Let Us Pray

Lectio Divina

This ancient prayer of the Church is a slow praying of the Scriptures, in which we listen for what the Holy Spirit wants us to hear.

Gather and begin with the Sign of the Cross.

Leader: Come Holy Spirit. Open our ears;

All: open our minds; open our hearts; open our hands.
Based on Mark 8:22–25

Read Matthew 17:1–8
First Reflection
Read Matthew 17:1–8
Second Reflection
Read Matthew 17:1–8
Third Reflection

Leader: At the Savior's command
and formed by divine teaching,
we dare to say:

All: Our Father,
who art in heaven …

Sing "Open My Eyes"

Open my eyes, Lord.
Help me to see your face.
Open my eyes, Lord.
Help me to see.
© 1988, 1999, Jesse Manibusan.
Published by spiritandsong.com®,
a division of OCP. All rights reserved.

FAMILY+FAITH
LIVING AND LEARNING TOGETHER

YOUR CHILD LEARNED >>>

This chapter explains the Great Commandment in relationship to the Ten Commandments and Jesus' New Law, and explores how the Precepts of the Church guide the faithful.

Scripture

 Read **Mark 12:28–31** to find out what Jesus says is the first of all Commandments.

Catholics Believe

- Jesus brings a New Law of love and freedom rooted in the Great Commandment and Ten Commandments.
- The Beatitudes and the Precepts of the Church help the faithful live holy and dutiful lives.

To learn more, go to the *Catechism of the Catholic Church #1716–1729, 1970–1974, 2041–2043, 2055* at **usccb.org**.

People of Faith

This week, your child learned about Blessed Pier Giorgio Frassati, a young Italian student whose life prompted Pope Saint John Paul II to call him "a man of the Beatitudes."

CHILDREN AT THIS AGE >>>

How They Understand the Great Commandment

The Great Commandment of Jesus makes sense to your child, who is capable of seeing how all of the other Commandments fit into these larger categories. At a time when rules are sometimes seen by the middle-school student as stifling his or her independence, the Great Commandment can be a useful shorthand to encourage critical thinking and self-reflection on moral issues.

CONSIDER THIS >>>

What makes you lovable?

Do you find it hard to answer that question? Knowing why we are lovable might seem to fly in the face of humility. Yet, knowing ourselves as a beloved child of God is the very core of our faith. You were created by love, in love. How could you be more loved? As Catholics, we know that "human life, as a profound unity of physical and spiritual dimensions, is sacred. It is distinct from all other forms of life, since it alone is imprinted with the very image of its Creator" (*USCCA p. 310*).

LET'S TALK >>>

- Ask your child to explain the Great Commandment.
- Think of a moral issue you have recently discussed with your child. How can the Great Commandment aid in the discussion?

LET'S PRAY >>>

 Blessed Pier Giorgio, help us to live the Great Commandment in our lives as you did in yours. Amen.

For a multimedia glossary of Catholic Faith Words, Sunday readings, seasonal and Saint resources, and chapter activities go to **aliveinchrist.osv.com**.

Chapter 13 Review

A Work with Words Circle True if a statement is true, and circle False if a statement is false. Correct any false statements.

1. Jesus said to love your enemies and pray for those who hate you. **True/**~~**False**~~

_____

2. Following rules is at the heart of the Great Commandment of love. **True/**~~**False**~~

_____

3. The Beatitudes are more than laws; they are a call to a way of life and a source of hope in difficult times. **True/**~~**False**~~

_____

4. The Sermon on the Mount is the revelation of Jesus in glory to the Apostles Peter, James, and John. **True/**~~**False**~~

_____

5. The Precepts of the Church are teachings meant to help you grow in the love of God and neighbor. **True/**~~**False**~~

_____

B Check Understanding Read Matthew 5:3–10. List five of the groups of people who are blessed, according to the Beatitudes. Explain what each Beatitude you've listed means, and give an example of how you can live it today.

6. _____

_____

7. _____

_____

8. _____

_____

9. _____

_____

10. _____

_____

Go to **aliveinchrist.osv.com** for an interactive review.

Justice and Peace

 Let Us Pray

Leader: Lord God, help us work hard for justice
so that all people may live in peace.

"The LORD does righteous deeds,
brings justice to all the oppressed."
Psalm 103:6

All: Lord God, help us work hard for justice
so that all people may live in peace. Amen.

Scripture

Learn to do good. Make justice your aim: redress the wronged, hear the orphan's plea, defend the widow.   **Isaiah 1:17**

? What Do You Wonder?

- What is the difference between what's fair and what's just?

- Why is working for justice linked to peace and acting as a peacemaker?

Seeking Justice

What does it mean to act justly?

The search for justice is a response to the natural moral law, rules about goodness that are written in our hearts and are natural to follow. The natural moral law expresses the God-given human dignity, or inner worth, of all persons. Anything that robs us of that dignity is unjust. Unborn children, the elderly, family members, enemies, people who live in other lands, people who are poor, even criminals in prison—all are humans with God-given dignity.

Justice means giving God and other people what is due to them. It is one of the **virtues** that help you grow in love for God and others. We learn about virtues and the Christian life in the Beatitudes, including "just" living.

God's **grace** helps you live a virtuous life. The Ten Commandments, the Beatitudes (see next page), and the Great Commandment of love help you understand how to act justly. Yet there are those who disobey God's law and ignore Jesus' example of loving others. As a consequence, many people still suffer injustice.

Scripture

The Beatitudes

"Blessed are the poor in spirit,
    for theirs is the kingdom of heaven.
Blessed are they who mourn,
    for they will be comforted.
Blessed are the meek,
    for they will inherit the land.
Blessed are they who hunger and thirst for righteousness,
    for they will be satisfied.
Blessed are the merciful,
    for they will be shown mercy.
Blessed are the clean of heart,
    for they will see God.
Blessed are the peacemakers,
    for they will be called children of God.
Blessed are they who are persecuted for the sake of
    righteousness,
    for theirs is the kingdom of heaven."

Matthew 5:3–10

Catholic Faith Words

justice giving God what is due him. This virtue also means giving each person what he or she is due because that person is a child of God.

virtues good spiritual habits that strengthen you and enable you to do what is right and good. They develop over time with our practice and openness to God's grace.

grace God's free, loving gift of his own life and help to do what he calls us to do. It is participation in the life of the Holy Trinity.

Share Your Faith

Reflect Think about an unjust action that you have witnessed or experienced. Write about why it was unjust and how it made you feel.

_____

_____

_____

Share With a partner, brainstorm when or why actions are unjust.

Peace

What is the relationship between peace and justice?

Where there is an absence of justice, there is no **peace**. Only people and nations who live in justice will know real peace.

The Law addressed issues of peace and justice among the Israelites, such as paying workers their wages on time. But not everyone listened. About eight centuries before Christ, three prophets spoke of people living without justice and peace. God said through the prophets that the people would bear the consequences of their sin, but he would never stop loving them.

Three Prophets

Hosea reported that lying, murder, stealing, and adultery had replaced fidelity and mercy. Yet he prophesied that one day God would heal the sinners and love them freely. "I will be like the dew for Israel: he will blossom like the lily…" (**Hosea 14:6**).

Amos observed that the weak were trampled down, that the just were oppressed, and that bribery was everywhere. Yet Amos also pointed out that one day God would restore his People, Israel, and return them to their land. The prophet Micah reminded people that the path to righteousness was simple.

© Our Sunday Visitor

Catholic Faith Words

peace a state of calm or harmony when things are in their proper order and people settle problems with kindness and justice

common good the good of everyone, with particular concern for those who might be most vulnerable to harm

social sin unjust structures that can occur as the result of personal sin. One person's sin can cause others to sin, and the sin can spread through a whole society.

Underline the words in Micah's message that state what the Lord requires of you.

📖 Scripture

What the Lord Requires

"You have been told, O mortal, what is good, and what the LORD requires of you: Only to do justice and to love goodness, and to walk humbly with your God." Micah 6:8

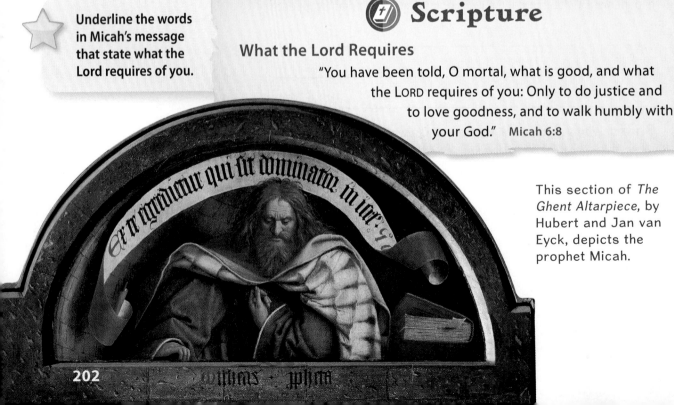

This section of *The Ghent Altarpiece,* by Hubert and Jan van Eyck, depicts the prophet Micah.

Justice Seekers and Peacemakers

Today, the Church continues the work of the Old Testament prophets. The Church helps you understand the responsibility you have to work for justice and peace as Jesus did. We come to the realization that when we love God with our whole heart, we instinctively reach out in love to others. There are certain areas that need your close attention.

The failure to give others what is due them is an injustice and goes against the **common good**. When personal sin leads whole communities or societies to make such choices, the sin grows. This kind of sin can be called **social sin**. Racism, sexism, and terrorism are examples of social sins. Wherever there is hatred, envy, prejudice, or division between people, there is no real peace. A just world is a sign of the Kingdom of God.

The Common Good

Life

Your duty as a Christian citizen is to protect all human life and work for peace, striving to heal injustices that threaten human life.

Dignity

Your duty is to work with those in authority to build a society in which the dignity of all people is respected. Christians must work to reject and counteract prejudice and discrimination.

Basic needs

Your duty is to care for those who are poor and to see that they have adequate food, shelter, and clothing.

Connect Your Faith

Listen to the Prophets Match what each prophet teaches about living with peace and justice.

Hosea	One day God would restore his People, Israel, and return them to their land
Amos	The path to righteousness is simple
Micah	One day God would heal the sinners and love them freely

Our Catholic Life

What does it mean to promote human dignity?

A just world is a sign of the Kingdom of God. Justice begins when you recognize the dignity, or inner worth, of each person.

God created each of us, and he has a plan for our lives. We are all valuable to him and each other. When you respect and promote human dignity, you honor God, in whose image and likeness humans are created.

Mark a Y next to what you can do to respect yourself, and an O next to what you can do to respect others.

Y or O

[Y] Remember that God created you in his image and likeness. **(See Genesis 1:27.)**

[O] Be honest and kind in your communications. **(See Ephesians 4:25, 32.)**

[Y] Make time to talk with God in prayer. **(See Sirach 37:15.)**

[Y] Develop an honest, healthy view of yourself. **(See Romans 12:3.)**

[O] Stand up for the rights of others. **(See Proverbs 31:8–9.)**

[Y] Practice moderation, or balance, in the way you eat, dress, exercise, and rest. **(See 1 Timothy 4:7–8.)**

[O] Avoid stereotyping and prejudice. **(See James 2:1–9.)**

[OY] Insist on respect for your body and the bodies of others. **(See 1 Corinthians 6:19–20.)**

People of Faith

Blessed Maria Vicenta, 1867–1949

July 30

Blessed Maria Vicenta was born in Mexico. She was known for her devotion to the Infant Jesus. After she recovered from a serious illness, she decided to dedicate her life to God by helping those who were poor and sick. She knew that every person has an inner worth that must be respected. To help do that, she founded the Servants of the Holy Trinity and the Poor. The Servants cared for the wounded during the Mexican Revolution and opened seventeen hospitals, clinics, and nurseries. Blessed Maria and her sisters worked to create a society in which the dignity of all was important.

Discuss: How do you show that you value the dignity of each person you meet?

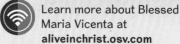

Learn more about Blessed Maria Vicenta at **aliveinchrist.osv.com**

Live Your Faith

Think of the person whom you chose for your word map in the activity on page 193. Recall some specific actions of this person.

Takes lead, Cares for others, loving to everyone.

Write one way you will try to follow that person's example this week.

I will try to be kinder to my classmats

♡ Let Us Pray

Litany of Justice and Peace

This litany prayer helps us to voice our prayers of intercession, asking God's help to make us his instruments of bringing peace and justice to all the world.

Gather and begin with the Sign of the Cross.

Leader: God our Father, you have called us as one family to care for one another, to live in peace, and to be concerned for each other because we are one.

Side 1: Jesus, friend of the poor,

All: help us to bring justice to the world.

Side 2: Holy Spirit, who enables us to do what seems impossible,

All: help us bear peace to the world.

Side 1: Jesus, Herald of the Good News,

All: help us to bring justice to the world.

Side 2: Holy Spirit, who gives us confidence,

All: help us bear peace to the world.

Side 1: Jesus, who said yes to the Father,

All: help us to bring justice to the world.

Side 2: Holy Spirit, source of all unity,

All: help us bear peace to the world.

Leader: For what particular situations in our local area, in our world, can we pray today for peace and justice?

All: Help us bear peace to the world. Amen.

 Sing "Raise Your Voice for Justice"

FAMILY+FAITH
LIVING AND LEARNING TOGETHER

YOUR CHILD LEARNED >>>

This chapter explores the virtues of peace and justice and the common good, and explains social sin, human dignity, and natural moral law.

Scripture

 Read **Isaiah 1:17** to find out what it means to be just and to learn to do good.

Catholics Believe

- God's grace makes it possible for us to live a life of virtue, respecting the human dignity of all.

- Justice is giving what is due to God and others. Where justice is absent, peace is not possible.

To learn more, go to the *Catechism of the Catholic Church #1807, 1939–1942, 2304–2306* at **usccb.org**.

People of Faith

This week your child learned about Blessed Maria Vicenta, who cared for the wounded of the Mexican Revolution.

CHILDREN AT THIS AGE >>>

How They Understand Justice The social perspective of your child is still somewhat limited. What is fair and just in matters concerning himself or herself can sometimes be limited to what he or she wants in the situation. Still, when children this age step back from this to view larger issues in society and in the world as a whole, they have a strong sense of justice and a desire to do what they can to make the world a better place.

CONSIDER THIS >>>

When have you seen or read something that made you ask, "How can we have let that happen?"

When communities of people act together in sin or allow sin to happen, the result can be horrendous. Racism, sexism, terrorism, and lack of respect for human life are all examples of what can happen when people look away or participate in what may seem small ways. As Catholics, we know that "sins give rise to social situations and institutions that are contrary to the divine goodness. 'Structures of sin' are the expression and effect of personal sins. They lead their victims to do evil in their turn. In an analogous sense, they constitute 'social sin'" (*CCC, 1869*).

LET'S TALK >>>

- Ask your child to share one important message of the prophets.

- Talk with your child about what it means to treat people with dignity.

LET'S PRAY >>>

 Merciful God, help us follow the example of Blessed Maria Vicenta by doing our part to respect the dignity of everyone we meet. Amen.

 For a multimedia glossary of Catholic Faith Words, Sunday readings, seasonal and Saint resources, and chapter activities go to **aliveinchrist.osv.com**.

Chapter 14 Review

A **Work with Words** Complete each sentence with the correct term.

1. Where there is an absence of justice, there is not full

    _____.

2. The search for justice is a response to the _____ God

    writes in our hearts.

3. The prophet _____ called on the people to do the

    right thing, love goodness, and walk humbly with God.

4. _____ means giving God and people what is due to them.

5. _____ are habits of goodness that help you grow in love

    of God and others.

B **Check Understanding** Use the terms from the Word Bank to write
a summary of the chapter.

6–10. <u>Bring social sin down in the world. Bring up</u>
<u>justice and peace. Human dignity is important</u>
<u>and and we deserve it. Be the graces the world</u>
<u>needs.</u>

_____

_____

_____

_____

_____

_____

_____

_____

Word Bank
. . . .

human
dignity

justice

peace

social sin

grace

© Our Sunday Visitor

Go to **aliveinchrist.osv.com**
for an interactive review.

Sin and Forgiveness

♥ Let Us Pray

Leader: God of mercy, thank you for your forgiveness and love.

"Bless the LORD, my soul;
Who pardons all your sins,
   and crowns you with mercy and
   compassion." **Psalm 103:2a, 3a, 4b**

All: God of mercy, thank you for your forgiveness and love. Help me become as compassionate and big-hearted as you. Amen.

🖪 Scripture

Peter approaching [Jesus] asked him, "Lord, if my brother sins against me, how often must I forgive him? As many as seven times?" Jesus answered, "I say to you, not seven times but seventy-seven times." **Matthew 18:21–22**

❓ What Do You Wonder?

- Was Jesus serious about forgiving everyone all the time?
- How do you know that Jesus forgives your sins?

Your Relationship with God

What does Jesus teach about sin and forgiveness?

Sin is an offense against God and disrupts the harmony of his plan for creation. Sin affects your relationship with God and others. Sin can be mortal (serious) or venial (less serious).

A **venial sin** weakens but does not destroy your relationship with God. The Sacrament of Penance and Reconciliation is a means of healing for those who have fallen into venial sin. Venial sins for which you are not sorry can move you gradually toward a decision to commit mortal sin.

Mortal sin is a deliberate and freely chosen act. It is a very serious sin by which someone completely turns away from God. The conditions of mortal sin are these:

- The matter must be serious.
- The person must know that the action is serious and sinful.
- The person must freely choose to do the sinful action.

The primary reason for the Sacrament of Reconciliation is the confession and forgiveness of mortal sins. If left unrepented, mortal sin puts a person in danger of Hell after death.

➔ **How could a venial sin lead to more serious sin?**

© Our Sunday Visitor

Catholic Faith Words

sin an offense against God as well as against reason, truth, and conscience

venial sin a sin that weakens a person's relationship with God but does not destroy it

mortal sin a very serious sin by which someone turns completely away from God

God's Mercy

In the Parable of the Unforgiving Servant, Jesus teaches an important lesson about God's mercy and forgiveness.

Scripture

The Parable of the Unforgiving Servant

There once was a king who decided to settle accounts with his servants. One servant owed him a huge amount. The king ordered the man to be sold, along with his family and possessions, in payment of his debt. Hearing this, the servant begged the king's mercy and the king forgave him his debt.

The forgiven debtor then found a fellow servant who owed him a much smaller amount. He demanded that the other man pay everything he owed. The fellow servant fell to his knees and begged for mercy. Instead of finding mercy, the man was thrown into jail until he paid the debt.

When the king found out about the incident, he said to the forgiven debtor, "I forgave you your entire debt because you begged me to. Should you not have had pity on your fellow servant, as I had pity on you?" Then the king sent the debtor to prison until he paid back what he owed.

Jesus then said to his disciples, "So will my heavenly Father do to you, unless each of you forgives his brother from his heart."

Based on Matthew 18:23–35

Share Your Faith

Reflect What lesson about God's mercy and forgiveness did Jesus teach in this parable?

_____

_____

Share With a partner, list ways to show forgiveness to others.

_____

_____

_____

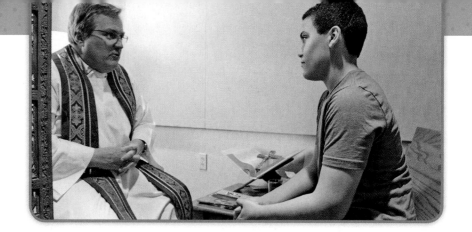

Making Things Right

How can you inform your conscience?

In your heart God has written an inner law to help you recognize good and evil. And your **conscience** acts as a wise adviser. Your conscience is your free will and right reason, or good sense, working to help you make good choices. You should always obey the certain judgment of an informed conscience.

Your informed conscience is like a fine tool. It is meant to be maintained and used. You maintain it by listening with your mind and heart to the Word of God, the teaching of the Church, the advice of wise people, and the prompting of the Holy Spirit.

Penance and Reconciliation

When you sin, the Church provides a way for you to experience God's forgiveness through the Sacrament of Penance and Reconciliation. The Church encourages us to go to confession when we've committed venial sin, but we must receive the Sacrament when in the state of mortal sin.

Catholic Faith Words

conscience the God-given ability that helps us judge whether actions are right or wrong. It is important for us to know God's laws so our conscience can help us make good decisions.

sacramental seal the rule that a priest is not to share anything he hears in confession

Celebrating the Sacrament

- Carefully examine your conscience, deciding in what ways you have failed to love God and others.

- Confess any sins you have committed since your last confession and accept a penance from the priest to make up for your sins.

- Pray an Act of Contrition to express your sorrow for sin and your intention to avoid sin.

- Receive absolution from the priest, who grants forgiveness of sin in God's name.

ACT OF CONTRITION

My God,
I am sorry for my sins with all my heart.
In choosing to do wrong and failing to do good,
I have sinned against you whom I should love above all things.
I firmly intend, with your help,
to do penance,
to sin no more,
and to avoid whatever leads me to sin.
Our Savior Jesus Christ suffered and died for us.
In his name, my God, have mercy.

Amen

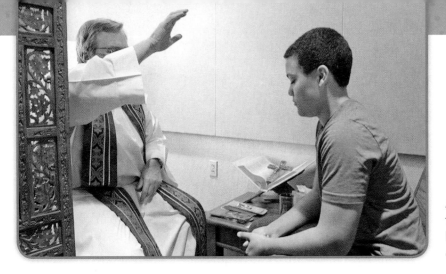

After you have confessed, the priest extends his hand and absolves you of sin.

Effects of the Sacrament

The Sacrament of Penance and Reconciliation provides you with many benefits. The effects of the Sacrament include:

- Your full friendship with God is restored or healed.
- You are reconciled with the Church and freed from the threat of Hell.
- You are given peace and strength to do what is right and good.

Any sin confessed in the Sacrament can never be told to anyone by the priest. This is called the **sacramental seal**, or seal of confession.

Connect Your Faith

Describe Reconciliation Circle the words or phrases that reflect your experience of the Sacrament of Reconciliation.

relief end of hurting God

grace making amends starting over

healing

friendship peace freedom

Add words or phrases of your own.

_____

Our Catholic Life

How can I keep a clear conscience?

Your conscience is a gift from God that helps you to know the difference between right and wrong. A well-formed conscience helps you to know the will of God and act according to his will. If you continue to go against your conscience, it grows insensitive to God's guidance and direction. On the other hand, when you do your best to form your conscience and follow it, you will enjoy the peace and joy that come from a good conscience.

Informing your conscience helps you make good moral choices. Here are some steps to follow.

Check off what you are doing now, and draw a star next to something you want to work on this week.

Informing Your Conscience

THINK

| *Think about choices and results before you act.* | ☐ Pause to think through your choices before deciding on one. |

COMPARE

| *Compare your choice with teachings of Jesus and the Church.* | ☐ Call to mind the command to love God and your neighbor with all your heart. |
| | ☐ Think of the Ten Commandments, the Beatitudes, and the teachings of the Church. |

TALK

| *Talk about your choice with a wise person.* | ☐ Seek out the advice of someone whose judgment you can trust. |

PRAY

| *Pray to the Holy Spirit for help.* | ☐ Pray for the Holy Spirit's help so that your choice is the correct one and so that it makes you a more loving person. |

People of Faith

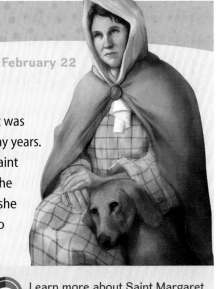

Saint Margaret of Cortona, 1247–1297

As a young girl, Saint Margaret wanted to do whatever she liked, even if it was wrong or sinful. She ran away from home and lived a very bad life for many years. Then one day, one of her closest friends was murdered. This so shocked Saint Margaret that she confessed her sins and immediately changed her life. She lived with the nuns at a convent, although she didn't become a nun, and she worked with the sick and poor. Saint Margaret had a dog that she loved so much that when she died, a statue of her dog was put on her tomb.

Discuss: When you do something wrong, do you tell God that you are sorry?

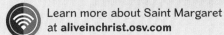

Learn more about Saint Margaret at **aliveinchrist.osv.com**

Live Your Faith

Role-Plays on Conscience Read the following situations, and write how you would respond in each.

1. You find yourself with some friends in a local store. Two of your friends plan to steal something while the store clerk is helping the others. What do you do?

   _____

   _____

   _____

   _____

2. During study hall, two classmates start to argue and hit each other out of view of the study hall monitor. You see this happening. What do you do?

   _____

   _____

   _____

   _____

Role-play one of the situations in a small group, and act out a conclusion. Discuss how an informed conscience would react in each situation.

Let Us Pray

The Jesus Prayer

Gather and begin with the Sign of the Cross.

All: Sing "You Alone"

You alone are holy,
you alone are Lord.
You alone are worthy to be honored and adored.
Mercy you have given, kindness you have shown.
Love is you alone.

Place yourself in a position of prayer, and breathe deeply and quietly. Now combine your focused breathing with an ancient prayer called the Jesus Prayer.

As you breathe in, silently pray, "Lord Jesus Christ."
As you breathe out, silently pray, "Son of God."
As you breathe in, silently pray, "have mercy on me."
As you breathe out, silently pray, "a sinner."

All: God our Father, you do not want to lose anyone to sin.
Help us do good and avoid evil.
If we fail, guide us to your forgiveness
in the Sacrament of Penance
and Reconciliation.
We ask this through Jesus,
your Son, who lives and
reigns with you and the
Holy Spirit now and forever.
Amen.

FAMILY+FAITH
LIVING AND LEARNING TOGETHER

© Our Sunday Visitor

YOUR CHILD LEARNED >>>

This chapter examines mortal and venial sin and explains the need for an informed conscience and the effects of the Sacrament of Penance and Reconciliation.

Scripture

Read **Matthew 18:21–22** to find out what Jesus has to say about forgiveness.

Catholics Believe

• Your conscience helps you know when you have sinned.

• Through the Sacrament of Reconciliation, God forgives sins and restores us to his friendship.

To learn more, go to the *Catechism of the Catholic Church #1440–1445, 1777–1782, 1849–1850* at **usccb.org**.

People of Faith

This week your child learned about Saint Margaret of Cortona, a reformed sinner, who was known for her work with the poor and for loving her dog.

CHILDREN AT THIS AGE >>>

How They Understand Sin and Forgiveness Most children this age are ready to grow when it comes to taking personal responsibility for their behavior and being accountable to others. One factor that can motivate them is their desire for new freedom and independence. It's important for your child to know that increased freedom will come naturally as he or she shows greater responsibility. Your child's ability to recognize when he or she has wronged someone and to both ask for and receive forgiveness is an important part of this process of maturity.

CONSIDER THIS >>>

How important is it to deal with something small before it turns into something bigger?

We understand what that means when it comes to our house or car maintenance. Yet, how often do we apply that understanding to sin? When we give in to temptation and choose to sin it can be the beginning of a pattern that leads us to even more grave sin. As Catholics, we know that "sins are rightly evaluated according to their gravity. The distinction between mortal and venial sin, already evident in Scripture (cf. 1 John 5:16-17), became part of the tradition of the Church. It is corroborated by human experience" (*CCC, 1854*).

LET'S TALK >>>

• Ask your child to explain what Jesus taught about sin and forgiveness.

• Share a time when you struggled to rely on your conscience as your guide but in the end did so.

LET'S PRAY >>>

Saint Margaret, help us always to be willing to confess our sins and ask for God's forgiveness. Amen.

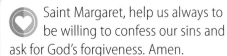

For a multimedia glossary of Catholic Faith Words, Sunday readings, seasonal and Saint resources, and chapter activities go to **aliveinchrist.osv.com**.

Chapter 15 Review

A **Work with Words** Fill in the circle next to the correct answer.

1. Deliberate and serious acts by which a person turns away from God are _____.
   - ○ mortal sins
   - ○ crimes
   - ○ venial sins

2. Sins that weaken but do not destroy a person's relationship with God are _____.
   - ○ mortal sins
   - ○ crimes
   - ○ venial sins

3. The God-given ability that helps us judge whether actions are right or wrong is _____.
   - ○ natural law
   - ○ conscience
   - ○ Sacrament

4. A priest keeps secret what he hears in confession because of the _____.
   - ○ covenant
   - ○ sacramental seal
   - ○ anointing

5. Jesus preached this parable about forgiveness: the Parable of the _____.
   - ○ Good Shepherd
   - ○ Mustard Seed
   - ○ Unforgiving Servant

B **Check Understanding** Name five effects of the Sacrament of Penance and Reconciliation.

6. _____
   _____
   _____
   _____

7. _____
   _____
   _____
   _____

8. _____
   _____
   _____
   _____

9. _____
   _____
   _____
   _____

10. _____
    _____
    _____
    _____

Go to **aliveinchrist.osv.com** for an interactive review.

Unit Review

A **Work with Words** Use the clues provided to solve the puzzle.

Across

4. unjust structures in society

5. destroys a person's relationship with God

7. ability to judge right and wrong

9. inner worth of a person

10. a state of calm when things are in their proper order

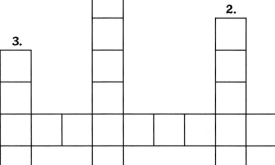

Down

1. Jesus' teachings about true happiness and living for God's Kingdom

2. weakens your relationship with God

3. giving God and others what is due to them

6. Jesus' New Law

8. Gift of the Holy Spirit prompting you to love

B Check Understanding Match each description in Column 1 with the correct term in Column 2.

Column 1

Column 2

11. The revelation of Jesus in glory to the Apostles Peter, James, and John

life

12. Gift of the Holy Spirit

Precepts of the Church

13. What you have a duty to protect

Transfiguration

14. Forgiveness and friendship with God restored

charity

15. Some of the minimum requirements given by Church leaders for deepening your relationship with God and the Church

Penance and Reconciliation

C Make Connections Write a response to each question or statement.

16. How would you describe justice?

_____

_____

_____

_____

_____

_____

17. In your own words, explain the Great Commandment.

_____

_____

_____

_____

_____

_____

18. Give two examples of a venial sin and two examples of a mortal sin.

_____

_____

_____

_____

_____

19. How does knowing that humans are made in the image and likeness of God help promote human dignity?

_____

_____

_____

_____

_____

20. In your life, what helps you most in informing your conscience?

_____

_____

_____

_____

_____

Sacraments

Our Catholic Tradition

- The mission of the Church is to proclaim the Gospel in word and deed to all people. (CCC, 849)

- The Sacraments of Initiation give Catholics new life and the strength to accomplish their mission of loving God and serving others. (CCC, 1212)

- The Sacraments at the Service of Communion—Holy Orders and Matrimony—help bishops, priests, deacons, and married couples live out their mission by following their vocation of service to others. (CCC, 1534)

How do the Sacraments of Initiation set you on the path of your vocation?

© Our Sunday Visitor

CHAPTER 16

Baptized for Mission

 Let Us Pray

Leader: You summon us to mission, Lord. Call us on account of your reign.

"Your reign is a reign for all ages,
    your dominion for all generations.
The LORD is trustworthy in all his words,
    and loving in all his works." **Psalm 145:13**

All: You summon us to mission, Lord. Call us on account of your reign.

 Scripture

For to this you have been called, because Christ also suffered for you, leaving you an example that you should follow in his footsteps. **1 Peter 2:21**

? What Do You Wonder?

- What does Baptism have to do with marriage or priesthood?

- How will you know what God wants you to do with your life?

223

The Apostles' Mission

How did the Apostles carry out Jesus' mission?

The word *mission* comes from a Latin word meaning "to send," and includes the idea of being sent to accomplish specific tasks. Jesus told his Apostles to continue his mission. He kept his promise and sent the Holy Spirit to them at Pentecost. Then they were ready to carry out Jesus' mission. One day, God sent an angel with a message to the Apostle Philip. This is his story.

Catholic Faith Words

conversion the continual process of becoming the people God intends us to be through change and growth. It is a response to God's love and forgiveness.

 Scripture

Philip and the Ethiopian

The angel instructed me to set out walking from Jerusalem. Soon I spotted a chariot, and the Spirit told me to catch up with it.

In the chariot, I saw a man from Ethiopia who was reading from the scroll of the prophet Isaiah. "Do you understand what you are reading?" I asked the man.

"How can I, unless someone instructs me?" the man answered, gesturing to me to climb into the chariot. When I sat down with the man, I saw that he was reading a passage about the Servant of the Lord. I explained that the Servant of the Lord was Jesus. I told the man the Good News of Jesus.

When we came to a pool of water, the man cried out, "Look, there is water. What is to prevent my being baptized?" So I baptized him in the pool. Then the Spirit led me away. The Ethiopian continued on his way, praising God.

Based on Acts 8:26–39

1. Underline what Philip shared with the Ethiopian.

2. Circle how the Ethiopian responded.

© Our Sunday Visitor

God's Mission for You

The story of Philip and the Ethiopian offers an example of continuing Jesus' mission. Like Philip, you are called to take any opportunity to share the Good News. Through Philip, the Ethiopian experienced **conversion**, a process of change and growth. After being baptized, he began his own mission, "rejoicing and praising God."

Jesus gave us the Holy Spirit to help us on our mission. Through the liturgy and Sacraments of the Church, you experience Jesus' presence and receive God's grace. The Holy Spirit is with you on this mission, which has the ultimate goal of life and happiness with God. The Kingdom of God is already present, but its fullness will come at the end of time.

Through the Sacrament of Baptism, we put on Christ and become members of his Church. In the early Church, Baptism, Confirmation, and Eucharist were celebrated together. A person was baptized and sealed with the Spirit, and then joined the assembly at Eucharist for the first time. These Sacraments are called the Sacraments of Initiation because they mark the entry into the Christian life. Celebrating these Sacraments together has again become the norm for adults and for some children entering the Church today.

The Church baptizes in the names of the three Divine Persons of the Holy Trinity. Those who are baptized enter into the very life of God, who is love. All of the Sacraments offer a share into the mystery that is God—Father, Son, and Holy Spirit.

Share Your Faith

Reflect Imagine that you have been asked to explain *mission* to a friend. What would you say?

Share Use the letters in the word *mission* to begin a word or phrase that explains what you would tell someone about our faith.

M _____

I _____

S _____

S _____

I _____

O _____

N _____

Sacraments of Initiation

How do you carry out the mission of Jesus today?

People of Jesus' time heard many stories involving water and new life. At creation, the Spirit moved over the waters. At the time of Noah and the great flood, water brought about a new beginning. When Moses and the Israelites crossed the Red Sea, their passage was a sign of their delivery from slavery.

In the Gospel according to Mark, Jesus began his ministry by being baptized by John with water. This was not the Sacrament as you know it today, although it had some of the same elements. Then, as now, it was a sign of conversion. Jesus submitted to John's baptism to show the people the importance of conversion.

Baptism

Baptism marks the beginning of your mission as a disciple of Jesus. This Sacrament gives you a permanent and unrepeatable seal that marks you for Christ. Baptism takes away Original Sin and all personal sin, and makes a person a child of God and a member of the Church. You are called by your Baptism to **evangelization**, or proclaiming and sharing the Good News. You are called to give witness to your faith through your words and actions.

➡ **Why is Baptism the beginning of our Christian mission?**

Confirmation

Confirmation perfects the grace of Baptism. You are given the strength to carry out your mission of sharing the Good News in word and action. Confirmation does this by an outpouring of the Gifts of the Holy Spirit, which seals or confirms you in Christ and unites you more closely with Jesus and the Church.

Catholic Faith Words

evangelization giving witness to the faith by proclaiming the Good News of Christ through words and deeds in a way that invites people to accept the Gospel

Eucharist the Sacrament in which Jesus gives himself and the bread and wine become his Body and Blood

transubstantiation the process by which the power of the Holy Spirit and the words of the priest transform the bread and wine into the Body and Blood of Christ

Real Presence the phrase used to describe that Jesus is really and truly present in the Eucharist—Body, Blood, Soul, and Divinity

Tabernacle the special place in the church where the Blessed Sacrament is reserved after Mass for those who are ill or for Eucharistic Adoration

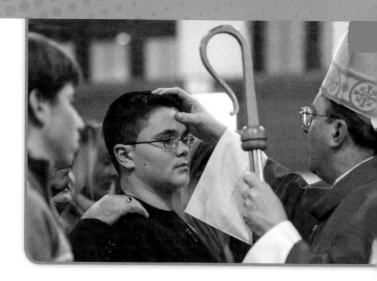

In Confirmation, a bishop, or sometimes a priest, anoints your forehead with Sacred Chrism. This anointing is combined with the laying on of the bishop's or priest's hand and the words, "Be sealed with the Gift of the Holy Spirit." Confirmation, like Baptism, gives you a permanent spiritual mark. For this reason, you celebrate each of these Sacraments only once in your life.

Eucharist

The final Sacrament of Initiation is the **Eucharist**. In the Eucharist, we remember, give thanks for, and share in the life, Death, and Resurrection of Jesus. At the altar, you are united with the People of God. You offer yourself to God and participate in Jesus' sacrifice. Responding to Jesus' assurance that his Body and Blood give life, you receive him in the Eucharist. The power of the Holy Spirit and the words of the priest transform the bread and wine into the Body and Blood of Jesus through **transubstantiation**. The Bread of Life nourishes you for your mission to announce the Good News and give glory to God. The Eucharist foretells eternal life in Heaven. Catholics show love and respect for the **Real Presence** of Jesus by receiving Holy Communion with reverence. Outside of Mass we honor and respect the real presence of Christ by visiting and praying before the Blessed Sacrament in church. The Body of Christ, not consumed in the Mass, is reserved in the **Tabernacle**.

Connect Your Faith

Learning More In each of the boxes, write something new you learned about the Sacrament.

	Baptism
	Confirmation
	Eucharist

Our Catholic Life

How can you be an agent of love for God?

God asks you to be an agent of his love. You will be working with the people and communities who surround you every day. The goal of your mission is to communicate the truth about God's love. Here is how to accomplish that mission.

1. Learn as much as you can about God's love and how to recognize it. Become familiar with the story of salvation revealed in the Bible. The Bible will be your map and your compass.

2. Get to know other people involved in mission. The Church gathers daily to celebrate the Eucharist. If you can, go to Mass one day during the week. At the next Sunday Mass, make a special effort to introduce yourself to others.

3. Identify your God-given gifts and talents and ways they can be used to share God's love with others.

_____

_____

_____

4. Work closely with your guide, the Holy Spirit. You won't accomplish your mission without him. Pray to him frequently because he can provide what you need to complete your mission.

5. Learn as much as you can about Jesus, the person who is sending you on this mission. Jesus gave his life to save all people from the power of sin and everlasting death. He is still active in this mission today through the Holy Spirit.

> **List some of your interests and talents above.**

© Our Sunday Visitor

People of Faith

November 18

Saint Rose Philippine Duchesne, 1769–1852

Rose Duchesne lived her baptismal call as a religious sister. Born in France, she cared for those who were sick, educated children who were neglected, and sheltered priests during the French Revolution. In 1818 she left France for the United States. She established convents and schools in Missouri and Louisiana. But she wanted to work with Native Americans. Finally, when she was quite old, she went to the Potawatomi tribe at Sugar Creek, Kansas. They called her "woman who prays always" because she spent so much of her free time in prayer.

Discuss: How does prayer help you participate in Jesus' mission?

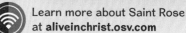

Learn more about Saint Rose at **aliveinchrist.osv.com**

Live Your Faith

Choose one thing you do well from the list you made of your interests and talents, and write or draw how you will use that God-given ability this week to accomplish your mission and to benefit others.

Let Us Pray

Celebration of the Word

Gather and begin with the Sign of the Cross.

Leader: Through Baptism, Confirmation, and Eucharist, Jesus sends us on a mission of evangelization. Listen as Jesus sends his disciples on such a mission.

Reader 1: A reading from the holy Gospel according to Luke.

Read Luke 9:1–6.

The Gospel of the Lord.

All: Praise to you, Lord Jesus Christ.

Reader 2: The spirit of the Lord GOD is upon me,
because the LORD has anointed me;
He has sent me to bring good news to the afflicted,
to bind up the brokenhearted,
To proclaim liberty to the captives,
release to the prisoners,

Reader 3: To announce a year of favor from the LORD
and a day of vindication by our God;
To comfort all who mourn.   Isaiah 61:1–2

Leader: Let us pray.

Bow your heads as the leader prays.

All: Amen.

▶ Sing "Go Make a Difference"

Go make a diff'rence.
We can make a diff'rence.
Go make a diff'rence in the world.
Text: Based on Matthew 5:13–16. Text and music
© 1997, Steve Angrisano and Thomas N. Tomaszek.
Published by spiritandsong.com®, a division of OCP.
All rights reserved.

FAMILY+FAITH
LIVING AND LEARNING TOGETHER

YOUR CHILD LEARNED >>>

This chapter defines evangelization and explains how the Eucharist nourishes us to announce the Good News.

Scripture

 Read **1 Peter 2:21** to find out what Jesus commissioned the disciples to do.

Catholics Believe

• The mission of the Church is to announce the Good News of God's Kingdom.

• Through the Sacraments of Initiation, Catholics are given new life and are called to spread the Good News.

To learn more, go to the *Catechism of the Catholic Church #849–856, 1212–1213, 1285* at **usccb.org**.

People of Faith

This week, your child learned about Saint Rose Philippine Duchesne, who was called "woman who prays always" by the Potawatomi tribe she served.

CHILDREN AT THIS AGE >>>

How They Understand Mission Many sixth-graders have not considered themselves "missionaries," but the Church teaches that all baptized persons are called to spread the Gospel to others. Your child will most often do this by example, but may at other times need the words to articulate what he or she believes and why. Developing these skills and connecting them with the Sacraments of Initiation is a way to strengthen the positive identity of your child at a time when identity development is becoming more important.

CONSIDER THIS >>>

How do you feel when you witness your child doing something loving?

Perhaps a parent's greatest reward is seeing our children live what we have been trying to teach them or model for them. As Catholics, we know that "God's people also share in Christ's role as prophet. This means both teaching and witnessing God's Word in the world. A real prophet, by teaching and good example, leads others to faith. St. Francis of Assisi once wrote, 'Preach always. Sometimes use words'"(*USCCA, p. 117*).

LET'S TALK >>>

• Ask your child to tell you how the Sacraments give us a mission and how they help us accomplish it.

• Share with your child a story from the day of their First Communion.

LET'S PRAY >>>

 Saint Rose, pray for us that we may be courageous in living out our mission to share the Good News of Jesus with others. Amen.

For a multimedia glossary of Catholic Faith Words, Sunday readings, seasonal and Saint resources, and chapter activities go to **aliveinchrist.osv.com**.

Chapter 16 Review

A **Work with Words** Complete each sentence with the correct term from the Word Bank.

Word Bank

Word Bank

Tabernacle

Baptism

evangelization

Sacred Chrism

Confirmation

Real Presence

Initiation

Sacraments

Eucharist

transubstantiation

1. The Sacraments of _____ are the foundation for Christian living.

2. Jesus really and truly present in the Eucharist—Body, Blood, Soul, and Divinity is called _____ .

3. Through the Sacrament of _____, a person begins the mission of a disciple.

4. _____ is blessed oil used for anointing in the Sacraments of Baptism, Confirmation, and Holy Orders.

5. Giving witness to your faith by proclaiming the Good News of Jesus is called _____.

6. Like Baptism, _____ gives the recipient a permanent spiritual mark.

7. The _____ is a foretaste of eternal life in Heaven.

8. The special place in the church where the Blessed Sacrament is reserved for those who are ill or for Eucharistic Adoration is called the _____.

9. The power of the Holy Spirit and the words of the priest transform the bread and wine into the Body and Blood of Jesus through _____.

10. Through the Seven _____ of the Church, we experience Jesus' presence and grace.

© Our Sunday Visitor

Go to **aliveinchrist.osv.com** for an interactive review.

Lives of Service

 **Let Us Pray**

Leader: Gracious God, make us all your servants.

"Gladden the soul of your servant;
    to you, Lord, I lift up my soul." **Psalm 86:4**

All: Gracious God, make us all your servants. May we be
"Christ" to one another. Amen.

Scripture

As each one has received a gift, use it to serve one another as good stewards of God's varied grace. Whoever preaches, let it be with the words of God; whoever serves, let it be with the strength that God supplies, so that in all things God may be glorified through Jesus Christ, to whom belong glory and dominion forever and ever. Amen. **1 Peter 4:10–11**

© Our Sunday Visitor

? What Do You Wonder?

- Why are our talents and abilities referred to as gifts?

- How does your life give glory to God?

In this painting, how are the disciples reacting to Jesus washing their feet? What might they have thought and felt?

Called to Serve

What is the meaning of the word vocation?

Serving others is an essential part of being a baptized person. Jesus placed great importance on it. At his Last Supper, Jesus knew that his Death was near. Knowing that he would not have another chance to teach his disciples before he went to the Cross, Jesus did a surprising thing.

 **Scripture**

The Washing of the Disciples' Feet

Jesus got up from the table and poured water into a basin. He then knelt to wash his disciples' feet. His disciples were very surprised at first. When it was Peter's turn, he objected by saying, "You will never wash my feet."

Jesus told him, "Unless I wash you, you will have no inheritance with me."

At this remark Peter looked serious and replied, "Master, then not only my feet, but my hands and head as well."

Then Jesus returned to his seat at the table. He asked his disciples, "Do you realize what I have done for you?" Then he explained, "If I, therefore, the master and teacher, have washed your feet, you ought to wash one another's feet." **Based on John 13:1–15**

➜ Explain to a partner what Jesus wanted his disciples to understand when he washed their feet.

The Cost of Serving Others

In Jesus' time, people who were poor walked barefoot, and those of a higher class wore sandals. Washing the feet of guests when they entered a home was a job for servants—the owner of the house would not do it. It was shocking for Jesus' disciples to see him do such a thing.

Jesus' action was a sign that his disciples needed to be purified before they could enter his Kingdom, just as you were purified by your Baptism. The washing of the disciples' feet was also a reminder that serving others would not always be easy. The disciples would have to humble themselves, just as Jesus would be humbled by his Passion and Death. Serving others involves helping others even when it is inconvenient or difficult to do so.

Your Vocation

Today, followers of Jesus usually are not asked to wash people's feet, but all of us are called to love and serve God and our neighbor. This is part of our **vocation**, God's plan for us and the purpose for which he made us.

When you are older, you may decide to live out your vocation by answering God's call to the ordained priesthood, to religious life, to marriage, or, perhaps, to the committed single life.

You may not yet know the vocation to which God is calling you. By praying, learning more about Jesus, and looking at the gifts and talents God has given you, you will discover your vocation.

> ### Catholic Faith Words
>
> **vocation** the purpose for which God made us and a particular way to answer his call, whether as a lay person (married or single), a member of a religious community, or a member of the ordained ministry

Share Your Faith

Reflect Recall the list you made of your talents and gifts.

Share Choose a life's work that would use those talents and serve God, and write it here.

_____

Then write two ways that you could serve others through this work by using these talents and gifts.

_____

_____

Living the Call

How do people live out their baptismal call?

Everyone who is baptized is called to continue the mission of Jesus by serving others. But some are called to ordained ministry through the Sacrament of Holy Orders.

Holy Orders confers a sacred power, through the laying on of hands by the bishop, for serving the faithful by teaching, leading the people in worship, and pastoral governing. Bishops, priests, and deacons all share in this Sacrament of Holy Orders. Ordained men are marked forever as Christ's representatives.

A **bishop** serves the Church as the pastor and teacher of his diocese. All the bishops work together with the Pope for the good of the whole Church and make up the **Magisterium**, or the teaching authority of the Church.

Priests assist the bishop within a diocese. As pastor of a parish, a priest shares the bishop's work in the diocese. Priests act *in persona Christi*, as a representative of Christ, and preside in celebrations of the Sacraments for the parish.

Permanent deacons are ordained ministers who serve the diocese and parish by assisting in liturgical roles and by doing works of charity. Married men can be called to this ministry.

Consecrated Life

Some priests live in religious communities in what is called **consecrated religious life**. Members of these communities dedicate themselves to serving God by following the charism, or special grace, of the community and its founder. There are also many communities of religious sisters and brothers. Members of religious communities may teach, care for the sick, work as missionaries, or do other good works.

Members of religious communities profess in public to live three vows, or sacred promises, that are found at the heart of the Gospel—poverty, chastity, and obedience. These vows are also called the evangelical counsels.

Catholic Faith Words

Holy Orders the Sacrament in which a baptized man is ordained to teach the faithful, lead divine worship, and govern the Church; ordained ministers serve as bishops, priests, or deacons

Magisterium the teaching office of the Church, which is all of the bishops in union with the Pope. The Magisterium has the teaching authority to interpret the Word of God found in Scripture and Tradition.

consecrated religious life a state of life lived in community and characterized by the vows of poverty, chastity, and obedience

The Evangelical Counsels

Poverty	The choice to live a simple life and to share material possessions in community.
Chastity	The choice to maintain the right balance of body and spirit in human sexuality. This is also a virtue that requires the proper integration of sexuality according to one's state of life. For men and women religious, this means living a celibate life.
Obedience	The choice to follow and obey God's will as it is expressed through the guidance of the community's leaders, the charism of the community, and the individual's conscience.

Those who accept the call to ordained priesthood or consecrated religious life choose lives of service for the sake of God's People. Because they are human, they can make mistakes. But they are always worthy of respect, because of their human dignity and their willingness to make a difficult and lifelong commitment in service to God's People.

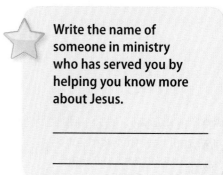

Write the name of someone in ministry who has served you by helping you know more about Jesus.

_____

_____

Connect Your Faith

Living Vows Explain how to live each of these vows in your own words.

Poverty _____

_____

_____

Chastity _____

_____

Obedience _____

_____

_____

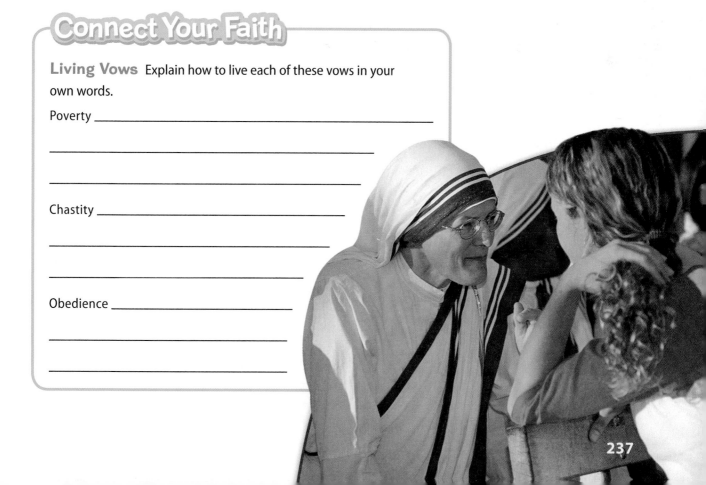

Our Catholic Life

How can you follow the example of Jesus in serving God and others?

Jesus taught his disciples a great deal about service. His words can help you today as you work to serve God and others.

In the Gospels, Jesus speaks words of great wisdom. He teaches what it means to be a servant. Here are a few Scripture passages in which Jesus tells how to serve.

In the second column, tell how the words of Jesus in each passage help you serve.

© Our Sunday Visitor

The Wisdom of Jesus

"I no longer call you slaves, because a slave does not know what his master is doing. I have called you friends, because I have told you everything I have heard from my Father."

John 15:15

_____

_____

_____

"If anyone wishes to be first, he shall be the last of all and the servant of all."

Mark 9:35

_____

_____

"For I was hungry and you gave me food, I was thirsty and you gave me drink, a stranger and you welcomed me, naked and you clothed me, ill and you cared for me, in prison and you visited me... whatever you did for one of these least brothers of mine, you did for me."

Matthew 25:35–36, 40

_____

_____

_____

_____

People of Faith

July 31

Saint Ignatius of Loyola, 1491–1556

Saint Ignatius was a soldier. While recovering from a wound, he read a book about the life of Christ and decided to become a priest. He founded an order of priests called the Society of Jesus, also called the Jesuits. Saint Ignatius wrote a book called *Spiritual Exercises*, which people still use today as a way to help others experience Jesus' love. His motto was: "Do everything for the honor and glory of God." The Jesuits are famous for their learning and teaching. They continue to spread the Good News of Jesus in parishes, high schools, and universities.

Discuss: How do you use your call to share the love of Jesus with people?

Learn more about Saint Ignatius at **aliveinchrist.osv.com**

Live Your Faith

Explain what is happening in these images. Describe how the people are serving others. Then name one thing you will do this week to serve others in your parish or community.

Let Us Pray

Prayer of Petition

Gather and begin with the Sign of the Cross.

Leader: God our Father, bless all who serve you and others.

Reader 1: A reading from the Letter to the Hebrews.

Read Hebrews 5:1–6.

The word of the Lord.

All: Thanks be to God.

Reader 2: We ask that your ministers may grow to a greater love of Jesus.

All: Lord, hear our prayer.

Reader 3: We ask that the Holy Spirit may strengthen their hearts and enlighten their minds.

All: Lord, hear our prayer.

Reader 4: We ask that through their efforts and ours, in the power of the Holy Spirit, your Kingdom will continue to grow.

All: Lord, hear our prayer.

Leader: Let us pray.

Bow your heads as the leader prays.

All: Amen.

 Sing "I Will Choose Christ"

I will choose Christ,
I will choose love,
I choose to serve.
I give my heart, I give my life,
I give my all to you.

FAMILY+FAITH
LIVING AND LEARNING TOGETHER

YOUR CHILD LEARNED >>>

This chapter defines vocation as the purpose for which God made us and a particular way to answer his call, and explains that Holy Orders confers a sacred power for serving the faithful.

Scripture

 Read **1 Peter 4:10–11** to find out about God's gifts to us and how we are intended to use them.

Catholics Believe

- All of the baptized are called to follow Christ by serving others.
- Ordained men serve God through preaching the Word and through celebrating the Sacraments.

To learn more, go to the *Catechism of the Catholic Church #897–900, 1548–1553* at **usccb.org**.

People of Faith

This week, your child learned about Saint Ignatius of Loyola. His motto was: "Do everything for the honor and glory of God."

CHILDREN AT THIS AGE >>>

How They Understand Service to Others Sixth-graders enjoy helping others, especially when they feel that they have made a unique contribution no one else could have made. Still, their limited ability to know what something feels like for someone else may cause them to miss opportunities to serve others if no one points out these opportunities to them.

CONSIDER THIS >>>

Do you think it is more difficult to hear God's call in the world today?

Despite the "noise" of our culture, God continues to call each baptized person in a unique way to respond to Jesus' invitation to service. We call this a vocation. As Catholics, we know that "ordination to the priesthood is always a call and a gift from God. Christ reminded his Apostles that they needed to ask the Lord of the harvest to send laborers into the harvest. Those who seek the priesthood respond generously to God's call using the words of the prophet, 'Here I am, send me (Is. 6:8)'" (*USCCA, p. 269*).

LET'S TALK >>>

- Ask your child to explain the word *vocation*.
- Share with your child about a time when you felt God was calling you or your family to serve him and others.

LET'S PRAY >>>

 Saint Ignatius, pray for us that we may do everything for God's honor and glory. Amen.

 For a multimedia glossary of Catholic Faith Words, Sunday readings, seasonal and Saint resources, and chapter activities go to **aliveinchrist.osv.com**.

Chapter 17 Review

A **Work with Words** Match each description in Column 1 with the correct term in Column 2.

Column 1

Column 2

1. A call to love and serve God

Magisterium

2. Marked forever as Christ's representatives

Holy Orders

3. A state of life often lived in community

vocation

4. The teaching authority of the Church

consecrated religious life

5. Confers sacred power for serving the faithful by teaching, leading worship, and pastoral governing

ordained men

B **Check Understanding** Circle True if a statement is true, and circle False if a statement is false. Correct any false statements.

6. All baptized people share in the Sacrament of Holy Orders. **True/False**

_____

7. Jesus taught that if anyone wants to be first, he or she must be a servant of all. **True/False**

_____

8. Among their works of service, members of religious communities teach, care for the sick, and work as missionaries. **True/False**

_____

9. At the Last Supper, Jesus taught the disciples how to serve by showing them how to prepare a meal. **True/False**

_____

10. Members of religious communities take vows of poverty, chastity, and obedience. **True/False**

_____

Go to **aliveinchrist.osv.com** for an interactive review.

Sharing God's Love

 Let Us Pray

Leader: God of love, help us become witnesses of your great love in the world.

"Wherever you go I will go,
    wherever you lodge I will lodge.
Your people shall be my people
    and your God, my God." **Ruth 1:16**

All: God of love, help us become witnesses of your great love in the world.

 Scripture

Have you not read that from the beginning the Creator "made them male and female" and said, "For this reason a man shall leave his father and mother and be joined to his wife, and the two shall become one flesh"? So they are no longer two, but one flesh. Therefore, what God has joined together, no human being must separate. **Matthew 19:4–6**

? What Do You Wonder?

- What do Catholics believe is different, or special, about marriage?
- How will you know whom to marry?

Together in Holiness

How is marriage a Sacrament?

Good marriages are based on friendship. In the New Testament, marriage is an image of Christ's relationship with the Church. Jesus used wedding images in some of his parables. He also performed his first miracle at a wedding.

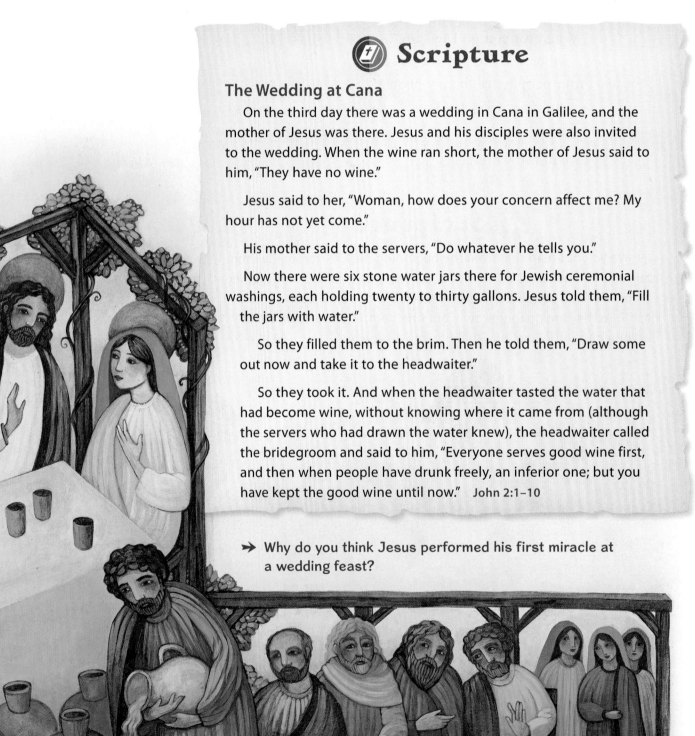

✝ Scripture

The Wedding at Cana

On the third day there was a wedding in Cana in Galilee, and the mother of Jesus was there. Jesus and his disciples were also invited to the wedding. When the wine ran short, the mother of Jesus said to him, "They have no wine."

Jesus said to her, "Woman, how does your concern affect me? My hour has not yet come."

His mother said to the servers, "Do whatever he tells you."

Now there were six stone water jars there for Jewish ceremonial washings, each holding twenty to thirty gallons. Jesus told them, "Fill the jars with water."

So they filled them to the brim. Then he told them, "Draw some out now and take it to the headwaiter."

So they took it. And when the headwaiter tasted the water that had become wine, without knowing where it came from (although the servers who had drawn the water knew), the headwaiter called the bridegroom and said to him, "Everyone serves good wine first, and then when people have drunk freely, an inferior one; but you have kept the good wine until now." John 2:1–10

➡ Why do you think Jesus performed his first miracle at a wedding feast?

© Our Sunday Visitor

Matrimony

Jesus' presence at the wedding at Cana showed his appreciation for marriage. Jesus taught that marriage is from God and cannot be broken by human choices. He said, "What God has joined together, no human being must separate" (Mark 10:9).

Because of Jesus' teaching, the Church recognizes marriage as a Sacrament and gives it the name **Matrimony**. Marriage is a lifelong partnership of service with two purposes. It helps people grow together in holiness and love, and it creates the proper place for welcoming children and educating them in the practice of the faith. Together a family is called the **domestic Church**.

Sacrament of Service

Matrimony is called a Sacrament at the Service of Communion. Married people share a unique covenant and have special responsibilities. A husband and wife pledge to live their lives in loving friendship and service to each other and to the community, and to be open to any children God gives them. By their mutual love and fidelity, they build up the whole community of faith and become a sign of salvation to all who witness their self-giving love.

Catholic Faith Words

Matrimony a Sacrament at the Service of Communion in which a baptized man and a baptized woman make a permanent covenant of love with each other and with God

domestic Church a name for the Catholic family, because it is the community of Christians in the home. God made the family to be the first place we learn about loving others and following Christ.

Share Your Faith

Reflect In a small group, brainstorm the qualities of a strong marriage.

Share Choose what you consider to be the three most important qualities of a strong marriage, and write them on slips of paper. Work with a partner and use the slips of paper to create a paper chain.

Pope Francis describes families as "...caring for one another... husbands and wives first protect one another, and then, as parents, they care for their children, and children themselves, in time, protect their parents."

A Domestic Church

How is the family a domestic Church?

During Pope Saint John Paul II's visit to the United States in 1987 he spoke about the importance of families. He said that the life of the parish greatly depends on the commitment and involvement of its families. The family is the basic unit of society and of the Church. The Pope, however, was very realistic when he said that some families are healthy and filled with the love of God, some families have little energy for the Spirit, and some families have broken down altogether.

The Church has a concern for all families, and she ministers to them in the name of Jesus. Families are so important that they are called domestic Churches. A domestic Church is a church of the home, a family community of faith, hope, and charity. New members of the Church emerge from the family and, in the family, faith in Jesus is first nourished by word and example. In his 1981 letter on the family, Pope Saint John Paul II said, "The family, called together by word and Sacrament as the Church of the home, is both teacher and mother, the same as the worldwide Church."

➡ **In what ways is a family a domestic Church?**

Catholic Faith Words

temperance is the Cardinal Virtue that helps us use moderation, be disciplined, and have self-control

chastity a moral virtue and Fruit of the Holy Spirit that helps us express sexuality in the right ways for our call in life. In religious life or Holy Orders, chastity includes being celibate.

modesty a moral virtue and one of the Fruits of the Holy Spirit that helps us to dress, talk, and move in appropriate ways

Sharing God's Love

The families that come from the union of marriage are meant to be living signs of faith for the Church and the world. With God's grace, husbands and wives follow Christ together in love, just as others may be called to do in Holy Orders, consecrated religious life, or a committed single life.

No matter what vocation of love and service to God and others you follow, you are required to live the virtues related to sexuality—**temperance, chastity,** and **modesty**—and to honor the Ninth Commandment. In doing so, purity of heart is achieved with God's grace, discipline, and prayer.

Connect Your Faith

Write a Postcard
Design and write a postcard for a couple, a single person, or a religious brother or sister you know who is a sign of God's love to others. Describe the good example that he or she shows. Send the postcard to the person.

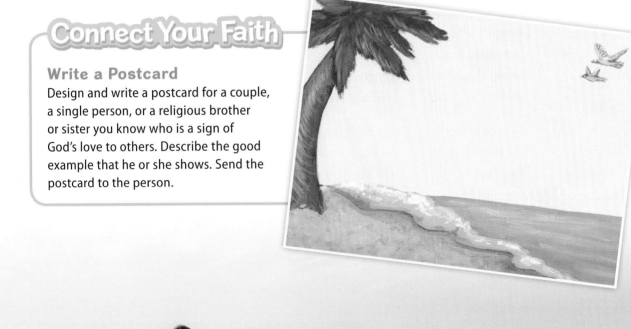

Our Catholic Life

How can you help promote harmony within your family?

The Letter to the Ephesians was written to a small community of faith that in many ways resembled a family. It faced challenges that many families face today. Outside pressures troubled the community. There was also anger and fighting among its members. Harmony was replaced by confusion.

The Letter to the Ephesians offered wise advice to the community in the city of Ephesus—advice that you can use to help promote harmony within your own family.

Ways to Harmony

"Put away falsehood; speak the truth."	*Remove "all bitterness, fury, anger, shouting, and reviling."*	*"Be kind to one another, compassionate, and forgiving."*	*"Live as children of light."*	*"Honor your father and mother."*
Families that respect the truth and allow their members to be _____ are usually healthy families. Always try to speak the truth.	Reviling is the use of abusive language. _____ and abuse tear families apart. Practice forgiveness.	There may be problems in your family, but your kindness, compassion, and _____ will go a long way toward easing these problems.	Take time to _____ for your family members. The light of Jesus and the Holy Spirit will help you bring light to the family.	The _____ Commandment is the first to carry a promise. The promise is "that it may go well with you and that you may have a long life on earth."

Based on Ephesians 4:25, 31, 32; 5:8; 6:2

Fill in the missing words to complete the explanation. If you need some help, read the passage from Ephesians in the New Testament.

People of Faith

July 13

Saint Henry II, 972–1024

Saint Henry is the only King of Germany to become a Saint. As a young boy, he thought he might become a priest, but instead God wanted him to become the ruler of the Holy Roman Empire. He and his wife Cunegond used their position and wealth to help as many people as they could. They gave away much of their fortune to help the poor. Saint Henry traveled throughout his kingdom trying to establish peace. He and Cunegond are buried together in Bamberg Cathedral in Germany.

Discuss: How does your family work for justice?

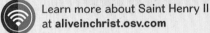 Learn more about Saint Henry II at **aliveinchrist.osv.com**

Live Your Faith

Draw or write ways in which marriage is a service in the circles below.

 **Let Us Pray**

Prayer of Blessing

Gather and begin with the
Sign of the Cross.

Leader: God our Father, we
ask your blessing on all
married couples.

Reader 1: May the peace of Christ live always in the hearts and homes
of all married couples.

Reader 2: May they be ready and willing to comfort all who come
to them in need, and may they enjoy the blessings promised
to the compassionate.

Reader 3: May their children bring them happiness, and may their
generous love for their children be returned to them over
and over again.

Reader 4: May they find happiness and satisfaction in their work.

Reader 5: May the Lord bless them with many happy years together
so that they may enjoy the rewards of a good life.

Leader: Let us pray.

Bow your heads as the leader prays.

All: Amen.

 Sing "Somos el Cuerpo de Cristo/We Are the Body of Christ"
Somos el cuerpo de Cristo.
We are the body of Christ.
Hemos oído el llamado;
we've answered "Yes" to the call of the Lord.
© 1994, Jaime Cortez. Published by OCP. All rights reserved.

FAMILY+FAITH
LIVING AND LEARNING TOGETHER

YOUR CHILD LEARNED >>>

This chapter identifies Matrimony as the Sacrament in which a baptized man and woman make a permanent covenant of love with each other and with God, and discusses the family as a domestic Church.

Scripture

 Read **Matthew 19:4–6** to find out what Jesus says about marriage.

Catholics Believe

- Matrimony helps a man and woman grow in love and holiness and prepare a home for children.
- The Church celebrates marriage through the Sacrament of Matrimony.

To learn more, go to the *Catechism of the Catholic Church* *#1612–1617, 1646–1651, 2204–2206* at **usccb.org**.

People of Faith

This week, your child learned about Saint King Henry II, who used his power and wealth to help the poor of his kingdom.

CHILDREN AT THIS AGE >>>

How They Understand Marriage A sixth-grader's understanding of marriage is strongly related to their experience of marriage in the home. Children with single or divorced parents or children who live with couples whose marriages involve much conflict can still learn about healthy marriage. By emphasizing God's love for us and his desire for our happiness, adults can help children understand that even in our brokenness and our sinfulness, God is always urging us to love as he loves.

CONSIDER THIS >>>

Are you aware that your child is the visible sign of the invisible love between you and your spouse?

Our Catholic faith teaches that God's love made visible in your commitment to each other is now "enfleshed" in your child. Your child is a sign of your participation in God's ongoing process of giving life. As Catholics, we know that "the couple's joyful acceptance of children includes the responsibility to serve as models of Christian commitment for their children and helps them grow in wisdom and grace. In this way, the family becomes a 'domestic church'" *(USCCA, p. 286)*.

LET'S TALK >>>

- Ask your child to describe purity of heart.
- Talk about the importance of temperance and practicing the virtues of chastity and modesty.

LET'S PRAY >>>

 Saint Henry, help all married couples live out their vocation and raise healthy, happy families. Amen.

For a multimedia glossary of Catholic Faith Words, Sunday readings, seasonal and Saint resources, and chapter activities go to **aliveinchrist.osv.com**.

Chapter 18 Review

A Work with Words **Fill in the circle next to the correct answer.**

1. Jesus' first miracle in the Gospel according to John was _____.
   - ○ walking on water
   - ○ turning water into wine
   - ○ the multiplication of loaves

2. The Sacrament that unites a baptized man and woman is _____.
   - ○ Matrimony
   - ○ Eucharist
   - ○ Holy Orders

3. The two purposes of marriage are to help people grow together in holiness and love and to create a place for welcoming _____.
   - ○ strangers
   - ○ pets
   - ○ children

4. _____ said: "The family, called together by word and Sacrament as the Church of the home, is both teacher and mother, the same as the worldwide Church."
   - ○ Saint Peter
   - ○ Jesus
   - ○ Pope Saint John Paul II

5. The basic unit of society and the Church is the _____.
   - ○ marriage
   - ○ family
   - ○ single life

B Check Understanding **Circle the choice that best completes each sentence.**

6. The cardinal virtue of **(temperance, modesty)** helps you use moderation, be disciplined, and have self-control.

7. To live in harmony, a family should practice living as **(children of darkness, children of light)**.

8. A **(domestic, foreign)** Church is a church of the home.

9. The moral virtue of **(chastity, modesty)** leads you to dress, talk, and move in appropriate ways.

10. In Holy Orders, chastity includes being **(celibate, married)**.

Go to **aliveinchrist.osv.com** for an interactive review.

Unit Review

A **Work with Words** Complete each sentence with the correct term from the Word Bank.

Word Bank

Baptism   mission   Matrimony   consecrated

vocation   Sacrament   domestic   Sacred Chrism

Reconciliation   ordained   evangelization   Magisterium

1. A call to love and serve God is a _____.

2. A sending forth to share the Good News of Jesus and God's Kingdom is known as a _____.

3. _____ is a Sacrament of Service in which a man and woman make a covenant of love with each other and with God.

4. _____ is blessed oil used for anointing in the Sacraments of Baptism, Confirmation, and Holy Orders.

5. _____ is giving witness to the faith by proclaiming the Good News of Jesus Christ to the world through words and deeds.

6. Families are the order God created and are so important that they are called _____ Churches.

7. The _____ ministry of bishops, priests, and deacons includes leading the celebration of the Sacraments and governing the faithful.

8. _____ religious life is lived in community and characterized by profession of vows.

9. The _____ is the teaching authority of the Church.

10. Catholics become members of Christ's Church through _____.

B **Check Understanding** Fill in the circle next to the correct answer.

11. Jesus fulfills the ministry of priest, prophet, and _____.

○ author

○ teacher

○ king

○ father

12. Which one of these leads you to dress, talk, and move in appropriate ways?

○ fortitude

○ modesty

○ chastity

○ patience

13. In the Gospel according to John, Jesus performed his first miracle in _____.

○ Cana

○ Galilee

○ Bethlehem

○ Bethany

14. _____ is the virtue that helps you use moderation in your life.

○ Chastity

○ Temperance

○ Purity of heart

○ Love

15. Jesus submitted to John's baptism to show the importance of _____.

○ holy water

○ symbols

○ John

○ conversion

C Make Connections **Write a response to each question.**

16. What are some examples of different missions?

_____

_____

_____

_____

17. What does Real Presence mean?

_____

_____

_____

_____

18. What does Jesus mean when he says "If anyone wishes to be first, he shall be the last of all and the servant of all"?

_____

_____

_____

_____

19. Why is it important to honor your father and mother?

_____

_____

_____

_____

20. What kinds of sacrifices do people who accept the call to ordained priesthood or religious life make?

_____

_____

_____

_____

Kingdom of God

Our Catholic Tradition

- When we celebrate the Eucharist, we are connected through the Communion of Saints to the living Christian faithful and those who have died in Christ. (CCC, 1370)

- The Church is called to work for the unity of all Christians and to reunite the Body of Christ. (CCC, 820)

- We know that God will triumph over evil when Christ comes again in glory. (CCC, 677)

How does the Communion of Saints express God's plan, his desire for all people?

© Our Sunday Visitor

The Communion of Saints

 **Let Us Pray**

Leader: Help us be devoted, O Lord, to you and to one another.

"The heavens praise your marvels, LORD,
 your loyalty in the assembly of the holy
  ones." **Psalm 89:6**

All: Faithful Lord, keep us one in communion, unfailing in charity, and constant in prayer. Include us all in the great circle of Saints. Amen.

 **Scripture**

"To all the beloved of God … called to be holy. Grace to you and peace from God our Father and the Lord Jesus Christ. First, I give thanks to my God through Jesus Christ for all of you, because your faith is heralded throughout the world."

Romans 1:7–8

? What Do You Wonder?

- How do the Saints in Heaven help you to live your life as a disciple?

- Why do you pray for others—living and dead?

The Church Community

What is the Communion of Saints?

Isn't it great when you feel like you belong? Whether you are part of a sports team, a scout troop, or your family, belonging helps us feel valued and secure. A community gives us a sense of oneness, a sense of unity.

The members of the first Christian community were joined to one another by bonds of faith, hope, and charity. They knew this was the way to live as Jesus did. Things were generously shared and distributed according to need. Here is a biblical description of life in the early Church.

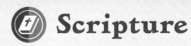

Scripture

Communal Life

They devoted themselves to the teaching of the apostles and to the communal life, to the breaking of the bread and to the prayers... All who believed were together and had all things in common; they would sell their property and possessions and divide them among all according to each one's need. Every day they devoted themselves to meeting together in the temple area and to breaking bread in their homes. They ate their meals with exultation and sincerity of heart, praising God and enjoying favor with all the people. And every day the Lord added to their number those who were being saved. **Acts 2:42–47**

Catholic Faith Words

Communion of Saints when referring to holy persons, the Communion of Saints includes the pilgrim Church on Earth, those being purified in Purgatory, and the blessed already in Heaven

Heaven the full joy of living eternally in God's presence

Purgatory a state of final cleansing after death and before entering into Heaven

Hell eternal separation from God because of a choice to turn away from him and not seek forgiveness

All the Faithful

The first community of Christians was very small, but the Church today has grown to include many members all over the world. You are still connected today to the early Christians.

The Church itself is often referred to as a **Communion of Saints**. This expression refers first to the holy things, above all the Eucharist, by which the unity of the faithful is represented and brought about. The term also refers to the communion among all the faithful who are living today and those who have died and are in **Heaven** or **Purgatory**. The Communion of Saints is bound together by the love of the Holy Trinity.

At death, some people are not ready for Heaven and God's eternal friendship. However, they have not broken their relationship with God and are not to be separated from God in **Hell**. These souls need final purification in Purgatory. Purgatory is a state of final cleansing that helps the soul prepare for life with God.

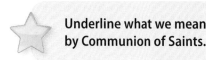

Underline what we mean by Communion of Saints.

As a member of the Communion of Saints, you are encouraged by the Church to pray for the souls in Purgatory.

Two very special days celebrated in the Church year are All Saints Day on November 1, and All Souls Day on November 2. All Saints Day is a Holy Day of Obligation. It honors all who live now with God in Heaven. On All Souls Day, the Church prays for those who have died in friendship with God but are undergoing final purification before enjoying eternal happiness with him in Heaven.

Share Your Faith

Reflect Review the stories of the people of faith about whom you have read in this book.

Share With a partner, choose two of these people and discuss the qualities that made them people of faith. Write some qualities you would like to develop.

_____

_____

Saint Ignatius of Loyola

Charity and Prayer

What do charity and prayer have to do with the Communion of Saints?

One virtue that links you directly with the Communion of Saints and the Trinity is charity. It is the Theological Virtue by which you love God above all things and by which you love others because you love God. It is one of the three virtues that relate directly to your relationship with God. Charity calls you to live as the Trinity lives, in perfect love.

In the Scripture account of the first Christians, you saw an example of people practicing charity. Out of charity, you use your resources—your time, your money, and your talents—to show your love of God by helping others in need. Charitable people show care for the physical needs of others through the **Corporal Works of Mercy**, such as feeding the hungry or visiting the sick. They also address the spiritual needs of others by performing the **Spiritual Works of Mercy**.

One way the Church provides for the physical and spiritual needs of her members is through the Sacrament of the Anointing of the Sick, which is part of the Church's pastoral care of the sick. Through this Sacrament, an elderly or very sick person is anointed by the priest with the oil of the sick, which has been blessed by a bishop, and strengthened by prayer and the grace of the Holy Spirit.

The celebration of this Sacrament includes the laying on of hands by the priest, a prayer, and the anointing itself on the hands and forehead of the recipient. The priest offers this prayer:

Through this holy anointing,
may the Lord in his love and mercy help you
with the grace of the Holy Spirit.

May the Lord who frees you from sin
save you and raise you up.

from Pastoral Care of the Sick: Anointing, #124

© Our Sunday Visitor

Intercessory Prayer

Praying for others is one of the Works of Mercy. A prayer of **intercession**, or intercessory prayer, is interceding, or stepping between, God and others to ask God's help for them. You can pray for those who are close to you; for those around the world who suffer from hunger, poverty, disease, and war; and for those who have died and are not yet with God in Heaven.

You can pray by using your own words to ask God's help for whatever you or others need. You can also use such traditional prayers as litanies. You can pray out loud or in silence, at Mass or in a peaceful place. Others in the Communion of Saints will also intercede with God for you. You can ask Mary, the Mother of God, and all the Saints to present your prayers before God.

Personal Prayer

Every member of the Communion of Saints is important. As you grow stronger in your own relationship with God, you make the whole Communion of Saints stronger. One way to create stronger bonds is through your personal prayer.

One form of personal prayer is reflection. When you reflect on God, you use your mind, imagination, and emotions to listen to him and deepen your faith. For example, you can read from the Bible and ask the Holy Spirit to help you understand what God is saying to you as you reflect on the Scripture passage. Other thoughts and worries may enter your mind and distract you from prayer. Gently turn away from them and back to God.

© Our Sunday Visitor

S. JOSEPH.

> ### Catholic Faith Words
>
> **Corporal Works of Mercy** actions that show care for the physical needs of others
>
> **Spiritual Works of Mercy** actions that address the needs of the heart, mind, and soul
>
> **intercession** a form of prayer that involves praying to God on behalf of another; also called intercessory prayer

Connect Your Faith

Design a Prayer Card Make a list of family members, both living and dead. Then design a prayer card to remind yourself to pray for them. Keep it with you every day.

Our Catholic Life

What are some ways in which you can intercede for others?

Intercessory prayer is praying to God for the needs of others. The Bible has many examples of these kinds of prayers. When you pray for others and their needs, you serve them. There are many ways in which you can pray for the needs of others. Here are some steps to follow.

In the space provided, write who or what you would pray for in each category.

© Our Sunday Visitor

Praying for Others

Pray for people you know who are in need of God's blessing.	**Pray for the issues of your nation and the world.**
• Remember those among your family and friends who are sick, troubled, or lonely.	• Ask for peace in countries torn by war.
• Keep in mind Jesus' teaching that you should remember your enemies when you pray.	• Pray for those who have been affected by natural disasters.
• _____	• _____
Pray for the needs of your community.	**Offer a prayer for the Church.**
• Ask for God's blessing on people who are poor and homeless.	• Pray for Church leaders, that they may continue to be guided by the Holy Spirit.
• Pray for justice where there is division or unrest.	• Ask for God's mercy on those who have died, as well as on those who are living.
• Pray for the strengthening of families.	• Pray for the work of the Church everywhere.
• _____	• _____

People of Faith

October 5

Saint Mary Faustina Kowalska, 1905–1938

Saint Mary Faustina was born in Poland. She was the third of ten children. When she was twenty, she entered the Congregation of Sisters of Our Lady of Mercy. While praying one night, she had a vision of Jesus as the "King of Divine Mercy." He told her that she was to tell the whole world that God was merciful and kind. She had a picture of Jesus painted showing red and white rays of light coming from his heart. She told us all to pray, "Jesus, I trust in you." She is sometimes called the "Apostle of Divine Mercy."

Discuss: How do you show your trust in Jesus?

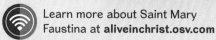 Learn more about Saint Mary Faustina at **aliveinchrist.osv.com**

Live Your Faith

Develop prayers for your community and for the Church using the suggestions from the previous page. Pray both together to form one intercessory prayer.

Community:

_____

_____

_____

_____

Church:

_____

_____

_____

_____

_____

_____

_____

_____

Let Us Pray

Litany of the Saints

Gather and begin with the Sign of the Cross.

Leader: Holy Mary, Mother of God,

All: Pray for us.

Leader: Saint John the Baptist,

All: Pray for us.

Leader: Saint Mary Magdalene,

All: Pray for us.

Leader: Saint Ignatius,

All: Pray for us.

ST FRANCISCO DE ASIS

Leader: Saint Francis of Assisi,

All: Pray for us.

Leader: All holy women and men,

All: Pray for us.

Leader: Lord, be merciful,

All: Lord, save your People.

Leader: By your Death and rising to new life,

All: Lord, save your People.

Leader: By your gift of the Holy Spirit,

All: Lord, save your People. Amen.

▶ Sing "For All the Saints"

© Our Sunday Visitor

FAMILY+FAITH

LIVING AND LEARNING TOGETHER

YOUR CHILD LEARNED >>>

This chapter explores the Works of Mercy, explains intercessory prayer and reflection, and identifies the Communion of Saints.

Scripture

Read **Romans 1:7** to find out what Saint Paul says about our call to be Saints.

Catholics Believe

- Members of the Communion of Saints can intercede for others.
- The Communion of Saints includes all holy persons, both living and dead, who are united in the Eucharist.

To learn more, go to the *Catechism of the Catholic Church #946–948, 2634–2638* at **usccb.org**.

People of Faith

This week, your child learned about Saint Mary Faustina Kowalska, the founder of the Divine Mercy devotion.

CHILDREN AT THIS AGE >>>

How They Understand the Saints Saints can be important heroes to children this age, especially when they are exposed to young people who showed extraordinary virtue, such as Saint Dominic Savio or Saint Maria Goretti. A large part of identity development for the middle school child is dependent upon the examples and mentors the child chooses, and there is no better place to turn than to the Saints. It is also important for children this age to learn that God wishes for all of us to be Saints. Holiness is possible for each person.

CONSIDER THIS >>>

Do you believe that love is stronger than death?

When someone we love dies, often the only thought that gets us through the grief of loss is the belief that he or she now lives in the arms of God. All members of the Church, both living and dead, are included in the Communion of Saints. The act of praying for the living and the dead is a sign of connection among all believers. As Catholics, we know that "the Church assists those in Purgatory through prayer and especially the Eucharist in their final process of purification. Offering Masses for the deceased is a most powerful way of aiding them" *(USCCA, p. 154).*

LET'S TALK >>>

- Ask your child to describe the Communion of Saints.
- Talk about how your family honors— throughout the year and especially on All Saints Day or All Souls Day—family members and others who have died.

LET'S PRAY >>>

"For the sake of His sorrowful Passion, have mercy on us and on the whole world." (Divine Mercy prayer)

For a multimedia glossary of Catholic Faith Words, Sunday readings, seasonal and Saint resources, and chapter activities go to **aliveinchrist.osv.com**.

Chapter 19 Review

A Work with Words **Complete each statement.**

1. Love of God and neighbor is called _____.

2. _____ is a form of prayer in which you use your mind, imagination, and emotions to listen to God and deepen your faith.

3. The state of final cleansing after death and before entering into Heaven is called _____.

4. _____ is eternal separation from God because of a choice to turn away from him and not seek forgiveness.

5. Charitable people provide for the spiritual needs of others by performing _____.

6. When you ask God's help for others, you _____ for them.

7. _____ is the full joy of living eternally in God's Presence.

B Check Understanding **Write a summary of the chapter, using the terms from the Word Bank.**

8–10. _____

_____

_____

_____

_____

_____

_____

_____

_____

_____

_____

Word Bank

communal life

intercessory prayer

Communion of Saints

early Christians

Go to **aliveinchrist.osv.com** for an interactive review.

CHAPTER 20

Christian Unity

 Let Us Pray

Leader: Draw near, O Lord of all, bind us together in truth and love.

"The LORD is near to all who call upon him, to all who call upon him in truth." **Psalm 145:18**

All: Draw near, O Lord of all, bind us together in truth and love.

 Scripture

…preserve the unity of the spirit through the bond of peace: one body and one Spirit, as you were also called to the one hope of your call; one Lord, one faith, one baptism; one God and Father of all, who is over all and through all and in all. **Ephesians 4:3–6**

? What Do You Wonder?

- Why is there disunity among Christians today?
- How did this disunity come about?

Unity and Division

What did Jesus teach about unity?

In the garden, on the night before he died, Jesus prayed to the Father that his disciples would be one.

Highlight how Jesus described the unity he prayed for.

 Scripture

The Prayer of Jesus

Later in the garden, Jesus prayed… "Behold, the hour is coming and has arrived when each of you will be scattered to his own home and you will leave me alone. … In the world you will have trouble, but take courage, I have conquered the world."

Then Jesus prayed, "Holy Father, keep them in your name that you have given me, so that they may be one just as we are. … I pray not only for them, but also for those who will believe in me through their word, so that they may all be one, as you, Father, are in me and I in you, that they also may be in us, that the world may believe that you sent me." Based on John 16:32–33, 17:11, 20–21

One of the most precious gifts of the Church is the unity that comes from Jesus. The Church has one Lord, one faith, and one Baptism. Jesus formed his followers into one Body and gave that Body the life of one Spirit.

The Story Continues

Before the Last Supper was over, Judas had left to arrange for Jesus' arrest. Like the history of the Israelites, the history of the Church is a story of heroes and holiness. But there are also times of sin and failure along the way. As time went on, other people tested the unity of the Church. Because of this, Paul wrote to the Corinthians, urging them to be united in the same mind and purpose. (See 1 Corinthians 1:10–13.)

More Divisions

In A.D. 1054, a **schism**, or division, occurred between the Church in the East and the Church in the West. Leaders quarreled about authority, Church practices, and Church teaching. The Great Schism, as it was called, continues to this day. The Eastern Orthodox Churches remain divided from the Catholic Church.

In the 1500s the Catholic Church experienced another separation. A priest named Martin Luther spoke out against some practices of the Church that he believed could confuse believers. His action led to the **Protestant Reformation**. Luther and several other Christian leaders and groups separated from the authority of the Pope. The unity of the Church in the West was shattered. Despite improvements, Protestants and Catholics are still separated today.

> ## Catholic Faith Words
>
> **schism** a break or division
>
> **Protestant Reformation** a sixteenth-century religious separation from the Catholic Church that began with Martin Luther's preaching against what he felt were errors in the Church

Share Your Faith

Reflect Create a timeline or other visual summary of the events in Church history, including the divisions you have read about. Choose an image that symbolizes the events.

Share Explain your symbol to a partner. Then discuss why you think unity was so important to Jesus.

New Hope

What is ecumenism?

Today there are many different Protestant communities. These communities have their own organization, worship, and set of beliefs. Since the Protestant Reformation, these communities have continued to subdivide. These splits have occurred because people have disagreed about such issues as biblical interpretation, authority, and worship.

Division among Christians has been a sad reality for a long time. For centuries various groups ignored the love and unity in Jesus that was their bond as Christians.

In the early 1900s, representatives of many Christian groups gathered to talk about working in harmony. Realizing that they had neglected working for unity in Jesus, they began the ecumenical movement. The word **ecumenism** comes from a Greek biblical phrase that means "the whole household of God." The purpose of this organized effort is to bring Christians together in a spirit of cooperation and to work together in hope to restore unity among Christians.

➜ **How can you be respectful of other people's beliefs?**

© Our Sunday Visitor

Catholic Faith Words

ecumenism an organized effort to bring Christians together in cooperation as they look forward in hope to the restoration of the unity of the Christian Church

Ecumenism Today

The ecumenical movement was one of the important issues Catholic bishops from around the world discussed during the Second Vatican Council. This Church council took place in Rome between 1962 and 1965. The bishops agreed that unity among Christians was Christ's desire for the Church, and that the divisions between Christians should not be ignored.

The bishops outlined steps Christians could take to encourage the spirit of ecumenism. Unity would be possible only if Christians from different groups began to talk to one another. Christians should join together for prayer and acts of service. Churches should focus on what unites them rather than on what divides them. As Saint Paul tells us, "as a body is one though it has many parts, and all the parts of the body, though many, are one body, also in Christ" (1 Corinthians 12:12).

We can work with other Christians to further the unity for which Jesus prayed. We can open doors to understanding by respecting the views of others while holding fast to our own. Place your hope for unity in the power of the Holy Spirit. Pray to make Christianity one, as Jesus and the Father are one.

➡ **When and where did Catholic bishops discuss and outline steps toward ecumenism?**

Connect Your Faith

A Poem for Unity Write a poem about the unity you would like to see in the Church. Use the following pattern:

Unity

Two adjectives that describe unity: _____

Three words with –ing endings that describe unity: _____

A short sentence about unity: _____

One word that is a synonym for unity: _____

Our Catholic Life

How can the Church work toward greater unity among Christians?

The Catholic bishops at the Second Vatican Council described seven steps the Church could take toward greater unity among Christians. Here are the steps the bishops outlined for the Church, as well as some actions you can take.

Check off things you can do to work toward unity.

Steps to Unity

The Church must renew herself.	Stay informed. Continue to learn about Jesus and the Church.	☐
The members of the Church must practice conversion of heart.	Grow in holiness. Accept the challenge to grow in your faith.	☐
All Christians must pray together.	Pray for unity with other Christians, including Protestant Christians.	☐
Christians should come to know one another as brothers and sisters.	Learn how other Christians worship and live their faith.	☐
Both priests and lay people should learn about the spirit of ecumenism.	Don't assume that everyone has learned about ecumenism. Spread the word among family and friends.	☐
Christians from different communities should meet and talk about what they hold in common.	Under the guidance of your teacher and pastor, invite speakers from other Christian communities to talk with your group about what they hold in common with Catholics.	☐
Christians should cooperate in service projects.	Plan a service project with a group from a Protestant community.	☐

Parish councils meet to discuss how a parish can help its members and the community.

People of Faith

Saint Charles Borromeo, 1538–1584

Saint Charles was born into a wealthy Italian family. His uncle was Pope Pius IV. Charles became a priest, then a bishop, and finally a cardinal. He worked hard to correct the problems that had caused Protestants to separate from the Church during the Protestant Reformation. He believed that many of the problems and divisions happened because priests needed more education. He built many schools to train priests so they could be better teachers. He also helped write an important Catechism explaining what the Catholic Church teaches. When he had free time, Saint Charles liked to play pool!

Discuss: How do you accept those whose beliefs differ from yours?

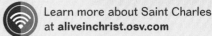
Learn more about Saint Charles at **aliveinchrist.osv.com**

Live Your Faith

Fill in the street signs with the signs of Christian unity you see in your community. Write about one you would especially like to participate in.

I would like to...

_____

_____

_____

_____

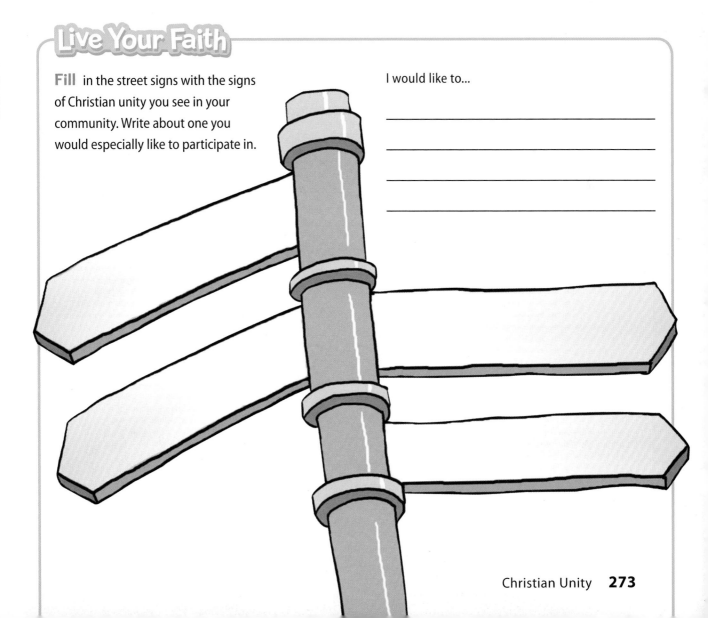

Christian Unity   **273**

Let Us Pray

Prayer of Petition

Gather and begin with the Sign of the Cross.

Leader: Lord, give us the strength to live in a manner worthy of the call we have received.

All: Lord, show us how to be one.

Leader: Give us the grace to act with all humility and gentleness, with patience, bearing with one another through love.

All: Lord, show us how to be one.

Leader: Guide us so that we move toward unity and peace.

All: Lord, show us how to be one.

Leader: We are one body and have one Spirit and are called together with one hope.

All: Lord, show us how to be one.

Leader: You have given us one Lord, one faith, one Baptism, one God and Father of all, who is over all things, through all things, and in all things.

All: Lord, show us how to be one. Amen. **Based on Ephesians 4:1–6**

 Sing "One Spirit, One Church"

We are a pilgrim people.
We are the Church of God.
A fam'ly of believers,
disciples of the Lord.
United in one spirit,
ignited by the fire.
Still burning through the ages,
still present in our lives.

FAMILY+FAITH
LIVING AND LEARNING TOGETHER

YOUR CHILD LEARNED >>>

This chapter explores Jesus' desire for unity among his believers, explains ecumenism. and examines the Catholic Church's desire to reunite the Body of Christ.

Scripture

 Read **Ephesians 4:3–6** to find out what Saint Paul writes about the importance of unity.

Catholics Believe

- Catholics work toward the unity of all Christians, because God desires it.
- Today the ecumenical movement looks for ways to help all Christians work toward unity.

To learn more, go to the *Catechism of the Catholic Church #813–822* at **usccb.org**.

People of Faith

This week, your child learned about Saint Charles Borromeo, who is known for working to heal divisions within Christianity.

CHILDREN AT THIS AGE >>>

How They Understand Christian Unity Your child may have friends from school or other activities who belong to other Christian communities. He or she might be curious about what sorts of issues divide Christians and what things unite us as believers in Jesus. While our ability to worship together is sometimes limited, it is important to respect and recognize one another as believers in Jesus and to encourage one another to the extent possible.

CONSIDER THIS >>>

How do you show respect for people whose thinking is different from yours?

The first step in showing respect for another is an openness to listen. In order to begin to understand another's point of view or their beliefs we must begin with hearts open to receive what we do not understand. Ecumenism is the effort of various religions to listen to one another and work toward unity of belief. As Catholics, we understand that "ecumenism includes efforts to pray together, joint study of the Scripture and of one another's traditions, common action for social justice, and dialogue in which leaders and theologians of the different churches and communities discuss in depth their doctrinal and theological positions for greater mutual understanding, and 'to work for unity in truth' (UUS, nos. 18, 29). In dialogue the obligation to respect the truth is absolute" (*USCCA, p. 128*).

LET'S TALK >>>

- Ask your child to explain Jesus' desire for us all to be united.
- Talk about how your family respects people of other faiths.

LET'S PRAY >>>

 Saint Charles, pray for us that we may work toward the unity of all Christians. Help us accept those whose beliefs differ from our own. Amen.

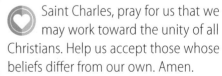 For a multimedia glossary of Catholic Faith Words, Sunday readings, seasonal and Saint resources, and chapter activities go to **aliveinchrist.osv.com**.

Chapter 20 Review

A **Work with Words** Fill in the circle next to the correct answer.

1. Jesus' prayer that "all may be one, as you, Father, are in me and I in you," is a prayer for _____.
   ○ unity
   ○ division
   ○ justice

2. The break that occurred between the Churches in the East and the West is called the _____.
   ○ Great Schism
   ○ Protestant Reformation
   ○ Second Vatican Council

3. In the sixteenth century, Martin Luther's words gave rise to the _____.
   ○ Great Schism
   ○ Second Vatican Council
   ○ Protestant Reformation

4. Since the Protestant Reformation, independent Christian groups; called _____ have formed.
   ○ Christian ecumenism
   ○ Christian communities
   ○ Christian schisms

5. In the 1960s, ecumenism was an issue discussed by bishops from around the world at the _____.
   ○ Council of Trent
   ○ Second Vatican Council
   ○ First Vatican Council

6. Unity among different groups is possible only through the power of the _____.
   ○ Holy Spirit
   ○ Pope
   ○ Church

7. The word _____ comes from a Greek biblical phrase that means "the whole household of God."
   ○ unity
   ○ ecumenism
   ○ denomination

8. In the First Letter to the _____, Paul urged Christians to be united in the same mind and purpose.
   ○ Thessalonians
   ○ Romans
   ○ Corinthians

9. During the Great Schism, leaders quarreled about _____, Church practices, and Church teaching.
   ○ authority
   ○ those who were poor
   ○ property

10. Jesus said, "In the _____ you will have trouble, but take courage, I have conquered the _____."
    ○ Church
    ○ home
    ○ world

Go to **aliveinchrist.osv.com** for an interactive review.

A New Creation

 **Let Us Pray**

Leader: O God, help us put our hope in you.

"I wait for the LORD,
  my soul waits
  and I hope for his word.
For with the LORD is mercy,
  with him is plenteous redemption."

Psalm 130:5, 7

All: O God, help us put our hope in you. Amen.

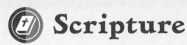 **Scripture**

Conducting yourselves in holiness and devotion, waiting for and hastening the coming of the day of God, ... [A]ccording to his promise we await new heavens and a new earth in which righteousness dwells. ... [G]row in grace and in the knowledge of our Lord and savior Jesus Christ. To him be glory now and to the day of eternity.

2 Peter 3:11b–12a, 13, 18

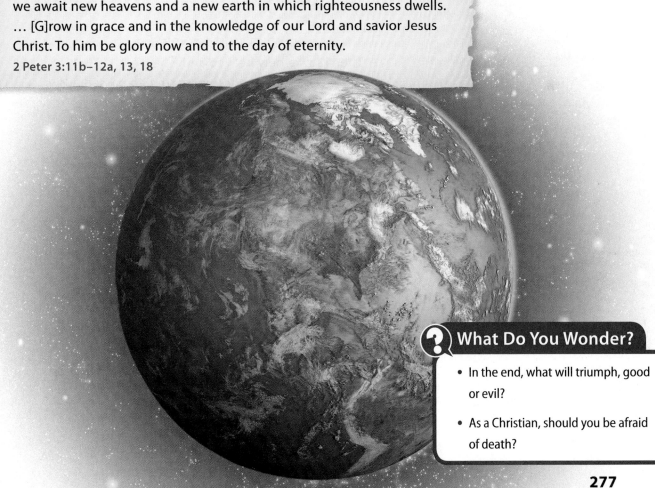

? What Do You Wonder?

- In the end, what will triumph, good or evil?

- As a Christian, should you be afraid of death?

277

The Triumph of Good

What is the Book of Revelation about?

The ultimate victory of good over evil will take place when Christ comes in glory. You can read about this victory in the Book of Revelation. To understand Revelation, you must not take the images and symbols literally. The symbols are meant not only to describe the end of the world, but also to give hope and assurance to Christians.

This book was written as a form of **apocalyptic literature**. The word *apocalyptic* refers to something that is revealed, or unveiled. The Book of Revelation unveils the reality of God. The author used symbols and numbers to unveil a message for his fellow Christians who were being oppressed and persecuted.

The message is simple: God will triumph over evil. He will give life to all who have died for their faith. Jesus will return and bring about a new world in which peace and justice last forever.

Catholic Faith Words

apocalyptic literature a type of writing that reveals what humans cannot see, including the spiritual world or future events

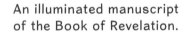

An illuminated manuscript of the Book of Revelation.

ⓣ Scripture

The New Heaven and the New Earth

Then I saw a new heaven and a new earth. The former heaven and the former earth had passed away, and the sea was no more. I also saw the holy city, a new Jerusalem, coming down out of heaven from God, prepared as a bride adorned for her husband. I heard a loud voice from the throne saying, "Behold, God's dwelling is with the human race. He will dwell with them and they will be his people and God himself will always be with them [as their God]. He will wipe every tear from their eyes, and there shall be no more death or mourning, wailing or pain, [for] the old order has passed away." **Revelation 21:1–4**

➔ What is the purpose of the symbols and images in the Book of Revelation?

➔ What is God's message for us today?

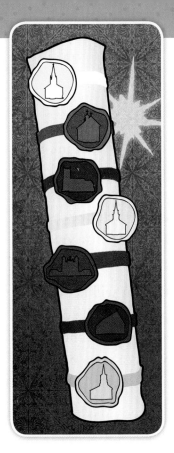

Unveiling the Future

Toward the end of the first century, the Roman Emperors Nero and Domitian ordered that Christians be persecuted. Many followers of Jesus grew fearful as they watched their friends and family members sent to their deaths. These Christians wanted assurance that their faithfulness would be rewarded. They found that assurance in the Book of Revelation.

The writer of Revelation received the revelation in visions. Someone "like a son of man," with a face as bright as the sun, spoke to him. He meant Jesus. The writer was given seven messages for seven churches. The messages were meant for the Church everywhere.

After these messages, Revelation describes many more visions. In one, the writer sees the greatness and glory of God. He meets "the Lamb who was slain," another image of Jesus. The Lamb is handed a scroll closed with seven seals. Each opened seal sets loose a frightening image of death. The opening of the seventh seal begins a new cycle of seven angels blowing trumpets. Each trumpet blast sends a new plague upon the Earth. The seventh trumpet, however, promises that God's new creation is coming soon. (See Revelation 5:6—11:19.) Other visions follow, but this promise is repeatedly made: God will triumph over evil. The old world is ending. A new world is coming.

Key to Revelation
Numbers
4 = the world
6 = imperfection
7 = perfection or completion
12 = Israel or the Apostles
666 = imperfection or evil
1,000 = a huge amount or a long time

Share Your Faith

Reflect What evils do you hope God will triumph over today?

Share In a small group, pray for God's victory over these evils. Then write a message to people your age about staying hopeful in the midst of the troubles of the world.

_____

_____

Hope for the Future

What is God's new creation?

The **Resurrection** of Jesus is the source of Revelation's hope and optimism. By his Resurrection, Jesus triumphed over death and transformed death into life. He changed the curse of death into a blessing. Those who are put to death for their faith will be raised from the dead. People who mourn those martyred are reassured by the Book of Revelation that death is not the end.

Because Jesus has been raised to new life, you will be raised, too. When you were baptized, you were raised from the death of sin to a new life with God the Father, the Son, and the Holy Spirit. After you die, having lived the promises of your Baptism, you will live with God forever.

Your body will someday die, just as Jesus' body died on the Cross. But your body will be raised to new life, just as Jesus was raised from the dead. In the Old Testament, God gradually revealed the reality of bodily resurrection. So when Jesus was raised from the dead, his followers were able to accept the reality of a living, breathing, triumphant Jesus returned from the dead in a glorified body.

→ **How does your belief in the Resurrection affect how you feel about loved ones who have died?**

Students stand in silent prayer at the Nativity Church in Bethlehem.

New Creation

Revelation's final vision is of a **new creation**. God promises that this new creation will include new Heavens and a new Earth ruled by God's justice. (See 2 Peter 3:13.) Good will be rewarded and evil punished. The righteous, those who seek God sincerely and respond to his grace, will reign with God forever.

The Reign of God has already begun with Jesus. It is present in the Church, the beginning of the new Jerusalem, which is the beginning of the Kingdom of God on Earth.

The Bible begins with the story of creation in Genesis, and ends with the story of the new creation in Revelation. These stories tell you that the world began and will end according to God's design.

© Our Sunday Visitor

Catholic Faith Words

Resurrection the event of Jesus being raised from Death to new life by God the Father through the power of the Holy Spirit

new creation the future of justice, love, and peace promised by God, in which good will be rewarded and evil punished

Connect Your Faith

The "New Jerusalem" Read Revelation 21:1–4. In a poem or drawing, tell or show what you think the "new Jerusalem" will look like.

Our Catholic Life

How can you have hope for the future?

Hope is a wish for something with an expectation that you may get it. You may hope for many things, such as good grades or a friendship with a particular person. The Theological Virtue of hope, however, is a gift from God by which you trust that he will grant you eternal life and the necessary grace to obtain it.

For a Christian, the great hope, the one that makes all the other hopes possible, is that you will see God in Heaven and enjoy life with him forever. Here are some ways to become a person of great hope.

Have faith

Faith makes it possible for you to hope for something that will last forever. Persevere. Keep your eyes fixed on Jesus. Like him, you will have trials as well as successes, sadness as well as happiness, setbacks as well as victories. "For the sake of the joy that lay before him [Jesus] endured the cross," and then he took his place next to his Father in Heaven. (See Hebrews 12:2.)

Remind yourself of God's friendship

In life and death you can truly rely on God's friendship. "For I am convinced that neither death, nor life, . . . nor present things, nor future things, . . . nor any other creature will be able to separate us from the love of God in Christ Jesus our Lord" (Romans 8:38–39).

Pray

Stay close to the source of hope. The virtue of hope is not something you give yourself. It is a gift that God gives you. Through your prayer, he increases your hope and makes you a stronger person.

Write one thing for which you hope and pray. Tell how the steps above help to guide your prayer.

_____

_____

_____

_____

People of Faith

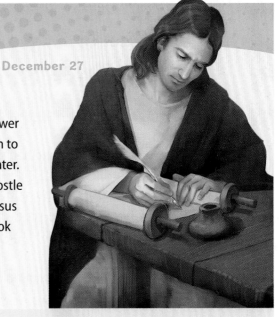

Saint John the Evangelist, c. 4–104

Saint John was the son of Zebedee and Salome. He was a follower of Saint John the Baptist and a fisherman until Jesus called him to be an Apostle. He joined Jesus with his brother James the Greater. Saint John was with Jesus for three years and was the only Apostle known to have been present at the crucifixion. At that time, Jesus placed Mary in his care. John is said to be the author of the Book of Revelation, the final book of the Bible, as well as the Gospel according to John, and three Epistles. He was the last of the Apostles to die, and was very old at that time.

Discuss: How do you follow Jesus today?

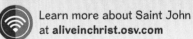

Learn more about Saint John at **aliveinchrist.osv.com**

Live Your Faith

Choose one or more of the symbols used in the Book of Revelation. Draw the symbol here, creating a positive message for the world today.

Let Us Pray

Reflective Scripture Prayer Service

As we pray with Scripture today, we will reflect on God's dream for us.

Gather and begin with the Sign of the Cross.

Leader: Lord, you said, "I am the Alpha and the Omega …
the one who is and who was and who is to come, the
almighty." **Revelation 1:8**

Reader: Read Revelation 21:1–5.
The Word of the Lord.

All: Thanks be to God.

Reflection

Leader: The Lord will destroy death and wipe away tears.

Side 1: "Holy, holy, holy is the Lord God almighty,

Side 2: who was, and who is, and who is to come."

Leader: The Lord will create a new Heaven and a new Earth.

Side 1: "Holy, holy, holy is the Lord God almighty,

Side 2: who was, and who is, and who
is to come." **Revelation 4:8**

 All: Sing "Holy God, We Praise
Thy Name"

FAMILY+FAITH
LIVING AND LEARNING TOGETHER

YOUR CHILD LEARNED >>>

This chapter defines apocalyptic literature, explains that the world began and will end according to God's design, and explores the resurrection of the body and life everlasting.

Scripture

 Read **2 Peter 3:11b–12a** to find out about a new Heaven and a new Earth.

Catholics Believe

- God will triumph over evil when Christ comes again in glory.
- In the new creation, God will reward good and punish evil.

To learn more, go to the *Catechism of the Catholic Church #1038–1041, 1042–1047* at **usccb.org**.

People of Faith

This week, your child learned about Saint John the Evangelist. John and his brother James both became Apostles of Jesus.

CHILDREN AT THIS AGE >>>

How They Understand the New Creation and the End of Time Your child may not think about the end of time very often, but children this age are often curious about what Heaven will be like. Their strong sense of justice also makes the idea of a final reward for good and punishment of evil very attractive to them. As they consider this, it is important that they reflect on what God has planned for their lives and how they can faithfully follow his plan and thus find lasting happiness.

CONSIDER THIS >>>

How do you remain hopeful in the midst of overwhelming evil?

Life can present us with experiences so filled with darkness that we struggle to hold on to hope. It is in those desperate moments that we need to put our hope in the name of the Lord. Through his Death and Resurrection Jesus teaches us the greatest truth: there is no evil that love cannot conquer. God can make all things good. As Catholics, we know that "God permits such moral evil in part out of respect for the gift of freedom with which he endowed created beings. But his response to moral evil is an even greater act of love through the sending of his Son who offers his life to bring us back to God" (*USCCA, p. 57*).

LET'S TALK >>>

- Ask your child to tell you about the Book of Revelation.
- Talk about how your family shows your belief that God will triumph over evil and good will reign.

LET'S PRAY >>>

 Dear Saint John, help us always to keep our hearts and minds focused on Heaven. Amen.

For a multimedia glossary of Catholic Faith Words, Sunday readings, seasonal and Saint resources, and chapter activities go to **aliveinchrist.osv.com**.

Chapter 21 Review

A **Work with Words** Match each description in Column 1 with the correct term in Column 2.

Column 1   Column 2

1. These people sincerely seek God   apocalyptic
and seek to do his will.

2. This word means "revealed" or   Resurrection
"unveiled."

3. A central message of this book is   Revelation
that God will triumph over evil.

4. The event of Jesus being raised from   the righteous
Death to new life by God the Father
through the power of the Holy Spirit.

5. This is the final vision in the Book   new creation
of Revelation.

B **Check Understanding** Complete each statement.

6. The writer of Revelation said that the revelation came to him

in _____.

7. When John wrote the Book of Revelation, he was on the island

of _____.

8. The Bible ends with the story of the new _____
in Revelation.

9. The Theological Virtue of _____ is a gift from God
by which you trust that he will grant you eternal life.

10. In the Book of Revelation, the number _____ is a
symbol for perfection or completion.

Go to **aliveinchrist.osv.com**
for an interactive review.

Unit Review

A Work with Words **Fill in the circle next to the correct answer.**

1. The Communion of Saints includes
   _____.

   ○ the pilgrim Church on Earth
   ○ those being purified in Purgatory
   ○ the blessed in Heaven
   ○ all of these

2. The action that is not part of the
   Sacrament of the Anointing of the
   Sick is _____.

   ○ anointing of hands and forehead
   ○ Act of Contrition
   ○ priest's laying on of hands
   ○ prayer for elderly or ill person

3. The full joy of living eternally in God's
   presence is _____.

   ○ Communion of Saints
   ○ Purgatory
   ○ Heaven
   ○ Hell

4. Because Jesus was raised to new life in
   the Resurrection, _____.

   ○ death has been defeated
   ○ everyone will go to Heaven
   ○ no one will physically die again
   ○ evil no longer exists

5. Ecumenism is an organized effort
   to _____.

   ○ stop world hunger
   ○ end all wars
   ○ bring all peoples together
   ○ bring Christians together

B Check Understanding **Match each description in Column 1 with the correct term in Column 2.**

Column 1	Column 2
6. Son of encouragement	Jesus
7. "I have conquered the world."	the Lamb
8. Arranged for Jesus' arrest	John
9. Wrote an apocalyptic book	Judas
10. Opens a scroll with seven seals	Barnabas

Complete each sentence with the correct word from the Word Bank.

11. The Book of Revelation presents the promise of a new

    _____.

12. Literature that is _____ includes a message
    that is revealed or unveiled.

13. Martin Luther's actions led to the Protestant

    _____.

14. The Church is often referred to as the _____
    of Saints.

15. Purgatory is a state of final _____ after death and before Heaven.

C **Make Connections** Write brief responses to these questions.

16. How would you describe the Works of Mercy?

    _____

    _____

    _____

    _____

    _____

17. What are some ways in which others can pray for you?

    _____

    _____

    _____

    _____

    _____

18. What do you look forward to in Heaven?

_____

_____

_____

_____

_____

_____

19. Why do you think God is able to overcome all evil?

_____

_____

_____

_____

_____

_____

20. How is reflection helpful to you in prayer?

_____

_____

_____

_____

_____

_____

Life and Dignity of the Human Person

In Scripture God tells us, "Before I formed you in the womb I knew you" (Jeremiah 1:5). God created each one of us. Every person is unique and unrepeatable. God has a special plan for each of our lives. He knows what he made us to be.

Because God made each of us, we should treat each person with dignity. Every life is valuable to God. We should take care of the bodies and minds God gave us and use them to do good things. We should be kind toward others and solve problems peacefully instead of fighting. If we see someone else being bullied, teased, or disrespected, we need to speak up and get help from an adult if necessary. We should help to protect others because every life is important to God.

Life and Dignity

It is important to respect the life and dignity of each person. Because all humans are created in the image of God, everyone has value and worth, including the unborn, the aged, and those who struggle with life-threatening or debilitating illnesses.

The Fifth Commandment tells us "You shall not kill." The Catholic Church has always been clear about protecting human life from the moment of conception to natural death.

The Church calls us to provide special protection to the unborn, who are among the most vulnerable and innocent. Abortion, the deliberate termination of a pregnancy by killing an unborn child, is a grave sin against the Fifth Commandment.

Through prayer and action, the Church calls governments to protect the right to life of all human beings, the unborn as well as the terminally ill and aged. And she provides prayer, guidance, and many types of support to those individuals facing difficult challenges in these areas.

What is true of the unborn is also true of persons who are sick, or who have serious disabilities. The value and dignity of every human life is a basic teaching of the Catholic Church.

≫ **What actions do you perform to show that you respect the dignity of other people?**

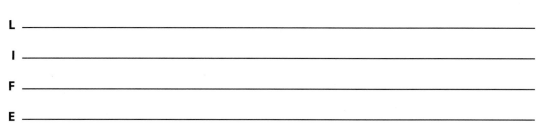

Dignity and Action

On each line, use the letter given to begin a phrase or sentence to describe why human life is so important and how we can protect it.

L ——————————————————

I ——————————————————

F ——————————————————

E ——————————————————

Call to Family, Community, and Participation

From the very beginning, God made people to be in relationship with one another. Scripture tells us, "The LORD God said: It is not good for the man to be alone. I will make a helper suited to him" (Genesis 2:18). God gave us communities so that we could take care of one another.

The family is a very special type of community. Our Church teaches that the family is the "school of holiness" and the "domestic Church." These names reflect the Catholic teaching that the family is where we learn who God is and how to live a Christian life. It is the first place where we learn what it means to live in a community. The family is where we learn how to love others.

Call to Community

For some people, their only goal in life is to look out for themselves. They argue that they have no obligation to worry about anyone else's problems. They brag that they do not need anyone's help to get by.

This is not the way God intended human life to be lived. He planned for you to be born into a community, the family. It is there that you were first introduced to the faith and values that will sustain you through life. God also brings you salvation as a member of a larger community—the Church.

Communities like the family, the Church, and the country you live in are precious. These communities form a framework that will enable you to lead a good life. In return, though, you have a duty to participate actively in these institutions. You need to accept responsibilities within your family, the Church, and your country.

Families and Society

In a small group, discuss some ways that families help society. Think about your family or one you know and what they do for their parish, communities, schools, and places of work. Fill in the chart below and then share your ideas with the larger group.

Involvement	
Name of FAMILY	_____
What they do for their PARISH	_____
What they do for their COMMUNITY	_____
What they do for their SCHOOL OR WORKPLACE	_____

Rights and Responsibilities of the Human Person

Because God made every person, everyone has rights and responsibilities. Rights are the freedoms or things every person needs and should have. Responsibilities are our duties, or the things we must do.

Jesus tells us to "love your neighbor as yourself" (Mark 12:31). The *Catechism* teaches that "respect for the human person considers the other 'another self'" (CCC, 1944). We respect the rights that come from their dignity as human beings. Everyone has a right to food, shelter, clothing, rest, and the right to see a doctor if they need one. We also have a responsibility to treat others well and work together for the good of everyone.

Catholic nurse and newborn babies in Nazareth Hospital, Israel.

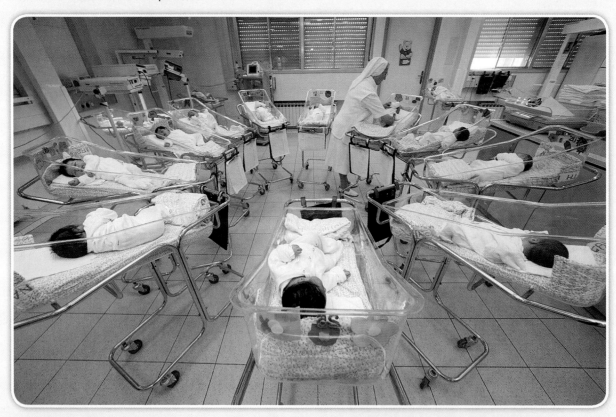

Rights and Responsibilities

Catholics are called to support the rights and responsibilities of all people. By doing so, the respect and dignity of every person is maintained. It is everyone's responsibility to reach out to others and to help those who are in need.

Those who are poor often face hunger and cold. But there are many other things about being poor that make life difficult. People who are poor worry about not having enough money to meet all their needs. It is difficult for them to feel secure.

One of the basic teachings of the Church is that people have a right to a decent life—to food, clothing, housing, education, and medical care. They also have the right to a job, which provides independence, security, and self-respect.

All people share the responsibility of seeing to it that everyone is provided with these things, and we all have a responsibility to provide these things for ourselves.

≫ **How are human rights and human responsibilities linked?**

Know Your Rights

In the puzzle below, find four words that tell about our human rights and responsibilities. Write the words on the lines next to the puzzle.

X	J	N	I	M	F	Z	W
F	R	E	S	P	E	C	T
N	V	G	E	F	J	Q	P
D	K	J	C	N	O	G	R
G	K	W	O	R	K	O	J
H	O	U	S	I	N	G	D

_____

_____

_____

_____

Option for the Poor and Vulnerable

In Scripture, Jesus says "whatever you did for one of these least brothers of mine, you did for me" (Matthew 25:40). Whatever we have done for people who are poor or needy, we have also done for him, and what we have not done for them, we haven't done for Jesus. This means we should treat people in need the same way we would treat Jesus himself. We should give special priority to people who are hungry, thirsty, homeless, or alone.

Saint Rose of Lima said, "When we serve the poor and the sick, we serve Jesus." Our Church teaches that we should have special love and care for those who are poor and put their needs first. This is called the preferential option for the poor. The *Catechism* teaches that "God blesses those who come to the aid of the poor and rebukes those who turn away from them … It is by what they have done for the poor that Jesus Christ will recognize his chosen ones" (CCC, 2443).

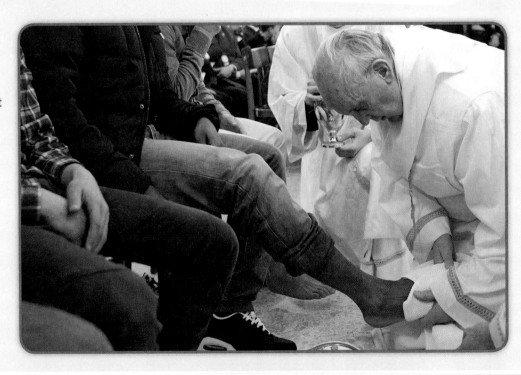

Pope Francis washes the feet of women as part of services on Holy Thursday.

Option for the Poor

Jesus challenged the beliefs of his society when he told those who were poor that they were blessed. His love for those who were disadvantaged both amazed and offended the rich and "respectable" people.

Every disciple of Jesus is called to love and serve those who are poor. As a Christian, you are called to examine your own life regularly to see whether you really must have everything you are tempted to buy. By denying yourself a few of these unnecessary things, you can assist people who desperately need your help.

Today's world is one of extremes. Tremendous wealth exists in many countries. However, extreme poverty exists in others. The Church insists that this situation is not morally acceptable. Recent Popes have taught that rich countries have the same kind of responsibility to poor countries that people who are wealthy have to those who are poor.

> ≫ **What things can Americans do to relieve poverty elsewhere in the world?**

Make a Plan

Brainstorm with your group some ideas about how you can raise money to help people in need in your community. Consider the people or groups that you can help, and how. Use these questions to help you brainstorm.

1. What program or service can we get involved in?

   _____

2. What are some fundraisers we can do?

   _____

3. What services or items can we sell?

   _____

4. What is the amount we can hope to raise?

   _____

The Dignity of Work and Rights of Workers

All adults have a right and responsibility to work. Work helps people earn money to buy food and other necessities. It also helps to give their lives meaning as they cooperate with God's creation. Everyone should have access to meaningful work, whether that work is within or outside the home.

Scripture and Catholic Tradition teach that workers deserve to be treated with justice by their employers. Scripture tells us that "you shall not exploit a poor and needy hired servant" (Deuteronomy 24:14). Workers have a right to a fair wage for their work (see Leviticus 19:13; Deuteronomy 24:15). When there is a conflict between workers and employers, workers have a right to get together and express their opinions. Workers and their employers should treat one another with respect and solve conflicts peacefully.

The Dignity of Work

Work is not just a means of earning money. Through their labor, humans are in partnership with God in his work of creation. Work produces order, usefulness, and beauty. The work that people do should enhance their dignity.

Sometimes a worker is deprived of his or her dignity by an employer. Individuals are often unable to negotiate their pay or working hours. They may be forced to work under conditions that endanger their health. This is why some workers form labor unions. Unions bargain with employers on behalf of all the workers in a particular factory or even in an entire industry. Solidarity in a labor union allows workers to ask that companies pay decent wages, maintain safe conditions at work, and give employees time off to be with their families.

For the past century, the Catholic Church throughout the world has supported the right of workers to form unions because these organizations are a powerful force to help workers receive the benefits necessary to live in dignity.

≫ **What are some things that make working enjoyable and pleasant for adults?**

Research an Occupation

Choose one type of work to research. Write a summary of your findings, explaining how the work done by people in this occupation is valuable to society. Report what you have learned to another group, to a group of parents, or to your local parish.

_____

_____

_____

_____

_____

_____

Solidarity of the Human Family

Our world includes people of different nations, races, cultures, beliefs, and economic levels. But God created each one of us. We are one human family. In fact, Scripture tells us that the differences that we see between ourselves and others are not important to God (see Romans 2:11). God calls everyone to be his children.

Because God created all people, we have an obligation to treat everyone with love, kindness, and justice. In the Beatitudes, Jesus says, "blessed are the peacemakers, for they will be called children of God" (Matthew 5:9). Working for justice between people will help us to live in peace with one another.

Solidarity

The word *catholic* comes from two Greek words that mean "according to the whole." When the early Christians described their church as the Catholic Church, they meant that the Church extended throughout the world and united people of every race and culture.

Solidarity is the unity that comes from recognizing that all of humanity is one family. It is a virtue that Catholics are called to practice in order to live up to the meaning of their name. Solidarity means recognizing that all men and women are brothers and sisters, whatever language they speak, or clothes they wear. When people anywhere experience injustice, you feel hurt. When people are suffering, even if it is on the other side of the globe, you recognize a responsibility to help them.

What happens in the world today affects people everywhere. Thanks to airplanes, television, and the Internet, no place is really that far away from any other. You can learn about the suffering of people in many different places and offer them real help. In doing so, you can show solidarity with the whole human community.

≫ **What are some things that would bring greater solidarity to the world?**

Draw a Poster

Using words and pictures, design a poster illustrating how we might have a relationship of solidarity with a group of people who are in need somewhere else in the world. For example, if an area has recently experienced a natural disaster, how can your community help them get aid? Include a map of the place and a map of your own community. Write some notes about your design and the message you want to share below.

_____

_____

_____

Care for God's Creation

When God created the world—the animals, plants, and all natural things—he looked upon what he had made and called it "very good" (Genesis 1:31). God made people the stewards of the "fish of the sea, the birds of the air, and all the living things that crawl on the earth" (Genesis 1:28). That means humans have a special responsibility to care for all of God's creation.

Catholic Tradition teaches us that God created the Earth and all living things for the common good—the good of everyone. God asks us to take care of the environment and all living things, so that they can be enjoyed by everyone today and in future generations. The *Catechism* teaches us that we owe animals kindness, because they give glory to God just by being what they were made to be.

Care for Creation

Like all the beautiful things on Earth, flowers are a gift of God the Creator. Gratitude to him is an appropriate response to their beauty. As one of God's stewards, you can help care for this natural beauty. By planting gardens, humans cooperate with God in making the world more beautiful. In this way, we act as good caretakers of creation.

God has provided all the resources that allow humans to lead rich and comfortable lives: the air they breathe and the water they drink, the soil and the plants that grow in it, the minerals under the ground, the animals, birds, insects, and fish. He wants humans to show their thankfulness for all of these resources by using them wisely and ensuring that they remain available for future generations.

≫ **Why is it necessary for humans to cooperate with God to preserve Earth's varied resources?**

Plan a Neighborhood Project

Discuss how your group can carry out a neighborhood improvement project. Together, decide on one project that the group can plan and complete. Write your notes below. Then create a calendar for your project.

1. Specific tasks that need to be done for this project:

_____

_____

2. Equipment required to do the project:

_____

3. Specific task assigned to you:

_____

Scripture

Catholic Bibles

Catholic Bibles have seven Old Testament books or parts of books not included in other Christian Bibles. When these books are included in a Protestant Bible, they are usually called the Apocrypha or Deutero-canonical Books. The word *apocrypha* comes from a Greek word that means "hidden things."

The apocryphal books are not found in the present Hebrew Bible but were included in an early Jewish canon that included Greek writings. Protestant Reformers of later centuries did not accept these books. Catholic translations of the Bible include The New American Bible Revised Edition and The New Jerusalem Bible. Some translations, such as The New Revised Standard Version, are accepted by Catholics and Protestants.

How to Better Understand Scripture

God is the author of Sacred Scripture. But he used human authors and inspired them to write the contents of the Bible, to convey the saving truth he wanted us to know.

Catholics understand the Bible is a religious book and not an eyewitness account of historical events. For this reason, Catholics read Scripture while taking into account the context in which the human authors were writing. They were writing for a particular time and place and for a particular group of people. They were also using particular literary forms.

You should always rely on the guidance of the Holy Spirit and the Church to help you understand the Word of God in Scripture.

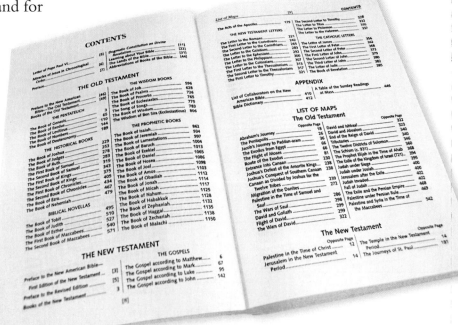

Gospel Formation

The Gospels according to Matthew, Mark, Luke, and John announce the Good News of Jesus to Christians today. These books were formed in three stages:

1. The life and teaching of Jesus

Jesus' whole life and teaching proclaimed the Good News of God's Kingdom.

2. Oral tradition

After the Resurrection, the Apostles preached the Good News. Then the early Christians passed on what Jesus preached. They told and retold the teachings of Jesus and the story of his life, Death, Resurrection, and Ascension.

3. The written Gospels

The stories, teachings, and sayings of Jesus were collected and written in the Gospels according to Matthew, Mark, Luke (the synoptic, or similar, Gospels), and John.

Titles of Jesus in Scripture

Jesus' followers used several different names for him. These names showed people's understanding of who Jesus was.

Christ	means "the anointed one" in the Greek language.
Jesus	Jesus' common Jewish name; it means "God saves."
Lord	is used to acknowledge Jesus' divinity.
Messiah	the Hebrew word for "the anointed one;" the Messiah fulfills Jewish hope.
Rabbi	means "teacher."

Mary in the Bible

- Luke 1:30: The Angel Gabriel visits Mary to announce her favor with God.

- Luke 1:39–40: Mary visits Elizabeth to help her during her pregnancy.

- Luke 2:1–7: Mary goes with Joseph to Bethlehem, where she gives birth to Jesus.

- Matthew 2:11: The Magi visit Jesus with Mary.

- Matthew 2:13, 20: Mary, Joseph, and Jesus flee to Egypt and then return to Nazareth.

- Luke 2:33–35: Mary and Joseph take the child Jesus to the Temple for presentation.

- Luke 2:41–47: Mary and Joseph find the boy Jesus teaching in the Temple.

- John 2:1–5: Mary is present at the wedding at Cana.

- Matthew 12:47–49, Mark 3:31–34, Luke 8:19–21: Mary comes to speak to Jesus when he is teaching his disciples.

- John 19:25: Mary is present at the foot of Jesus' Cross.

- Acts 1:14: Mary is in the upper room with the first community in Jerusalem.

The Rosary and Scripture

Early Christians used beads or knotted strings to keep count of prayers. As devotion to Mary increased, it became popular to create psalters or books dedicated to Jesus or Mary, using biblical scenes. The Rosary we know today developed from both of these practices. As you pray each decade of beads, you think of one mystery in the life of Jesus or Mary.

The Mysteries of the Rosary

The Joyful Mysteries
The Annunciation
The Visitation
The Nativity
The Presentation in the Temple
The Finding in the Temple

The Luminous Mysteries
The Baptism of Jesus
The Wedding at Cana
The Proclamation of the Kingdom
The Transfiguration
The Institution of the Eucharist

The Sorrowful Mysteries
The Agony in the Garden
The Scourging at the Pillar
The Crowning with Thorns
The Carrying of the Cross
The Crucifixion and Death

The Glorious Mysteries
The Resurrection
The Ascension
The Descent of the Holy Spirit
The Assumption of Mary
The Coronation of Mary in Heaven

© Our Sunday Visitor

Creed

A creed is a summary of the Christian faith. The word *creed* means "I believe." There are two main creeds in the Church: the Apostles' Creed and the Nicene Creed.

Apostles' Creed

This is one of the Church's oldest creeds. It is a summary of Christian beliefs taught since the time of the Apostles. This creed is used in the celebration of Baptism and is often used at Mass during the Season of Easter and in Masses with children. This creed is part of the Rosary.

I believe in God,
the Father almighty,
Creator of heaven and earth,
and in Jesus Christ, his only Son, our Lord,

At the words that follow, up to and including
the Virgin Mary, *all bow.*

who was conceived by the Holy Spirit,
born of the Virgin Mary,
suffered under Pontius Pilate,
was crucified, died and was buried;
he descended into hell;
on the third day he rose again from the dead;
he ascended into heaven,
and is seated at the right hand
of God the Father almighty;
from there he will come to judge
the living and the dead.
I believe in the Holy Spirit,
the holy catholic Church,
the communion of saints,
the forgiveness of sins,
the resurrection of the body,
and life everlasting. Amen.

Nicene Creed

This creed which is prayed at Mass was written over a thousand years ago by leaders of the Church who met at a city named Nicaea. It is a summary of basic beliefs about God the Father, God the Son, and God the Holy Spirit, the Church, and other teachings.

I believe in one God,
the Father almighty,
maker of heaven and earth,
of all things visible and invisible.

I believe in one Lord Jesus Christ,
the Only Begotten Son of God,
born of the Father before all ages.
God from God, Light from Light,
true God from true God,
begotten, not made, consubstantial
  with the Father;
through him all things were made.
For us men and for our salvation
he came down from heaven,

At the words that follow up to and including and became man, *all bow.*

and by the Holy Spirit was incarnate
  of the Virgin Mary,
and became man.

For our sake he was crucified under
Pontius Pilate,
he suffered death and was buried,
and rose again on the third day
in accordance with the Scriptures.
He ascended into heaven
and is seated at the right hand of
the Father.
He will come again in glory
to judge the living and the dead
and his kingdom will have no end.

I believe in the Holy Spirit, the Lord,
the giver of life,
who proceeds from the Father and
the Son,
who with the Father and the Son is
adored and glorified,
who has spoken through the prophets.

I believe in one, holy, catholic and
apostolic Church.
I confess one Baptism for the
forgiveness of sins
and I look forward to the resurrection
of the dead
and the life of the world to come.
Amen.

Marks of the Church

The Catholic Church is the Church founded by Christ and his Apostles. There are four marks, or essential characteristics, that distinguish Christ's Church and her mission: one, holy, catholic, and apostolic. These marks are mentioned in the Nicene Creed.

One

One means all the members are united as the Body of Christ, given life by the one Spirit. They acknowledge one Lord, one faith, one Baptism.

Holy

Holy means the Church is centered in God. It is Christ who, by his sacrifice, makes the Church holy.

Catholic

Catholic means universal. The Church has the fullness of faith and is the means of salvation for all. The Church is for all times and all people.

Apostolic

Apostolic means the Church is built on the foundation of the Apostles. It teaches the doctrine of Jesus as it has been handed down through the Apostles and their successors, the Pope and bishops.

The Church's Mission

The Church's mission is to proclaim and further God's Reign in the world. She continues the mission, or work, of Christ through the Holy Spirit, according to God's plan until Jesus comes again in glory. This work is done by all Catholics—clergy, laity, and religious.

Ecumenism is a movement that seeks to bring about the unity of all Christian churches. The word *ecumenism* comes from a scriptural phrase in Greek that means "the whole household of God."

When a Pope is elected, he is given a ring with a figure of Saint Peter fishing on it. This reminds the Pope that he is to be a leader of God's People as Peter was.

Life after Death

At the end of the Nicene Creed we profess, "and I look forward to the resurrection of the dead and the life of the world to come." The Church sometimes refers to teaching about this topic as the Last Things.

The Particular Judgment is the judgment made at the moment of a person's death. At this judgment the soul is rewarded with the blessings of Heaven, given a time of purification, or condemned to Hell.

- Heaven is the state of being happy with God forever. The souls of the just experience the full joy of living in God's presence forever.

- The final purification (Purgatory) is a time after death for those who are in God's friendship but need to be purified to be with him in Heaven. It is a state of final cleansing after death and before entering into Heaven.

- Hell is the state of eternal separation from God because of a choice to turn away from him and not seek forgiveness.

The Last Judgment is also called the General Judgment. This refers to God's final triumph over evil that will occur at the end of time when Christ returns and judges all the living and the dead. Then, all will fully see and understand God's plan for creation.

The new Heaven and new Earth is the Kingdom of God (or new Jerusalem) that will come in its fullness at the end of time.

Holy People from the Past

Fathers of the Church

Apostolic fathers were first- and second-century Christian writers who give us information about the early Christian Church. They are called apostolic because it is believed they had a historical connection to the Apostles. Saints Clement, Ignatius of Antioch, and Polycarp, the author of The Epistle of Barnabas and the Didache, which includes several important teachings of the early Church, are considered apostolic fathers. Saints Athanasius, Basil, Gregory of Nazianzus, John Chrysostom, Ambrose, Augustine, Gregory, Jerome, Justin Martyr, Irenaeus, and Cyprian are called fathers of the Church because of some of their great writings and teachings.

Saints

Saints are very holy people who committed their lives to God, did his work on Earth, and are now with him in Heaven. A Saint is a hero of the Church. The Church uses a process called canonization to declare a person a Saint.

Steps of Canonization

A person or group of people approach their bishop to suggest a candidate for sainthood. A committee creates a report on the candidate and sends it to the Congregation for the Causes of Saints.

1. The Congregation researches the candidate to verify that he or she practiced virtue. When the Pope accepts the Congregation's report, the candidate is termed "venerable," or "servant of God."

2. The second process is a very lengthy research of the life of the candidate. A "promoter of the cause" is authorized to examine the person's life, virtues, writings, reputation for holiness, and reported miracles. As a rule one miracle must be credited to the candidate's intercession with God. The venerable candidate is then "beatified" by the Pope. The person is designated as "blessed."

3. Canonization is the solemn declaration by the Pope that the candidate is a Saint. This declaration requires one more miracle.

Saint Joseph is the patron, among other things, of the Universal Church, workers, fathers, peace, a happy home, and charity to people who are poor. His feast day is March 19. For Sicilians this feast is the occasion for hospitality. The tradition includes inviting to the table all who come to the door. A statue of Saint Joseph, surrounded by flowers and candles, is placed on the table as a centerpiece. A priest blesses the food. Any food brought by guests is offered to people who are poor.

The Liturgical Year

The liturgical year is the Church's annual cycle of seasons and feasts that celebrates Christ's Paschal Mystery. It begins on the First Sunday of Advent and ends on the feast of Christ the King, the last Sunday of Ordinary Time. This feast honors Jesus' reign over all of Heaven and Earth. It affirms the messianic kingship of Christ who gave his life through his Death on the Cross.

Ordinary Time is the name given to the thirty-three or thirty-four weeks during the year apart from the Seasons of Advent, Christmas, Lent, and Easter. The term ordinary comes from the Latin word *ordinis*, which means "number." The Sundays of Ordinary Time are numbered consecutively. They are divided into two groups. The first group marks the time between Christmas and Lent. The second group marks the time between Easter and Advent. Ordinary Time celebrates the fullness of the Christian mystery. The Scripture readings for this time are about the words and actions of Jesus in his public life. They call members of the Church to discipleship. The liturgical color for Ordinary Time is green.

It is common in Latin America for the Last Supper to be reenacted in church during Triduum. The priest and twelve men—dressed as Jesus and the disciples—dramatize or act out the Last Supper as recorded in the Gospel.

Holy Days of Obligation

Catholics are required to attend Mass on Sunday unless a serious reason prevents them from doing so. Catholics also must go to Mass on certain holy days. In the United States the Holy Days of Obligation are the feasts of:

- Mary the Mother of God (January 1)
- the Ascension of the Lord (forty days after Easter or the Sunday nearest the end of the forty-day period)
- the Assumption of Mary (August 15)
- All Saints Day (November 1)
- the Immaculate Conception of Mary (December 8)
- Christmas (December 25)

Order of Mass

Introductory Rites

Entrance Chant

Greeting

Rite for the Blessing and Sprinkling of Water

Penitential Act

Kyrie

Gloria

Collect

Liturgy of the Word

First Reading

Responsorial Psalm

Second Reading

Gospel Acclamation

Dialogue at the Gospel

Gospel Reading

Homily

Profession of Faith

Prayer of the Faithful

Liturgy of the Eucharist

Preparation of the Gifts

Invitation to Prayer

Prayer over the Offerings

Eucharistic Prayer

Preface Dialogue

Preface

Preface Acclamation

Consecration

Mystery of Faith

Concluding Doxology

Communion Rite

The Lord's Prayer

Sign of Peace

Lamb of God

Invitation to Communion

Communion

Prayer After Communion

Concluding Rites

Greeting

Blessing

Dismissal

Devotions

Novena

A novena is a private devotion. The word novena comes from the Latin word *novem*, which means "nine." A novena is a prayer in honor of one of the three Persons of the Holy Trinity, the Blessed Virgin Mary, or one of the Saints that is repeated over the course of nine days, weeks, or months for a special intention.

Stations of the Cross

The practice of the Stations of the Cross began in the early Church. Pilgrims would visit the various sites in Jerusalem that were associated with Christ's suffering and Death. The Stations of the Cross focus on fourteen scenes of Christ's Passion.

First Station: Jesus is condemned to death on the Cross.

Second Station: Jesus accepts his Cross.

Third Station: Jesus falls the first time.

Fourth Station: Jesus meets his sorrowful mother.

Fifth Station: Simon of Cyrene helps Jesus carry his Cross.

Sixth Station: Veronica wipes the face of Jesus.

Seventh Station: Jesus falls the second time.

Eighth Station: Jesus meets and speaks to the women of Jerusalem.

Ninth Station: Jesus falls the third time.

Tenth Station: Jesus is stripped of his garments.

Eleventh Station: Jesus is nailed to the Cross.

Twelfth Station: Jesus dies on the Cross.

Thirteenth Station: Jesus is taken down from the Cross.

Fourteenth Station: Jesus is placed in the tomb.

Moral Law

There are four expressions of moral law:

1. Divine law is the plan of God's wisdom to direct all human activity to good.

2. Natural moral law is the law that is written in your heart that helps you know what is good and what is evil.

3. Revealed law is law as it is revealed in the Old and New Testaments.

4. Civil and Church laws are established by nations and by the Church to promote the common good and to guide the decisions of each person.

The Great Commandment

"You shall love the Lord, your God, with all your heart, with all your being, with all your strength, and with all your mind, and your neighbor as yourself." **Luke 10:27**

"You shall love the Lord, your God, with your whole heart, and with your whole being, and with your whole strength." **Deuteronomy 6:5**

"You shall love your neighbor as yourself." **Leviticus 19:18**

The Ten Commandments

See **Exodus 20:1–17**

1. I am the Lord your God. You shall not have strange gods before me.

2. You shall not take the name of the Lord your God in vain.

3. Remember to keep holy the Lord's Day.

4. Honor your father and your mother.

5. You shall not kill.

6. You shall not commit adultery.

7. You shall not steal.

8. You shall not bear false witness against your neighbor.

9. You shall not covet your neighbor's wife.

10. You shall not covet your neighbor's goods.

The Beatitudes

The Beatitudes are teachings of Jesus that show the way to true happiness and tell the way to live in God's Kingdom now and always. They are promises of blessing made by Jesus to those who faithfully follow his example. They give direction to the human heart for finding the happiness that can be found in God alone. They teach about God's Kingdom and the participation in eternal life to which all are called.

Jesus' Beatitudes are recorded in both the Gospel according to Matthew and the Gospel according to Luke. The Lucan account appears on this page. The account from the Gospel according to Matthew can be found on page 201.

Blessed are you who are poor,
  for the kingdom of God is yours.
Blessed are you who are now hungry,
  for you will be satisfied.
Blessed are you who are now weeping,
  for you will laugh.
Blessed are you when people hate you,
  and when they exclude and insult you,
  and denounce your name as evil
  on account of the Son of Man.
Rejoice and leap for joy on that day! Behold, your reward will be great in heaven.

Luke 6:20–23

Precepts of the Church

The Precepts of the Church are laws that name specific actions that all Catholics are obligated to carry out.

1. Take part in the Mass on Sundays and holy days. Keep these days holy and avoid unnecessary work.

2. Celebrate the Sacrament of Reconciliation at least once a year.

3. Receive Holy Communion at least once a year during Easter time.

4. Fast and/or abstain on days of penance.

5. Give your time, gifts, and money to support the Church.

Sin and Vice

Sin is a deliberate thought, word, deed, or omission contrary to the law of God.

It is a choice to disobey God. It is a deliberate choice, not a mistake or an accident.

Sin is original or personal. Original Sin is the sin committed by the first humans, which led to the sinful condition of the human race. All humans are born with Original Sin. And because of it, all people are inclined to commit personal sins which are personally chosen. These sins are either mortal or venial.

Mortal sin breaks your relationship with God. For a sin to be mortal, three conditions must be present: It must be a serious matter. You must understand what you are going to do (sufficient reflection). You must fully agree to do it (full consent of the act).

Venial sin hurts your relationship with God without breaking it. The effects of venial sin include a lessening of the love of God in your heart and a weakening of the power to resist sin. There are seven vices that the Church calls capital sins. They are also called the seven deadly sins. They are tendencies in a person that can lead to sin. The seven capital sins are pride, covetousness (desire), lust, anger, gluttony, envy, and sloth.

Grace and Virtue

Grace is God's free, loving gift of his own life and help to do what God calls us to do. It is participation in the life of the Holy Trinity.

Actual grace is the gift God gives you to do good and avoid evil. Sanctifying grace is a sharing in the life of God.

Theological Virtues

Faith (see Romans 1:17)
Hope (see Titus 3:6–7)
Charity (Love) (see John 15:9)

Cardinal Virtues

Prudence   Fortitude
Justice   Temperance

Gifts of the Holy Spirit

See Isaiah 11:2–3

Wisdom   Knowledge
Right judgment (Counsel) Reverence (Piety)
Understanding   Wonder and awe (Fear of the Lord)
Courage (Fortitude)

Fruits of the Holy Spirit

See Galatians 5:22–23

Charity
Kindness
Faithfulness
Joy
Goodness
Modesty
Peace
Generosity
Self-control
Patience
Gentleness
Chastity

| Works of Mercy | |
Corporal (for the body)	Spiritual (for the spirit)
Feed the hungry.	Warn the sinner.
Give drink to the thirsty.	Teach the ignorant.
Clothe the naked.	Counsel the doubtful.
Shelter the homeless.	Comfort the sorrowful.
Visit the sick.	Bear wrongs patiently.
Visit the imprisoned.	Forgive injuries.
Bury the dead.	Pray for the living and the dead.

Human Dignity

Human dignity is the worth each person has because he or she is made in the image of God. We are all equal in dignity, each and every one of us worthy of respect and love. Because of our common human dignity, people have basic human rights, such as the right to life, food, clothing, and shelter. No government or social group should fail to recognize those rights. These rights include the protection of the unborn, the elderly, the ill, and even those in prison.

The Catholic Church responds to human needs through the Corporal Works of Mercy, which include feeding the hungry, giving drink to the thirsty, clothing the naked, sheltering the homeless, and visiting the sick and imprisoned.

Justice and Peace

Justice is a Cardinal Virtue. It is the habit and practice of giving God what is due him. It also means to give each person what he or she is due because that person is a child of God.

Social justice is a part of this Cardinal Virtue. It is the part that urges individuals to seek the common good of the whole group rather than just one person's individual good.

Peace is a state of calm and harmony when things are in their proper order and people settle problems with kindness and justice. In the Catholic tradition, peace is not just the absence of conflict. It is the result of right relationships with God and with your neighbor.

Common Good

The common good refers to the good of everyone, with particular concern for those who might be most vulnerable to harm. It means all the conditions that allow people to become who God wants them to become. The common good includes peace, development of groups of people, and respect for every person. These conditions vary from society to society, which is why the Church does not recommend any one country's political or economic system. The Church evaluates each system on the basis of whether or not it provides the conditions for human fulfillment.

Basic Prayers

These are essential prayers that every Catholic should know. Latin is the official, universal language of the Church. As members of the Catholic Church, we usually pray in the language that we speak, but we sometimes pray in Latin, the common language of the Church.

Sign of the Cross

In the name of the Father,
and of the Son,
and of the Holy Spirit.
Amen.

Signum Crucis

In nómine Patris
et Fílii
et Spíritus Sancti.
Amen.

The Lord's Prayer

Our Father, who art in heaven,
hallowed be thy name;
thy kingdom come,
thy will be done
on earth as it is in heaven.
Give us this day our daily bread,
and forgive us our trespasses,
as we forgive those who trespass
against us;
and lead us not into temptation,
but deliver us from evil. Amen.

Pater Noster

Pater noster qui es in cælis:
santificétur Nomen Tuum;
advéniat Regnum Tuum;
fiat volúntas Tua,
sicut in cælo, et in terra.
Panem nostrum
cotidiánum da nobis hódie;
et dimítte nobis débita nostra,
sicut et nos
dimíttus debitóribus nostris;
et ne nos indúcas in tentatiónem;
sed líbera nos a Malo.

Glory Be

Glory be to the Father
and to the Son
and to the Holy Spirit,
as it was in the beginning
is now, and ever shall be
world without end. Amen.

Gloria Patri

Gloria Patri
et Fílio
et Spíritui Sancto.
Sicut erat in princípio,
et nunc et semper
et in sæcula
sæculorem.
Amen.

Elements of the Lord's Prayer

The Lord's Prayer is made up of the following parts: praise, hope (a yearning for the Kingdom of God), petition (asking for our needs to be met, and for forgiveness of sins), and a desire for goodness (freedom from testing or evil). There are actually seven petitions in this prayer.

The Lord's Prayer (Scriptural)

Our Father in Heaven,
hallowed be your name,
your kingdom come,
your will be done,
on earth as in heaven.
Give us today our daily bread;
and forgive us our debts,
as we forgive our debtors;
and do not subject us to the final test,
but deliver us from the evil one.
Matthew 6:9–13

The Seven Petitions of the Lord's Prayer

Hallowed be thy name.
Thy Kingdom come.
Thy will be done on earth as it is in Heaven.

May your name be held holy.
The first three petitions are more theological. They draw us toward the Father's glory, are for God's sake (thy name, thy Kingdom, thy will), and are already answered in Jesus' sacrifice.

Give us this day our daily bread.
Forgive us our trespasses,
as we forgive those who trespass against us.
Lead us not into temptation.
Deliver us from evil.

Give us the food we need.
Forgive us of our sins, as we will forgive those who sin against us.
The last four ask God for improvement in our human situation. With them we put our weaknesses and our poverty of spirit in his hands. We gain strength and richness of spirit in his grace (give us, forgive us, lead us not, deliver us).

The Hail Mary

Hail, Mary, full of grace,
the Lord is with thee.
Blessed art thou among women
and blessed is the fruit of thy womb,
    Jesus.
Holy Mary, Mother of God,
pray for us sinners,
now and at the hour of our death.
Amen.

Ave Maria

Ave, María, grátia plena,
Dóminus tecum.
Benedícta tu in muliéribus,
et benedíctus fructus ventris
    tui, Iesus.
Sancta María, Mater Dei,
ora pro nobis peccatóribus,
nunc et in hora mortis nostræ.
    Amen.

Angelus

The *Angelus* is a prayer honoring the Incarnation. It is given its name by the first word of the Latin version of the prayer: *Angelus Domini nuntiavit Maria,* "The angel of the Lord declared unto Mary." It is recited three times each day—morning, noon, and evening, at the sound of the Angelus bell. Each response, where shown, is followed by reciting the Hail Mary.

V. The angel spoke God's message to Mary,
R. and she conceived of the Holy
Spirit.
Hail, Mary …
V. "I am the lowly servant of the Lord:
R. let it be done to me according to
your word."
Hail, Mary …
V. And the Word became flesh,
R. and lived among us.
Hail, Mary …
V. Pray for us, holy Mother of God,
R. that we may become worthy of the
promises of Christ.
Let us pray.
Lord,
fill our hearts with your grace:
once, through the message of an angel
you revealed to us the Incarnation of
your Son;
now, through his suffering and death

lead us to the glory of his Resurrection.
We ask this through Christ our Lord.
Amen.

Prayers from the Liturgy

The Canticle of Zechariah

This hymn is sung during the Liturgy of the Hours, Morning Prayer.

Blessed be the Lord, the God of Israel;
he has come to his people and set them
     free.

He has raised up for us a mighty savior,
born of the house of his servant David.

Through his holy prophets he promised of
old
that he would save us from our enemies,
from the hands of all who hate us.

He promised to show mercy to our fathers
and to remember his holy covenant.

This was the oath he swore to our father
Abraham:
to set us free from the hands of our
enemies,
free to worship him without fear,
holy and righteous in his sight
all the days of our life.

Based on Luke 1:68–75

The Magnificat (Mary's Canticle)

This hymn is sung during the Liturgy of the Hours, Evening Prayer.

My soul proclaims the greatness of the
Lord,
my spirit rejoices in God my Savior;
for he has looked with favor on his lowly
servant.
From this day all generations will call me
blessed:
the Almighty has done great things for me,
and holy is his Name.
He has mercy on those who fear him
in every generation.
He has shown the strength of his arm,
he has scattered the proud in their conceit.
He has cast down the mighty from their
thrones,
and has lifted up the lowly.
He has filled the hungry with good things,
and the rich he has sent away empty.
He has come to the help of his servant
Israel
for he has remembered his promise of
mercy,
the promise he made to our fathers,
to Abraham and his children for ever.

Based on Luke 1:46–55

Act of Contrition

My God,
I am sorry for my sins with all my heart.
In choosing to do wrong
and failing to do good,
I have sinned against you
whom I should love above all things.
I firmly intend, with your help,
to do penance,
to sin no more,
and to avoid whatever leads me to sin.
Our Savior Jesus Christ
suffered and died for us.
In his name, my God, have mercy.

Jesus Prayer

Lord Jesus Christ, Son of God, have mercy on me, a sinner.

Prayer to the Holy Spirit

V. Come Holy Spirit, fill the hearts of
your faithful.
R. And kindle in them the fire of your love.
V. Send forth your Spirit and they shall be created.
R. And you will renew the face of the earth.

Eternal Rest

Eternal rest grant to them, O Lord,
and let perpetual light shine upon them.
May they rest in peace.
Amen.

Personal and Family Prayers

Morning Prayer

I arise today
through God's strength to pilot me,
God's might to uphold me,
God's wisdom to guide me,
God's eye to look before me,
God's ear to hear me,
God's hand to guard me,
God's way to lie before me,
God's shield to protect me,
God's hosts to save me from the
snares of the devil.
Saint Patrick's Breastplate

Evening Prayer

Lord, from the rising of the sun to its setting your name is worthy of all praise. Let our prayer come like incense before you. May the lifting up of our hands be as an evening sacrifice acceptable to you, Lord our God. Amen.

Act of Faith

O God, we firmly believe that you are one God in three Divine Persons, Father, Son, and Holy Spirit; we believe that your Divine Son became man and died for our sins, and that he will come to judge the living and the dead. We believe these and all the truths that the holy Catholic Church teaches because you have revealed them, and you can neither deceive nor be deceived.

Act of Hope

O God, relying on your almighty power and your endless mercy and promises, we hope to gain pardon for our sins, the help of your grace, and life everlasting, through the saving actions of Jesus Christ, our Lord and Redeemer.

Act of Love

O God, we love you above all things, with our whole heart and soul, because you are all good and worthy of all love. We love our neighbor as ourselves for the love of you. We forgive all who have injured us and ask pardon of all whom we have injured.

Devotional Practices

As the Mother of Jesus, the Son of God, Mary is called the Mother of God, the Queen of all Saints, and the Mother of the Church. There are many prayers and practices of devotion to Mary. One of the most revered is the Rosary. It focuses on the twenty mysteries that describe events in the lives of Jesus and Mary.

How to Pray the Rosary

1. Pray the Sign of the Cross and say the Apostles' Creed.

2. Pray the Lord's Prayer.

3. Pray three Hail Marys.

4. Pray the Glory Be.

5. Say the first mystery; then pray the Lord's Prayer.

6. Pray ten Hail Marys while meditating on the mystery.

7. Pray the Glory Be.

8. Say the second mystery; then pray the Lord's Prayer. Repeat 6 and 7 and continue with the third, fourth, and fifth mysteries in the same manner.

9. Pray the Hail, Holy Queen.

Hail, Holy Queen

Hail, Holy Queen, Mother of mercy,
hail, our life, our sweetness, and our hope.
To you we cry, the children of Eve;
to you we send up our sighs,
mourning and weeping in this land of exile.
Turn, then, most gracious advocate,
your eyes of mercy toward us;
lead us home at last
and show us the blessed fruit of your womb, Jesus:
O clement, O loving, O sweet Virgin Mary.

The Chaplet of Divine Mercy

1. Begin with the Sign of the Cross.

2. Pray the Our Father.

3. Pray the Hail Mary.

4. Say the Apostles' Creed

5. Then pray, on the large bead before each decade on the rosary:

Eternal Father,
I offer you the Body and Blood,
Soul and Divinity,
of Your Dearly Beloved Son,
Our Lord, Jesus Christ,
in atonement for our sins
and those of the whole world.

6. On the small beads of each decade say:

For the sake of his sorrowful Passion,
have mercy on us and on the whole world.

7. Then say three times:

Holy God,
Holy Mighty One,
Holy Immortal One,
have mercy on us
and on the whole world.

The Way of the Cross

The First Station: Jesus is condemned to death. **John 3:16**
"For God so loved the world that he gave his only Son, so that everyone who believes in him might not perish but might have eternal life."

The Second Station: Jesus bears his Cross. **Luke 9:23**
"Then he said to all, 'If anyone wishes to come after me, he must deny himself and take up his cross daily and follow me.'"

The Third Station: Jesus falls the first time. **Isaiah 53:6**
"We had all gone astray like sheep, all following our own way; but the LORD laid upon him the guilt of us all."

The Fourth Station: Jesus meets his Mother. **Lamentations 1:12**
"Come, all who pass by the way, pay attention and see: is there is any pain like my pain…"

The Fifth Station: Simon of Cyrene helps Jesus carry his Cross. **Matthew 25:40**
"And the king will say to them in reply, 'Amen, I say to you, whatever you did for one of the least brothers of mine, you did for me.'"

The Sixth Station: Veronica wipes the face of Jesus. **John 14:9**
"… 'Whoever has seen me has seen the Father'…"

The Seventh Station: Jesus falls a second time. **Matthew 11:28**
"Come to me, all you who labor and are burdened, and I will give you rest."

The Eighth Station: Jesus meets the women of Jerusalem. **Luke 23:28**
"Jesus turned to them and said, 'Daughters of Jerusalem, do not weep for me; weep instead for yourselves and for your children.'"

The Ninth Station: Jesus falls a third time. **Luke 14:11**
"For everyone who exalts himself will be humbled, but the one who humbles himself will be exalted."

The Tenth Station: Jesus is stripped of his garments. **Luke 14:33**
"In the same way, every one of you who does not renounce all his possessions cannot be my disciple."

The Eleventh Station: Jesus is nailed to the Cross. **John 6:38**
"Because I came down from heaven not to do my own will but the will of the one who sent me."

The Twelfth Station: Jesus dies on the Cross. **Philippians 2:7–8**
"…And found human in appearance, he humbled himself, becoming obedient to death, even death on a cross."

The Thirteenth Station: Jesus is taken down from the Cross. **Luke 24:26**
"Was it not necessary that the Messiah should suffer these things and enter into his glory?"

The Fourteenth Station: Jesus is placed in the tomb. **John 12:24**
"Amen, Amen, I say to you, unless a grain of wheat falls to the ground and dies, it remains just a grain of wheat; but if it dies, it produces much fruit."

Catholic Faith Words

A

anoint to use oil to mark someone as chosen for a special purpose. In biblical times, the priests, the kings, and sometimes the prophets were anointed as a sign of God's favor. **(122)**

apocalyptic literature a type of writing that reveals what humans cannot see, including the spiritual world or future events **(278)**

Apostolic Succession the term used to describe how the authority and power to lead and teach the Church is passed down from the Apostles to their successors, the bishops **(168)**

B

Beatitudes teachings of Jesus that show the way to true happiness and tell the way to live in God's Kingdom now and always **(192)**

Body of Christ a name for the Church of which Christ is the head. All the baptized are members of the body. **(179)**

C

charity the Theological Virtue of love. It directs us to love God above all things and our neighbor as ourselves, for the love of God **(192)**

chastity a moral virtue and Fruit of the Holy Spirit that helps us express our sexuality in the right ways for our call in life. In religious life or Holy Orders, chastity includes being celibate. **(246)**

Christ a title for Jesus, the One anointed by God as Messiah **(125)**

Church the community of all baptized people who believe in God and follow Jesus. The word is often used for the Catholic Church because we trace our origins back to the Apostles. **(158)**

common good the good of everyone, with particular concern for those who might be most vulnerable to harm **(202)**

Communion of Saints when referring to holy persons, the Communion of Saints includes the pilgrim Church on Earth, those being purified in Purgatory, and the blessed already in Heaven **(258)**

conscience the God-given ability that helps us judge whether actions are right or wrong. It is important for us to know God's laws so our conscience can help us make good decisions. **(212)**

consecrated religious life a state of life lived in community and characterized by the vows of poverty, chastity, and obedience **(236)**

conversion the continual process of becoming the people God intends us to be through change and growth. It is a response to God's love and forgiveness. **(224)**

Corporal Works of Mercy actions that show care for the physical needs of others **(261)**

covenant a sacred promise or agreement between God and humans **(75)**

D

Decalogue another name for the Ten Commandments; the summary of laws that God gave to Moses on Mount Sinai. They tell us what must be done to live by God's covenant. **(109)**

Divine Revelation the process by which God makes himself known. The chief sources of Divine Revelation are Sacred Scripture and Sacred Tradition. **(55)**

domestic Church a name for the Catholic family, because it is the community of Christians in the home. God made the family to be the first place we learn about loving others and following Christ. **(245)**

ecumenism an organized effort to bring Christians together in cooperation as they look forward in hope to the restoration of the unity of the Christian Church **(270)**

Epistles letters written by Paul and several of the other Apostles to new Christian communities that they established. There are twenty-one letters in the New Testament. **(176)**

Eucharist the Sacrament in which Jesus gives himself and the bread and wine become his Body and Blood **(226)**

evangelization giving witness to the faith by proclaiming the Good News of Christ through words and deeds in a way that invites people to accept the Gospel **(226)**

exile the time when Judah, the southern kingdom, was conquered by the Babylonians (586 B.C.). As a result, the people of Judah were sent into Babylon, away from their homeland. **(142)**

Exodus the Israelites' journey from slavery in Egypt to freedom in the Promised Land, accomplished and directed by God **(98)**

faith the Theological Virtue that makes it possible for us to believe in God and the things that he has revealed to us. Faith leads us to obey him. It is both a gift from him and something we choose. **(90)**

faithfulness the loyalty and steadfastness that God shows to all humans, even when they sin. God's offer of friendship is never withdrawn. **(75)**

Gospel a word that means "Good News." The Gospel message is the Good News of God's Kingdom and his saving love. **(158)**

grace God's free, loving gift of his own life and help to do what he calls us to do. It is participation in the life of the Holy Trinity. **(201)**

Heaven the full joy of living eternally in God's presence **(258)**

Hell eternal separation from God because of a choice to turn away from him and not seek forgiveness **(258)**

Holy Orders the Sacrament in which a baptized man is ordained to teach the faithful, lead divine worship, and govern the Church; ordained ministers serve as bishops, priests, or deacons **(236)**

Holy Trinity the mystery of one God in three Divine Persons: Father, Son, and Holy Spirit **(166)**

human dignity the worth each person has because he or she is made in the image of God **(64)**

Incarnation the mystery that the Son of God took on a human nature in order to save all people **(144)**

intercession a form of prayer that involves praying to God on behalf of another; also called intercessory prayer **(261)**

justice giving God what is due him. This virtue also means giving each person what he or she is due because that person is a child of God. **(201)**

Kingdom of God God's rule of peace, justice, and love that exists in Heaven, but has not yet come in its fullness on Earth **(110)**

Magisterium the teaching office of the Church, which is all of the bishops in union with the Pope. The Magisterium has the teaching authority to interpret the Word of God found in Scripture and Tradition. **(236)**

Marks of the Church the essential characteristics that distinguish Christ's Church and her mission: one, holy, catholic, and apostolic **(179)**

Matrimony a Sacrament at the Service of Communion in which a baptized man and a baptized woman make a permanent covenant of love with each other and with God **(245)**

Messiah the promised one who would lead God's People. The word *Messiah* means "God's anointed," or "God's chosen one." Jesus is the Messiah. **(144)**

mission a job or purpose. The Church's mission is to announce the Good News of God's Kingdom. **(168)**

modesty a moral virtue and one of the Fruits of the Holy Spirit that helps us to dress, talk, and move in appropriate ways **(246)**

morality living in right relationship with God, yourself, and others. It is putting your beliefs into action. **(192)**

mortal sin a very serious sin by which someone turns completely away from God **(210)**

natural moral law rules about goodness that are written in our hearts and are natural to follow. However, our awareness of natural law can be clouded by Original Sin. **(109)**

new Adam a title for Jesus. By his obedience to the Father, and willingness to give his life, Jesus made amends for Adam's disobedience, overcame sin, and brought us eternal life. **(76)**

New Commandment Jesus' command for his disciples to love one another as he has loved us **(110)**

new creation the future of justice, love, and peace promised by God, in which good will be rewarded and evil punished **(281)**

New Testament the second part of the Bible, about the life and teaching of Jesus, his followers, and the early Church **(158)**

Old Testament the first part of the Bible, about God's relationship with the Hebrew people before Jesus was born. It includes the laws, history, and stories of God's People. **(64)**

Original Holiness the state of goodness that humanity enjoyed before our first parents, Adam and Eve, chose to sin against God **(67)**

Original Sin the sin of our first parents, Adam and Eve, which led to the sinful condition of the human race from its beginning **(76)**

Passover the Jewish holy day that celebrates God's leading the Israelites out of slavery in Egypt **(101)**

peace a state of calm or harmony when things are in their proper order and people settle problems with kindness and justice **(202)**

Precepts of the Church some of the minimum requirements given by Church leaders for deepening our relationship with God and the Church **(192)**

prophet a messenger from God who speaks the truth and calls the people to follow the laws of God's covenant and act with justice **(142)**

Protestant Reformation a sixteenth-century religious separation from the Catholic Church that began with Martin Luther's preaching against what he felt were errors in the Church **(269)**

providence God's loving care for all things; God's will and plan for creation **(67)**

psalms poems and hymns that were first used in the liturgy of the Israelites. Today, the psalms are also prayed and sung in the public prayer of the Church. **(125)**

Purgatory a state of final cleansing after death and before entering into Heaven **(258)**

Real Presence the phrase used to describe that Jesus is really and truly present in the Eucharist—Body, Blood, Soul, and Divinity **(226)**

Redeemer a title for Jesus, because by his Death on the Cross, he "bought back" the human race from the slavery of sin **(156)**

Resurrection the event of Jesus being raised from death to new life by God the Father through the power of the Holy Spirit **(281)**

Sabbath the seventh day of the week in the Jewish calendar. It is still observed by Jews as a day of rest, prayer, and worship. **(156)**

sacramental seal the rule that a priest is not to share anything he hears in confession **(212)**

Sacred Scripture the Word of God written by humans acting under the Holy Spirit's inspiration and guidance; another name for the Bible **(5, 55)**

Sacred Tradition God's Word to the Church, safeguarded by the Apostles and their successors, the bishops, and handed down verbally—in her Creeds, Sacraments, and other teachings—to future generations **(55)**

salvation the loving action of God's forgiveness of sins and the restoration of friendship with him brought by Jesus **(3, 90)**

Savior a title for Jesus, who came into the world to save all people who were lost through sin and to lead them back to God the Father **(101)**

schism a break or division **(269)**

Seven Sacraments effective signs of God's life, instituted by Christ and given to the Church. In the celebration of each Sacrament, there are visible signs and Divine actions that give grace and allow us to share in God's work. **(90)**

sin an offense against God as well as against reason, truth, and conscience **(210)**

social sin unjust structures that can occur as the result of personal sin. One person's sin can cause others to sin, and the sin can spread through a whole society. **(202)**

soul the spiritual part of a human that lives forever **(64)**

Spiritual Works of Mercy actions that address the needs of the heart, mind, and soul **(261)**

Tabernacle the special place in the church where the Blessed Sacrament is reserved after Mass for those who are ill or for Eucharistic Adoration **(226)**

temperance is the Cardinal Virtue that helps us use moderation, be disciplined, and have self-control **(246)**

temptation an attraction to sin, those actions and omissions that go against right reason and against God's law **(76)**

Transfiguration the revelation of Jesus in glory to the Apostles Peter, James, and John **(191)**

transubstantiation the process by which the power of the Holy Spirit and the words of the priest transform the bread and wine into the Body and Blood of Christ **(226)**

venial sin a sin that weakens a person's relationship with God but does not destroy it **(210)**

virtues good spiritual habits that strengthen you and enable you to do what is right and good. They develop over time with our practice and openness to God's grace. **(201)**

vocation the purpose for which God made us and a particular way to answer his call, whether as a lay person (married or single), a member of a religious community, or a member of the ordained ministry **(235)**

wisdom a gift from God that helps us see God's purpose and plan for our lives. Wisdom leads us to see things as God sees so that we might live holy lives. **(133)**

Index

Index

God, *continued*
  Laws of 109, 112, 134, 147, 190, 194, 200, 212, 317
  love of/for 3, 5, 6, 10, 16, 17, 66, 75, 77, 109, 110, 112, 159, 176, 193, 194, 200, 203, 212, 214, 222, 225, 228, 235, 243, 246, 247, 260, 315, 317, 319
  mercy of 211, 262, 263
  plan of 54, 55, 66, 90, 210, 281, 290, 293, 310, 315
  praising 2, 67, 92
  promise of 4, 32, 91, 108, 111, 120, 145, 281
  relationship with 3, 4, 74, 112, 210, 213, 259, 261, 282, 310, 317
  respect for 109, 112
  saving actions 4, 97, 102
  serving 10, 205, 236, 238, 247
  will of 124, 136
  wisdom of 131, 132, 136, 190, 315
  work of 42, 178, 299
  worshipping 157, 180
God the Father 42, 52, 77, 86, 112, 125, 280, 308
Good Friday 32, 126
Good News 2, 42, 154, 155, 158, 159, 160, 168, 169, 225, 226, 305
Gospel 155, **158**, 159, 222, 236, 329
Gospels, the (four) 5, 26, 58, 120, 154, 158, 159, 168, 238, 305
grace 11, 66, 101, **201**, 236, 281, 282, 321, 329
Great Commandment 110, 188, 189, 192, 193, 194, 195, 200, 315
"The Great Flood" 75
Great Schism 269
Gregory of Nazianzus, Saint 310
Gregory, Saint 310

H – I

Hail, Holy Queen 326
Hail Mary, the 322, 326
Heaven 41, 42, 111, 166, 227, **258**, 259, 261, 282, 306, 310, 311, 312, 329
Hebrews 4, 98, 108, 156
Hell 210, 213, **258**, 259, 310, 329
Henry II, Saint 249
Hilda of Whitby, Saint 113
Hildegard of Bingen, Saint 132
Historical Books (of the Bible) 4, 56
holiness 109, 245, 269, 272, 292, 311
holy 6, 109, 132, 192, 259, 311
holy (Mark of the Church) 178, 179, 309
Holy Communion 227, 317
holy days of obligation 259, 312, 317
Holy Orders, Sacrament of 222, **236**, 247, 329
Holy Saturday 32, 126
Holy Spirit 2, 42, 46, 91, 101, 102, 111, 112, 125, 136, 145, 154, 159, 166, 168, 170, 179, 193, 212, 214, 224, 225, 227, 261, 271, 280, 304, 306, 308, 309
  coming of the 42
  Fruits/Gifts of 46, 47, 226, 318
  guidance of the 55, 228, 262
Holy Thursday 26, 32, 126
Holy Trinity **166**, 225, 259, 260, 314, 329
Holy Week 32
hope 246, 258
Hosea 4, 143, 202
human dignity **64**, 66, 68, 109, 112, 200, 203, 204, 237, 290, 291, 294, 295, 299, 319, 329

humans 4, 32, 55, 64, 66, 67, 68, 74, 75, 76, 77, 86, 92, 102, 156, 159, 204, 291, 299, 302, 303, 317
Ignatius of Antioch, Saint 310
Ignatius of Loyola, Saint 239
image and likeness 64, 66, 68, 109, 204, 291, 319
Incarnation **144**, 145, 322, 329
Initiation, Sacraments of 27, 222, 225, 226, 227
intercession **261**, 329
intercessory prayer 261, 262
Irenaeus, Saint 310
Isaac 89, 90
Isaiah, Book of 4, 143, 157, 190
Israelites 4, 33, 77, 100, 101, 109, 110, 122, 123, 202, 226

J

Jacinta Marto, Blessed 147
Jacob 90
James, Letter of Epistle 5
James the Greater 283
Jeremiah 4, 42, 143, 190
Jerome, Saint 310
Jesse 124
Jesus Christ 4, 5, 22, 42, 58, 77, 100, 110, 112, 120, 144, 147, 154, 156, 157, 168, 169, 171, 177, 178, 179, 190, 191, 192, 203, 205, 224, 227, 244, 245, 246, 268, 270, 272, 278, 279, 280, 283, 296
  anointed one 125, 145
  baptism of 166, 226, 306
  belief in 169, 170
  birth of 17, 22, 125, 158, 306
  coming of 16
  death of 26, 33, 38, 101, 158, 159, 166, 234, 235, 280, 305, 314
  divine and human 144, 145
  faith in 27, 170, 246
  faithful(ness) 111
  image of 279
  kingship 126, 127
  law of freedom 193
  life of 2, 5, 32, 127, 155, 156, 157, 158, 168, 226, 228, 235, 258, 269, 297, 305
  love of/for 86, 160, 192, 193, 297
  ministry of 156, 226
  mission of 46, 224, 225, 236
  new Adam 77
  parables of 56, 158, 211, 244
  promises of 55, 316
  sacrifice of 227, 321
  salvation 32, 33, 55, 91
  the Savior 27
  Second Coming 16, 17, 310
  suffering of 26, 314
  teachings of 86, 110, 125, 145, 169, 180, 188, 192, 214, 245, 262, 305, 306, 309, 312, 316
  titles of 305
  wisdom of 238
  witness to 145, 170
Jesus Prayer 324
Jewish faith and customs 10
Joachim 10
Job 4, 133, 135
John Chrysostom, Saint 310
John, Gospel according to 5, 38, 158, 283
John Neumann, Saint 161
John Paul II, Pope Saint 195, 246
John the Baptist 158, 166, 226
John the Evangelist, Saint 283
Joseph, husband of Mary 125, 306

Joseph, son of Jacob 56, 90
Joshua 4, 122
Judah, people of 143
Judas 166, 269
Jude, Saint 181
Judges 4, 122
justice 22, 110, 188, 199, 200, **201**, 202, 203, 204, 262, 278, 298, 300, 319, 330
Justin Martyr, Saint 310

K – L

Kingdom of God 3, 42, **110**, 126, 158, 192, 203, 204, 225, 235, 256, 281, 310, 316, 321, 330
Lamb of God 313
Last Judgment 310
Last Supper, the 33, 86, 101, 110, 234, 269
Law of Moses 191, 192
Lectio Divina 58, 196
Lent 25–30, 126, 312
letters of the New Testament. *See* Epistles
Life and Dignity 290–291
litany 80, 206, 264
Litany of the Saints 264
liturgical year 2, 16, 126, 312
liturgy 125, 225
Liturgy of the Hours, Evening Prayer 323
Liturgy of the Hours, Morning Prayer 323
"The Lord Is My Shepherd" 121
Lord's Prayer, the 23, 125, 313, 320, 326
Lord's Supper 32. *See also* Eucharist
Louis IX of France, Saint 127
love 9, 64, 110, 145, 190, 212, 227, 245, 300, 319
  the poor 205, 296, 297
  your family 194
  your neighbor 17, 110, 112, 160, 193, 194, 200, 212, 214, 228, 235, 292, 294, 315, 319
Luke, Gospel of 5, 158, 305
Luther, Martin 269

M

Magi 306
Magisterium **236**, 330
Magnificat, the 323
"Make Disciples of All Nations" 165
"The Man Born Blind" 26
Margaret of Cortona, Saint 215
Maria Vicenta, Blessed 205
Mark, Gospel of 5, 158, 226, 305
Marks of the Church 178, **179**, 309, 330
marriage 235, 244, 245, 247
martyr 169, 170, 280
Mary 46, 147, 155, 166, 283, 306, 314
  model of faith 10, 11
  Mother of God 11, 261, 326
  Mother of the Church 326
  presentation of 9, 10
  Queen of All Saints 326
Mary Faustina Kowalska, Saint 263
Mary Magdalene 38
Mary's Canticle 323
Mass 5, 27, 92, 112, 145, 178, 194, 227, 228, 261, 307, 308, 312, 317
  Order of 313
Matrimony, Sacrament of 222, **245**, 330
Matthew, Gospel of 5, 158, 305
Matthias, Saint 166
Maurin, Peter 145
mercy 202, 211, 260, 262
Messiah 22, 120, **144**, 145, 305, 330

Photo Credits:

iv ©Bill & Peggy Wittman; **vi** ©Neil Setchfield /The Art Archive at Art Resource, NY; **viii** ©The Crosiers/Gene Plaisted, OSC; **1** ©Steve Chenn/Corbis; **2** (bg) ©Photos.com/PhotoObjects.net/Thinkstock; **2** (inset) ©Map of the Holy Land (coloured engraving), Danckerts, Theodorus (1663-1727)/Vorontsov Palace, Crimea, Ukraine,Giraudon/The Bridgeman Art Library; **3** (t) ©Pascal Deloche/Godong/Corbis; **3** (b) ©Laura Doss/Corbis; **4** ©Hemera/Thinkstock; **5** (t) ©The Crosiers/Gene Plaisted, OSC; **5** (c) ©Plan of Ephesus and its Environs, from 'The Imperial Bible Dictionary', published by Blackie & Son, c.1880s (litho), Falkener, Edward (1814-96)/Private Collection/Ken Welsh/The Bridgeman Art Library; **5** (b) ©MBI/Alamy; **6** ©Kevin Dodge/Corbis; **7** (bg) ©Image Copyright Joan Kerrigan, 2012 Used under license from Shutterstock.com; **7** (inset) ©iStockphoto.com/Joseph C. Justice Jr.; **8** ©Eric Audras/PhotoAlto/Corbis; **9** ©Jorge Fernandez/Alamy; **11** ©Tim MacPherson/cultura/Corbis; **13** ©Image Copyright Philip Meyer, 2012 Used under license from Shutterstock.com; **14** ©Jorge Fernandez/Alamy; **15** ©Beau Lark/Corbis; **17** ©Bill & Peggy Wittman; **18** ©Image Copyright Philip Meyer, 2012 Used under license from Shutterstock.com; **19** ©Image Copyright Philip Meyer, 2012 Used under license from Shutterstock.com; **21** ©Bill & Peggy Wittman; **22** ©(bl) Bill & Peggy Wittman; **22** (br) ©Bill & Peggy Wittman; **23** ©Image Copyright Philip Meyer, 2012 Used under license from Shutterstock.com; **24** (t) ©Bill & Peggy Wittman; **24** (b) ©Bill & Peggy Wittman; **25** ©imagebroker.net./SuperStock; **27** ©Bill & Peggy Wittman; **28** ©Image Copyright Philip Meyer, 2012 Used under license from Shutterstock.com; **29** ©Image Copyright Philip Meyer, 2012 Used under license from Shutterstock.com; **30** (t) ©moodboard/Corbis; **30** (b) ©imagebroker.net./SuperStock; **31** ©Bill & Peggy Wittman; **32-33** ©Hemera Technologies/PhotoObjects.net/Thinkstock; **34** ©Image Copyright Philip Meyer, 2012 Used under license from Shutterstock.com; **35** ©Image Copyright Philip Meyer, 2012 Used under license from Shutterstock.com; **36** ©Bill & Peggy Wittman; **37** ©The Crosiers/Gene Plaisted, OSC; **39** ©Image Copyright Philip Meyer, 2012 Used under license from Shutterstock.com; **40** (t) ©Our Sunday Visitor; **40** (b) ©The Crosiers/Gene Plaisted, OSC; **41** ©Paul Burns/cultura/Corbis; **43** ©Image Copyright Philip Meyer, 2012 Used under license from Shutterstock.com; **44** (t) ©Bill & Peggy Wittman; **44** (b) ©Paul Burns/cultura/Corbis; **45** ©Domino/Digital Vision/Gettyimages; **46** (t) ©Bill & Peggy Wittman; **46** (b) ©The Crosiers/Gene Plaisted, OSC; **48** ©Image Copyright Philip Meyer, 2012 Used under license from Shutterstock.com; **49** ©Image Copyright Philip Meyer, 2012 Used under license from Shutterstock.com; **50** (t) ©Bill & Peggy Wittman; **50** (b) ©Domino/Digital Vision/Gettyimages; **52** (c) ©Kevin Dodge/Corbis; **52** (b) ©AP Photo/L'Osservatore Romano, ho; **53** ©redbrickstock.com/Alamy; **54** ©Marilyn Angel Wynn/Nativestock Pictures/Corbis; **55** ©Design Pics Inc./Alamy; **56** ©Sheila Shamel; **58** ©Myrleen Pearson/Alamy; **59** ©Mark Edward Atkinson/Blend Images/Corbis; **60** (bg) ©Image Copyright Joan Kerrigan, 2012 Used under license from Shutterstock.com; **61** (bl) ©Design Pics Inc./Alamy; **63** Exactostock/SuperStock; **64** ©Jose Luis Pelaez, Inc./Blend Images/Corbis; **65** ©The World's First Morning. 1961 (w/c on paper), Hadjikyriakos-Ghikas, Nikos (1906-94)/Benaki Museum/Athens/Greece/Bridgeman Art Library; **66** ©Shannon Fagan/Corbis; **67** ©Phillippe Lissak/Photononstop/Getty Images; **68** ©Brachat, Oliver/the food passionates/Corbis; **70** (bg) ©Image Copyright Joan Kerrigan, 2012 Used under license from Shutterstock.com; **70** (inset) ©Our Sunday Visitor; **71** ©Exactostock/SuperStock; **73** ©iStockphoto/Thinkstock; **76** ©Erik Isakson/Tetra Images/Corbis; **77** ©Our Sunday Visitor; **78** (l) ©Blend Images/SuperStock; **78** (cr) ©iStockphoto/Thinkstock; **78** (br) ©iStockphoto/Thinkstock; **79** ©Our Sunday Visitor; **80** ©Image Copyright Joan Kerrigan, 2012 Used under license from Shutterstock.com; **81** ©Our Sunday Visitor; **86** (c) ©Kharbine-Tapabor/The Art Archive at Art Resource, NY; **86** (b) ©Blake Kent/Design Pics/Corbis; **87** ©Exactostock/SuperStock; **90** ©PhotoStock-Isreal/Alamy; **91** ©Martin Barraud/OJO Images/Getty Images; **92** ©Our Sunday Visitor; **93** ©Jason Horowitz/Corbis; **94** (bg) ©Image Copyright Joan Kerrigan, 2012 Used under license from Shutterstock.com; **94** (inset) ©The Good Shepherd (oil on canvas), Champaigne, Philippe de (1602-74)/Musee des Beaux-Arts, Lille, France/ Giraudon/The Bridgeman Art Library; **95** ©Martin Barraud/OJO Images/Getty Images; **97** ©Skip Brown/National Geographic/Getty Images; **100** ©Chen Leopold/Photostock/Isreal/Alamy; **101** ©Our Sunday Visitor; **102** ©Blue Jean Images/Corbis; **103** ©West End 61/SuperStock; **104** (bg) ©Image Copyright Joan Kerrigan, 2012 Used under license from Shutterstock.com; **104** (inset) ©Theo Allofs/Corbis; **105** ©Our Sunday Visitor; **107** ©Gianni Dagli Orti/The Art Archive at Art Resource, NY; **108** (l) ©Tim Zurowski/All Canada Photos/Corbis; **108** (r) ©Hemera/Thinkstock; **109** ©Image Source/Corbis; **110** ©P. Deliss/Godong/Corbis; **111** ©Norbert Schaefer/Corbis; **112** ©Ryan McVay/Lifesize/Thinkstock; **114** ©Image Copyright Joan Kerrigan, 2012 Used under license from Shutterstock.com; **115** ©Image Source/Corbis; **120** (c) ©Clarence Holmes/age fotostock/SuperStock; **120** (b) ©Providence Collection/Licensed From Goodsalt.com; **121** ©Ocean/Corbis; **122** ©RubberBall/Alamy; **123** (t) ©The Crosiers/Gene Plaisted, OSC; **123** (c) ©Providence Collection/Licensed From Goodsalt.com; **123** (b) ©Jephthah: Greeted by his Daughter at Mizpath, Quellinus, Erasmus (1607-78)/Private Collection/Photo ©Christie's Images/The Bridgeman Art Library; **124** ©Lars Justinen/Licensed From Goodsalt.com; **125** ©Neil Setchfield/The Art Archive at Art Resource, NY; **128** ©Image Copyright Joan Kerrigan, 2012 Used under license from Shutterstock.com; **129** ©Lars Justinen/Licensed From Goodsalt.com; **133** ©MANDY GODBEHEAR/Alamy; **134** ©King Solomon holding the temple, 1890 (Stained glass), Burne-Jones, Sir Edward Coley (1833-98)/Leigh, Staffordshire, UK/Ann S. Dean, Brighton/The Bridgeman Art Library; **135** ©Job and his friends, English School, (20th century)/Private collection/Look and Learn/The Bridgeman Art Library; **136** ©Wessel du Plooy (Destonian)/Alamy; **138** (bg) ©Image Copyright Joan Kerrigan, 2012 Used under license from Shutterstock.com; **138** (inset) ©Hemera/Thinkstock; **139** ©MANDY GODBEHEAR/Alamy; **141** (bg) ©Scala/Art Resource, NY; **141** (fg) ©SuperStock; **142** ©Image Asset Management Ltd./SuperStock; **143** ©Dean Conger/Corbis; **144** ©Ain Vares/Licensed From Goodsalt.com; **145** (t) ©Tom Grill/Corbis; **145** (b) ©Associated Press; **146** ©Digital Vision/Thinkstock; **148** (bg) ©Image Copyright Joan Kerrigan, 2012 Used under license from Shutterstock.com; **148** (inset) ©iStockphoto.com/Thinkstock; **149** ©Scala/Art Resource, NY; **154** (c) ©Destinations/Corbis; **154** (b) ©Our Sunday Visitor; **155** (t) ©12 year old Jesus in the temple 1851 (Pastel and Gousche on paper) Menzel, Adolph Friedrich Erdmann Von (1815-1905)/Hamburger Kunsthalle, Hamburg Germany/Bridgeman Art Library; **155** (b) ©Fancy Collection/SuperStock; **157** ©Myrleen Pearson/Alamy; **158** (bl) ©Our Sunday Visitor; **158** (br) ©Our Sunday Visitor; **159** (bl) ©Our Sunday Visitor; **159** (br) ©Our Sunday Visitor; **160** ©Rubberball/Getty Images; **162** ©Image Copyright Joan Kerrigan, 2012 Used under license from Shutterstock.com; **165** ©Bill & Peggy Wittman; **166** The incredulity of St. Thomas, 1602-03 Oil on canvas, Caravaggio, Michelangelo Merisi da (1571-1610)/Schloss Sanssouci, Potsdam Brandenburg, Germany/Alinari/The Bridgeman Art Library; **167** ©Francis G. Mayer/Corbis; **169** (tr) ©Hulton-Deutsch Collection/Corbis; **169** (cr) ©Bettman/Corbis; **169** (bl) ©AP Photo/Dmitry Lovetsky; **169** (br) ©Alessandra Benedetti/Corbis; **170** ©Edvard March/Corbis; **171** ©Art Directors & TRIP/Alamy; **172** (bg) ©Image Copyright Joan Kerrigan, 2012 Used under license from Shutterstock.com; **172** (inset) ©Janet Hyun/Licensed From Goodsalt.com; **173** (bl) ©Hulton-Deutsch Collection/Corbis; **173** (br) ©AP Photo/Dmitry Lovetsky; **175** ©JLP/Jose L. Pelaez/Corbis; **176** (bl) ©Westend61 GmbH/Alamy; **176** (bg) ©iStockphoto.com/loops7; **176** (inset) ©Courtesy of Department of Telecommunications, Vatican; **177** ©JOHANNES EISELE/AFP/Getty Images; **178** ©Bill & Peggy Wittman; **179** ©Our Sunday Visitor; **180** ©Steve Hix/Somos Images/Corbis; **182** (bg) ©Image Copyright Joan Kerrigan, 2012 Used under license from Shutterstock.com; **182** (inset) ©TOPICMedia/H. Heine/Alamy; **183** ©JLP/Jose L. Pelaez/Corbis; **188** (c) ©Bill & Peggy Wittman; **188** (b) ©Myrleen Pearson/PhotoEdit; **189** ©Standard Publishing/Licensed From Goodsalt.com; **190** (t) ©Mark Hunt/Huntstock/Corbis; **190** (b) ©The Crosiers/Gene Plaisted, OSC; **191** ©Scala/Art Resource, NY; **192** ©iStockphoto.com/Dori OConnell; **193** ©Our Sunday Visitor; **194** ©blickwinkel/Alamy; **196** (bg) ©Image Copyright Joan Kerrigan, 2012 Used under license from Shutterstock.com; **196** (inset) ©Our Sunday Visitor; **197** ©iStockphoto.com/Dori OConnell; **199** ©Robin Nelson/PhotoEdit; **201** ©Golden Pixels LLC/Alamy; **202** ©Prophet Micah from the exterior of the right wing of the Ghent altarpiece, 1432. (Oil on panel) Eyck Hubert (c. 1370-1426) & Jan van (1390-1441)/St. Bavo Cathedral, Ghent, Belgium/Lukas - Art in Flanders VZW/Photo: Hugo Maertens/The Bridgeman Art Library; **203** ©iStockphoto.com/Jani Bryson; **204** Blend Images/Alamy; **206** ©Image Copyright Joan Kerrigan, 2012 Used under license from Shutterstock.com; **207** ©Golden Pixels LLC/Alamy; **209** (t) ©The Crosiers/Gene Plaisted, OSC; **209** (b) ©Our Sunday Visitor; **210** ©David Young -Wolff/PhotoEdit; **212** ©Our Sunday Visitor; **213** ©Our Sunday Visitor; **216** (bg) ©Image Copyright Joan Kerrigan, 2012 Used under license from Shutterstock.com; **216** (inset) ©Sheila Shamel; **217** ©David Young -Wolff/PhotoEdit; **222** (c) ©Beau Lark/Corbis; **222** (b) ©Bill & Peggy Wittman; **223** ©Bill & Peggy Wittman; **224** ©Hemera/Thinkstock; **226** ©Ambient Images Inc./SuperStock; **227** ©Bill & Peggy Wittman; **228** ©Jeff Greenberg/PhotoEdit; **230** (bg) ©Image Copyright Joan Kerrigan, 2012 Used under license from Shutterstock.com; **230** (inset) ©Bill & Peggy Wittman; **231** ©Ambient Images Inc./SuperStock; **233** ©Our Sunday Visitor; **234** ©Gianni Dagli Orti/The Art Archive at Art Resource, NY; **235** ©Floresco Productions/Cultura/Getty Images; **236** ©Bill & Peggy Wittman; **237** ©Bill & Peggy Wittman; **238** ©SW Productions/Design Pics/Corbis; **240** (bg) ©Image Copyright Joan Kerrigan, 2012 Used under license from Shutterstock.com; **240** (inset) ©Tony Anderson/Corbis; **241** ©Our Sunday Visitor; **243** ©Anderson Ross/Blend Images/Corbis; **245** (fg) ©Hemera/Thinkstock; **245** (bg) ©Bill & Peggy Wittman; **246** ©Design Pics/SuperStock; **247** ©Anouk de Maar/cultura/Corbis; **248** ©Don Hammond/Design Pics/Corbis; **250** (bg) ©Image Copyright Joan Kerrigan, 2012 Used under license from Shutterstock.com; **250** (inset) ©Bill & Peggy Wittman; **251** ©Anderson Ross/Blend Images/Corbis; **256** (c) ©Enigma/Alamy; **256** (b) ©The Crosiers/Gene Plaisted, OSC; **257** ©Bill & Peggy Wittman; **258** ©Design Pics Inc./Alamy; **259** ©Hilary Morgan/Alamy; **260** (t) ©Radius Images/Corbis; **260** (b) ©Comstock/Thinkstock; **262** ©Bill & Peggy Wittman; **261** ©INTERFOTO/Alamy; **264** (bg) ©Image Copyright Joan Kerrigan, 2012 Used under license from Shutterstock.com; **264** (inset) ©Blue Lantern Studio/Corbis; **265** ©Design Pics Inc./Alamy; **267** ©Henrik Sorenson/The Image Bank/Getty Images; **269** (t) ©The Crosiers/Gene Plaisted, OSC; **269** (b) ©OJO Images Ltd/Alamy; **270** ©Miguel Medina/AFP/Getty Images; **271** (l) ©Vladimir Wrangel/Alamy; **271** (r) ©Our Sunday Visitor; **272** ©Bill & Peggy Wittman; **274** (bg) ©Image Copyright Joan Kerrigan, 2012 Used under license from Shutterstock.com; **275** ©Henrik Sorenson/The Image Bank/Getty Images; **277** ©Denis Scott/Corbis; **278** ©St. John watches the angels turn the sea into blood, from the Lambeth Apocalypse c. 1260 (vellum), English School, (13th century)/Lambeth Palace Library, London, UK/The Bridgeman Art Library; **280** ©Ain Vares/Licensed From Goodsalt.com; **281** Antoine Gyori/AGP/Corbis; **282** ©Corbis RF Best/Alamy; **283** ©Corbis Cusp/Alamy; **284** (bg) ©Image Copyright Joan Kerrigan, 2012 Used under license from Shutterstock.com; **284** (inset) ©Bill & Peggy Wittman; **285** ©Antoine Gyori/AGP/Corbis; **290** ©KidStock/Blend Images/Gettyimages; **291** ©Photo by Alex Wong/Getty Images; **292** ©Our Sunday Visitor; **293** ©Derek Trask/Photolibrary/Getty Images; **294** ©P Deliss/Godong/Corbis; **295** ©Image Copyright Peter Baxter, 2012 Used under license from Shutterstock.com; **296** ©Osservatore Romano/Reuters; **297** ©Sean Sprague/The Image Works; **298** ©Ocean/Corbis; **299** ©George Doyle/Stockbyte/Thinkstock; **300** ©Photononstop/SuperStock; **301** ©Bill & Peggy Wittman; **302** ©Syracuse Newspapers/D Lassman/The Image Works; **303** ©Fancy Collection/SuperStock; **304** ©Sheila Shamel; **305** (t) ©Arte & Immagini srl/CORBIS; **305** (b) ©Lars Justinen/Licensed From Goodsalt.com; **306** ©Claudia Rehm/Westend61/Corbis; **307** (bg) ©Bill & Peggy Wittman; **307** (inset) ©SuperStock/Glowimages; **309** ©Eric Vandeville/Gamma-Rapho via Getty images; **310** ©The Crosiers/Gene Plaisted, OSC; **311** (t) ©The Crosiers/Gene Plaisted, OSC; **311** (c) ©The Crosiers/Gene Plaisted, OSC; **311** (b) ©The Crosiers/Gene Plaisted, OSC; **312** (t) ©Andres Aguirre/LatinContent/Getty Images; **312** (b) ©Ain Vares/Licensed From Goodsalt.com; **314** ©Bill & Peggy Wittman; **318** ©The Crosiers/Gene Plaisted, OSC; **319** ©AP Photo/Gregorio Borgia; **320** ©Myrleen Pearson/PhotoEdit; **322** ©Ocean/Corbis; **324** ©Image Copyright Zvonimir Atletic, 2012 Used under license from Shutterstock.com; **326** ©Bill & Peggy Wittman

Additional Acknowledgments

Music selections copyright John Burland, used with permission, and produced in partnership with Ovation Music Services, P.O. Box **402** Earlwood NSW **2206**, Australia. Please refer to songs for specific copyright dates and information.

Micah 4, 143, 202
ministry 157, 158, 226, 236
miracle 311
mission 42, 46, 79, 154, **168**, 169, 179, 224, 225, 226, 227, 228, 236, 309, 330
missionary 168
modesty **246**, 247, 330
Monica, Saint 93
moral law 315
morality **192**, 330
Morning Prayer 325
mortal sin **210**, 212, 317, 330
Moses 4, 33, 98, 99, 101, 108, 109, 110, 122, 191, 226

Naomi 57
natural moral law **109**, 200, 315, 330
new Adam **76**, 77, 330
New Commandment **110**, 111, 192, 330
new covenant 86, 101
new creation 279, 280, **281**, 330
new Earth 17, 281, 310
new Heaven 17, 281, 310
"The New Heaven and the New Earth" 278
new Jerusalem 281, 310
new law 190
New Testament 4, 5, 32, 58, 100, 120, **158**, 168, 171, 177, 180, 244, 330
Nicene Creed 178, 307, 308, 309, 310
Noah 75, 76, 77, 226
novena 314

obedience 74, 76, 112, 123, 236, 237
Old Testament 4, 5, 32, 33, 58, **64**, 86, 100, 120, 122, 133, 190, 203, 304, 330
one (Mark of the Church) 178, 309
Option for the Poor 296–297
Ordinary Time 9–14, 126, 312
Original Holiness 32, 66, **67**, 330
Original Sin **76**, 77, 226, 317, 330

Palm (Passion) Sunday 126
parables 56, 158. *See also individual parables*
Particular Judgment 310
Paschal Mystery 32, 159, 312
Passion, Lord's 32
Passover, the 100, **101**, 103, 330
patriarchs 90
Paul, Saint 5, 145, 158, 168, 169, 171, 178, 181, 271
peace 22, 110, 188, 199, **202**, 203, 213, 214, 262, 278, 300, 319, 330
"Peace Be With You" 37
penance 26, 212, 317
Penance and Reconciliation, Sacrament of 26, 188, 210, 212, 213, 317
Pentateuch, the 4
Pentecost 38, 42, 45–50, 126, 167, 224
People of God 3, 32, 77, 86, 109, 120, 124, 176, 202, 227, 237
Peter To Rot, Blessed 79
Peter, Saint 5, 154, 158, 168, 169, 191, 209
Philip 224, 225
Pier Giorgio Frassati, Blessed 195
Pius IV, Pope 273
Pius X, Saint 169
Polycarp, Saint 310

Pope 137, 169, 236, 269, 309, 311
  Benedict XVI 169
  Francis 169, 246, 319
  Pius IV 273
  Saint Pius X 169
poverty 145, 236, 237, 261, 297, 321
prayer 2, 6, 11, 26, 58, 91, 112, 159, 229, 247, 271, 291, 322
  of adoration 70, 91, 92
  of blessing 91, 92, 250
  daily 170, 323, 325
  forms of 92
  of intercession 92, 162, 261
  of petition 92, 172, 240, 274, 321
  of praise 91, 92, 104, 128, 138, 321
  of reflection/silence 28, 94, 148, 261, 284
  of thanksgiving 58, 91, 92
"The Prayer of Jesus" 216, 268
Prayer of the Faithful 29
Prayer to the Holy Spirit 324
Precepts of the Church 188, **192**, 193, 317, 331
priest(s) 27, 136, 176, 212, 213, 222, 226, 227, 235, 236, 239
"The Prodigal Son" 56
Promised Land 33
prophet 2, 32, 56, 120, 122, **142**, 143, 144, 146, 190, 191, 194, 202, 203, 331
Prophetic Books, the 4
Protestant Reformation **269**, 270, 273, 331
Proverbs, Book of 4, 133, 135
providence **67**, 331
psalms 4, 56, **125**, 133, 331
Purgatory **258**, 259, 310, 331

"The Quail and the Manna" 108
"The Raising of Lazarus from the Dead" 26
Real Presence **226**, 227, 331
Redeemer **156**, 331
Reign of God 56, 281, 309. *See also* Kingdom of God
religious communities 236
Resurrection 4, 22, 26, 33, 38, 77, 101, 126, 158, 159, 166, 227, 280, **281**, 305, 306, 331
Revelation, Book of 5, 56, 58, 278, 279, 280, 281, 283
Rights and Responsibilities 294–295
Rosary, the 147, 306, 307, 326
Rose of Lima, Saint 296
Rose Philippine Duchesne, Saint 229
Ruth, Book of 4, 56, 57

Sabbath **156**, 157, 331
sacramental seal **212**, 213, 331
Sacred Chrism 227
Sacred Scripture 2, 3, 4, **5**, 32, 52, **55**, 57, 58, 59, 60, 75, 91, 92, 100, 109, 132, 133, 136, 146, 156, 157, 158, 170, 171, 178, 181, 228, 261, 262, 281, 283, 304, 305, 306, 312, 331
Sacred Tradition 52, **55**, 57, 298, 302, 331
Saint 2, 6, 12, 93, 170, 261, 311, 314
salvation **3**, 4, 32, 33, 55, **90**, 91, 101, 132, 159, 179, 228, 245, 309, 331
  history **3**, 4, 32, 91

"The Samaritan Woman" 26
"Samuel Anoints David" 124
sanctifying grace 318
Sarah (Sarai) 32, 88, 89, 91
Saul, King of Israel 123, 124
Savior 27, 97, **101**, 331
schism **269**, 331
"Second Account of Creation" 65
Second Coming 16, 17
Second Vatican Council 271, 272
Sermon on the Mount 192
Service of Communion, Sacrament at the 245
seven capital sins 317
Seven Sacraments **90**, 91, 101, 225, 331
sign of peace 313
Sign of the Cross 320, 326
sin 27, 76, 77, 91, 102, 125, 156, 179, 180, 209, **210**, 212, 213, 269, 280, 317, 321, 331
  confession of 169
  consequences of 202
  effect of 75
  mortal **210**, 212, 317, 330
  personal 203, 226
  social **202**, 203, 331
  venial **210**, 212, 317
Solidarity 300–301
Solomon, Book of 131, 134, 142
Son of God 16, 145, 159, 280, 308, 326
soul **64**, 110, 176, 259, 310, 331
Sower, parable of the 56
Spiritual Works of Mercy 260, **261**, 331
Stations of the Cross 314
stewardship 67, 69, 303

Tabernacle **226**, 227, 331
temperance **246**, 247, 331
Temple 306
temptation **76**, 332
Ten Commandments 108, 109, 110, 113, 188, 190, 191, 200, 214, 315
Teresa Benedicta, Saint 103
Teresa of Ávila, Saint 59
Theological Virtues 318
Thomas Aquinas, Saint 137
Timothy, Saint 171
Torah 109
Tower of Babel, the 76
Transfiguration **191**, 306, 332
transubstantiation **226**, 227, 332
Triduum 31–36, 126

unity 178, 256, 258, 259, 269, 270, 271, 272, 301, 309
venial sin **210**, 212, 317, 332
virtue 132, 200, **201**, 247, 260, 311, 332
vocation 222, 234, **235**, 239, 247, 332
vows 236
"The Washing of the Disciples' Feet" 110, 234
Way of the Cross, the 327
"The Wedding at Cana" 244, 245, 306
wisdom 54, 55, 132, **133**, 134, 135, 136, 146, 238, 332
Wisdom Books 4, 134
"The Woman at the Well" 26
Word of God 2, 4, 55, 92, 145, 146, 176, 190, 212, 304
Works of Mercy 261
Zechariah 9